Better Homes and Gardens

BEDS & BORDERS

More than 90 Plant-by-Number Gardens You Can Grow

WILEY

John Wiley & Sons, Inc.

Beds and Borders: More Than 90 Plant-by-Number Gardens You Can Grow

Contributing Writer and Project Editor: Veronica Lorson Fowler
Contributing Designer: Sundie Ruppert
Editor, Garden Books: Denny Schrock
Editorial Assistant: Billie Wade
Contributing Copy Editor: Fern Bradley
Contributing Proofreaders: Kelly Roberson, Terri Frederickson,
 Barb Rothfus
Contributing Indexer: Ellen Sherron

Meredith® Books
Editorial Director: Gregory H. Kayko
Editor in Chief, Garden: Doug Jimerson
Editorial Manager: David Speer
Art Director: Tim Alexander
Managing Editor: Doug Kouma
Executive Director, Sales: Ken Zagor
Director, Operations: George A. Susral
Director, Production: Douglas M. Johnston
Business Director: Janice Croat
Vice President and General Manager, SIP: Jeff Myers
Book Production Manager: Doug Johnson
Imaging Center Operator: Mitch Barlow

John Wiley & Sons, Inc.
Publisher: Natalie Chapman
Executive Editor: Anne Ficklen
Assistant Editor: Charleen Barila
Production Director: Diana Cisek
Manufacturing Manager: Tom Hyland

This book is printed on acid-free paper.

Note to Reader: Due to differing conditions, tools, and individual skills,
Meredith Corporation assumes no responsibility for any damages, injuries
suffered, or losses incurred as a result of following the information
published in this book. Before beginning any project, review the
instructions carefully, and if any doubts or questions remain, consult local
experts or authorities. Because codes and regulations vary greatly, you
always should check with authorities to ensure that your project complies
with all applicable local codes and regulations. Always read and observe
all of the safety precautions provided by manufacturers of any tools,
equipment, or supplies, and follow all accepted safety procedures.

Better Homes and Gardens Magazine
Editor in Chief: Gayle Goodson Butler

Meredith Publishing Group
President: Jack Griffin
Excutive Vice President: Doug Olson

Meredith Corporation
Chairman of the Board: William T. Kerr
President and Chief Executive Officer: Stephen M. Lacy

In Memoriam: E.T. Meredith III (1933–2003)

Limit of Liability/Disclaimer of Warranty: While the publisher and
author have used their best efforts in preparing this book, they make
no representations or warranties with respect to the accuracy or
completeness of the contents of this book and specifically disclaim any
implied warranties of merchantability or fitness for a particular purpose.
No warranty may be created or extended by sales representatives or
written sales materials. The advice and strategies contained herein may
not be suitable for your situation. You should consult with a professional
where appropriate. Neither the publisher nor author shall be liable for any
loss of profit or any other commercial damages, including but not limited
to special, incidental, consequential, or other damages.

For general information on our other products and services or for
technical support, please contact our Customer Care Department within
the United States at (800) 762–2974, outside the United States at
(317) 572–3993 or fax (317) 572–4002.

Wiley also publishes its books in a variety of electronic formats. Some
content that appears in print may not be available in electronic books. For
more information about Wiley products, visit our web site at www.wiley.com.

Library of Congress Cataloging-in-Publication Data

ISBN: 978-0470-54027-5
Printed in the United States of America

10 9 8 7 6 5 4 3 2

How To Use This Book

Get started creating the garden of your dreams by understanding the elements in this book. Beautiful photos, helpful illustrations, and how-to planting diagrams set you on your way!

THE PHOTOGRAPH
A photograph of the garden shows you what the design will look like when it matures and is at its peak.

THE ILLUSTRATION
Each design has an illustration to help you visualize how the plants grow together. All plants are shown blooming together, although in reality they may bloom at separate times.

THE PLANTING DIAGRAM
Each design has a planting diagram that shows where to position each plant for correct spacing. Bright colors, varied shapes, and clear lettering makes it easy to turn the photograph into a beautiful garden.

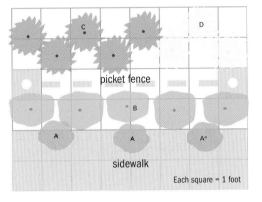

picket fence

sidewalk

Each square = 1 foot

PLANT LIST

A.	**3 Eging lobelias** (*Lobelia erinus*): Annual
B.	**5 Nasturtiums** (*Tropaeolum majus*): Annual
C.	**5 Star Gazer Oriental lilies** (*Lilium* 'Star Gazer'): Zones 4-8
D.	**3 Daylilies** (*Hemerocallis* hybrids): Zones 3-10

THE PLANT LIST
Each design includes a plant list to show you how many plants are needed. Use it as a shopping list when you purchase plants.

DESIGN TIP When you see this icon, you'll know that it's a tip on how to improve or adapt the design to your garden.

REGIONAL NOTE When you see this icon, you'll know there's information about how plants perform in different climates.

HOW-TO Some of the projects in this book call for step-by-step information. The How-To icon means you'll get solid, detailed information on how to complete a project.

MONEY SAVER These tips tell you how to stretch your garden budget.

WORK SAVER These tips help you find ways to create the design faster or save work in maintaining the garden.

ADAPT PLANS FREELY
Each locale is different; climates differ; and the tastes of every gardener are different. Use these designs and the Regional Notes as starting points. Then add, substract, or substitute plants at will. Have fun with them!

LESS IS MORE
This garden grows well with minimal watering in the eastern two-thirds of the U.S. In the western third of the country, you can substitute more drought-tolerant plants such as agastaches, penstemons, sedums, salvias, and yarrows.

PLANT SUPERSTARS
In some cases, plants in the design deserve a closer look. You'll get good tips on growing and using the featured plant or plants.

'Star Gazer' Oriental Lily

PLANT SUPERSTAR
STAR GAZER LILY

Many Oriental lilies are fragrant, but 'Star Gazer' is outstanding in that department. It has gained much attention in recent years in part because of its deep, rich scent. Add the fact that it has deep pink petals with red freckles and white edging, and its popularity is understandable. 'Star Gazer' makes an excellent cut flower. Include just one or two in an arrangement because indoors, the scent can be overpowering. (Tip: The stamens are coated with deep golden pollen that can stain tablecloths, clothing, and hands. Trim them off when cutting lilies for indoors.)

However, outside it's impossible to have too many of these spicy, sweet-scented flowers. Cluster them in groups for best visual effect and to help them support each other. In rich soils you may need to stake them.

Most Oriental lilies have excellent fragrance. They need full sun and deep, well-drained, fertile soil—work in plenty of compost. Grow them with moderate moisture and excellent drainage or they'll rot. Plant bulbs in fall (the most economical way to plant these gems) or purchase them as nursery-grown blooming pots in the spring.

After bloom time, cut the stalks back to remove spent flowers, but allow the foliage to die back completely before removing it.

GARDEN SMARTER
FRONT-YARD FLOWERS

What makes an ideal front-yard flower? It should possess the following characteristics:

It always looks good. Front-yard flowers should look good all growing season long. This can be tough to accomplish with perennials. Look for perennials with attractive foliage as well as colorful blooms. Sedum is an excellent example of this. A plant such as Oriental poppy, which is gorgeous during its brief bloom but soon develops brown foliage, is better placed in out-of-the-way areas, surrounded by other foliage that covers it once it's through blooming.

GARDEN SMARTER
These tips provide background on design, plants, and techniques to help you better execute the design—and simply to garden better!

TABLE OF CONTENTS

Garden Skills To Get You Started

All gardens require a little fundamental care and know-how. Here's how to make sure your garden is launched with the best possible start!

Watering is a garden fundamental, but some methods are better than others. Water smart!

It all starts with the soil. Amend it with plenty of compost to ensure that your plants get a good start with strong growth.

SUN AND SHADE

Some plants thrive in full sun. Others like shade. Here's what defines different types:

Full sun: At least 6 hours of unfiltered, direct light a day. Many plants do better with more, especially in the northern half of the U.S., where the light is less intense. The widest variety of colorful plants thrives in full sun.

Part shade/part sun: 4 to 6 hours of direct light a day or several more hours of filtered light. In the southern half of the U.S., many plants that are described as needing full sun appreciate shade in the afternoon, especially if they like ample moisture.

Medium to full shade: 4 hours or less of direct, unfiltered light, or continual filtered light. Fewer colorful plants thrive in this deeper shade, but choose carefully and you can have a beautiful garden filled with interesting foliage and some colorful flowers.

WATER WISELY

Follow the 1-inch rule. Most lawns and plantings need 1 inch of water a week. You can get away with less by planting drought-tolerant species.

Set up a rain gauge. It's smart to place a rain gauge in the garden so you can monitor how much moisture is received.

Water correctly. Water the soil, not the foliage, because splashing water on leaves encourages fungal diseases. Water in the morning to give plants plenty of time to dry off. Conserve water by running sprinklers right before or after sunrise, never on a windy day.

Keep containers well watered. In hot weather, they may need watering twice a day. Avoid small pots, which can dry out quickly.

CREATE GOOD SOIL

Good soil is the basis for good gardens. Make yours better and you'll have healthier plants, fewer weeds, and efficient watering.

Amend the soil. Every time you create a new bed or add a new plant, amend the soil. Compost is by far the best amendment. Add 2 or 3 inches when you create a bed and 1 inch every year thereafter. Other sources of organic material are also very helpful. Add them in smaller quantities.

Consider raised beds. If you have severe clay, sandy soil, hardpan, or rocky conditions, raised beds are a boon. Creating a raised bed 5 or 6 inches high can make all the difference. Fill it with a blend of compost and best-quality topsoil, purchased from a reliable source.

PICK THE PERFECT PLANT

Choosing the right plants for your garden, your lifestyle, and your region is key to success.

Read the label. The plant label or catalog or web description provides vital information. Follow recommendations on hardiness zones (see page 216), moisture, soil, and light.

Consider all aspects. It's easy to choose a plant for its pretty flower. But also think about the plant's mature height and width, what the foliage looks through the year, how well-suited it is to your climate, if it needs staking or other pampering, and how pest- and disease-resistant it is.

Do a little research. A quick web search can tell you a lot and help you make smart decisions. Never plant something you know nothing about unless you're okay with gambling to possibly lose it.

Substitute freely. Use the planting lists in these plans as a starting point. Substitute, add, or substract plants depending on your budget, what you can get from friends, what you like, and what you can find in your local garden centers or online.

KNOW YOUR ZONE

The U.S. Department of Agriculture has divided the country into various zones based on average low winter temperatures. (See page 216.) In most of the country, this information is essential in choosing plants that will survive the winter in your region.

In the West heat and drought-tolerance, rather than cold-hardiness, are more important, so following zone recommendations is less essential.

MAINTAIN IT

Inspect often. A daily stroll through the garden keeps you aware of what maintenance needs to be done, and prompts you to do it sooner. Also, by taking a close look at your garden daily, you'll catch problems early for easier control.

Mulch. Spread 1 to 3 inches of mulch, such as shredded bark, on your garden. It conserves moisture, suppresses weeds, and limits the spread of disease.

Keep up with weeds. The most successful gardeners spend a few minutes every day weeding and watering. It's amazing what you can do in 10-minute increments.

Deadhead. Trim off spent blooms often to keep your garden neat and attractive and encourage more blooms.

Fertilize. Compost is a wonderful soil amendment. It helps plants on levels that chemical fertilizers can't touch. In addition to compost, you may want to sprinkle general-purpose slow-release fertilizer over your garden several times a year. Give container plantings regular applications of liquid fertilizer since frequent watering flushes out nutrients.

When shopping for plants, read labels carefully and be thoughtful about how the plant will work in your garden.

As your garden grows, it's essential to do continual maintenance to keep plants healthy and the garden attractive.

The Easiest Beds & Borders

Bigger is not always better. Sometimes it's the simplest gardens that are the most satisfying to plant and tend. *In this chapter, you'll find smaller gardens that use easy-to-find and even easier-to-grow plants that are sure to please, no matter what your skill level.*

Most plants in these garden designs, in fact, can be found for sale at supermarkets and discount garden centers. Pick them up while you're shopping for other things and you'll be on your way!

Beds and Borders For Beginners

All beds and borders, no matter how simple and no matter how complex, follow a few basic rules of landscape design.

Put taller plants in the back, middle-height plants in the center, and lower plants along the front.

As you flip through the following pages, you'll see many of the following principles at work. If you like, you can also use these ideas to tweak the designs you see in this book—or to create an entirely new design of your own. Some of the basics of bed and border planning include:

Think big. The larger the border, the more mixing and matching you can do to ensure that the bed will always have blooming plants that look good, regardless of season. A narrow strip just a foot or two wide provides limited options while a border 4 to 5 feet deep has more impact.

Arrange plants according to height. Place taller plants in the back, medium plants in the center, and low-growers (sometimes called edging plants) in the front.

Use a variety of plant shapes and sizes. Put a feathery plant, such as a fern, next to one with a large leaf, such as a hosta. Or contrast the mounded form of hosta with a spiky plant like liriope.

Consider the effect of foliage. Flowers are important, of course, but if you include plants with a variety of foliage colors and textures, your design will look good all season long—not just when the plants bloom.

Mix it up. Put fuzzy silver plants next to shiny deep green ones or toss in a plant with deep purple foliage for contrast. The mix of leaf colors keeps plant types distinct and prevents the bed from appearing brushy or indistinct.

Group plants according to their growing needs. Avoid mixing sun-lovers with plants that require shade. Instead, grow plants that demand lots of light together in sunny sites and combine shade-tolerant plants in low-light areas.

Likewise, avoid planting a drought-tolerant plant such as thyme in front of a moisture-lover such as ligularia. If you make one plant happy with the amount of water it receives, you may well kill the other one.

Cluster several plants of the same type together. Larger groups form pleasing drifts of color that create impact. Planting one or two plants here or there can create a busy or messy patchwork effect. The beauty of the plants may be lost in the chaos. A single impatiens plant looks straggly; 25 make a lush drift.

Keep a color scheme in mind. Design beds and borders that look great by limiting the palette of colors included in the garden. Choose a color scheme and stick to it. (See Chapter Four starting on page 73 for several gardens based on color schemes.)

Foliage has colors, too! This planting combines citrusy green hosta with rich purple coral bells and the blue-gray of bleeding heart.

For a more cohesive look, choose a color scheme for a flower bed. This planting of cosmos, salvia, and dusty miller (*left*) has a classic combo of pink, blue, and silver.

Avoid a patchwork effect, especially in large beds, by planting in groups of six, eight, or more plants, as shown here (*right*).

GARDEN SMARTER

WAXING AND WANING

One of the first lessons new gardeners learn is that every flowering plant has a peak bloom period, which varies from a few days to several weeks or even months.

Oriental poppies, for example, are the star of the garden when in bloom for a week or two in late spring. But by summer, the foliage turns brown and unattractive. (Tip: Tuck them in among other plants that will conceal the fading foliage.)

Perennial salvia, on the other hand, blooms for several weeks in early summer and will rebloom after the first flush of flowers if you remove the faded blooms. And its silvery gray foliage is attractive even when out of bloom.

Annuals that like warm weather—such as marigolds, petunias, and impatiens—usually take two to four weeks to get established. Once they fill in, they look good throughout the rest of the growing season until frost. (If you like, buy larger sizes for a full, lush garden from the get-go.)

Your role as a gardener is like that of a symphony conductor. Orchestrate the plants in your garden to provide color from early spring through fall frosts. Know your plants' peak bloom times and then design your beds and borders to create a harmonious landscape that always hits the right note.

This garden is filled with plants that are attractive most of the growing season. The ornamental grasses and cannas, for example, look good from the moment they emerge from the ground in spring.

Low-Growing Favorites

Brighten a spot by your back door or along a walk with easy color.

THREE DIFFERENT KINDS OF ANNUALS COMBINE IN THIS CHARMING PLANTING FOR BIG IMPACT.

Fill a sunny spot fast with these easy and easily available annuals. They're readily available at most garden centers and inexpensive. And it take very little time to plant them. If you like, substitute in different low-growing sun-loving annuals, such as sweet alyssum and petunias.

This planting loves full sun but needs only moderate water. It's a great solution for a sun-baked spot.

PLANT LIST

A. **5 Nasturtiums** (*Tropaeolum majus*) such as 'Whirlybird Orange': Annual

B. **7 African daisies** (*Osteospermum* hybrids) such as 'Soprano White': Zones 10–11, annual elsewhere

C. **5 Geraniums** (*Pelargonium* × *hortorum*): Zones 10–11, annual elsewhere

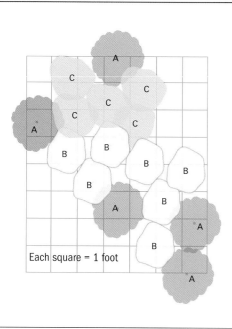

Each square = 1 foot

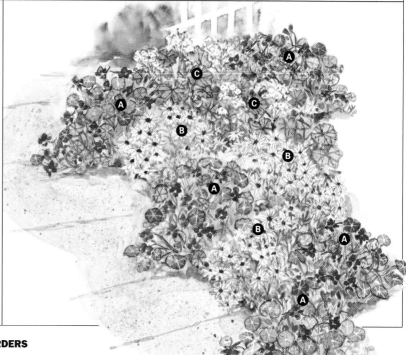

SUN GARDEN

Marvelous Mailbox

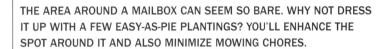

Use your mailbox as the focal point of this pretty little flower bed filled primarily with annuals.

THE AREA AROUND A MAILBOX CAN SEEM SO BARE. WHY NOT DRESS IT UP WITH A FEW EASY-AS-PIE PLANTINGS? YOU'LL ENHANCE THE SPOT AROUND IT AND ALSO MINIMIZE MOWING CHORES.

This plan calls for full sun, and the plantings are somewhat drought-tolerant once established. The pinks and the Dahlberg daisy will get rather scruffy-looking once summer heat hits. If desired, replace them with marigolds, petunias, or other warm-season annuals.

You could also easily adapt this planting plan to a lamppost, a birdhouse on a pole, or a flagpole. A pretty large-flowered clematis scrambles up the pole to soften the structure. The plan calls for a 'Ville de Lyon', but you could substitute nearly any clematis.

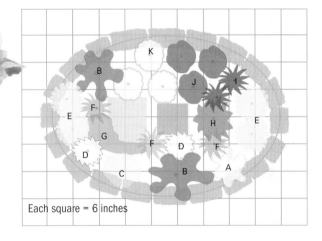

Each square = 6 inches

PLANT LIST

A. **1 Annual verbena** *(Verbena × hybrida)*: Zones 9–11, annual elsewhere

B. **2 Purple Wave petunias** *(Petunia* 'Purple Wave'*)*: Annual

C. **1 Dahlberg daisy** *(Dyssodia tenuiloba)*: Annual

D. **2 Impatiens** *(Impatiens walleriana)*: Annual

E. **4 Sweet alyssums** *(Lobularia maritima)*: Zones 10–11; annual elsewhere

F. **3 Dusty millers** *(Senecio cineraria* 'Silver Dust'*)*: Zones 7–11

G. **1 Clematis** *(Clematis* spp.*)*, such as 'Ville de Lyon': Zones 4–9

H. **1 Dahlia** *(Dahlia × hybrida)*: Annual

I. **2 China pinks** *(Dianthus chinensis)*: Annual

J. **3 Globe amaranths** *(Gomphrena globosa)*: Zones 9–11, annual elsewhere

K. **3 Geraniums** *(Pelargonium × hortorum)*: Annual

Formal Made Fun

A geometric garden doesn't have to be stuffy. Take a shape—in this case a rectangle—and outline it with a pretty edging flower.

A FORMAL GARDEN IN THE FRONT YARD IS ELEGANTLY WELCOMING. THIS GARDEN TAKES THE BEST QUALITIES OF FORMAL DESIGN—PLEASING SHAPES AND CLEAN LINES—AND MIXES THEM WITH CHEERFUL, AIRY PLANTINGS. A POT OUTFITTED WITH A POST AND TOPPED WITH A CASCADING BASKET IS AN UNEXPECTED TOUCH.

Fragrant white sweet alyssum edges this bed, which is planted entirely with annuals, ensuring color all growing season. Inside the ring of alyssum, a collection of blue mealycup sages, cosmos, petunias, and zinnias burst forth in bloom.

The container garden repeats the sweet alyssum edging, but in this case pairs it with bright yellow gazanias, which are wonderfully drought-tolerant, minimizing watering duties.

While this garden is rectangular, you could easily adapt it to a different shape that better suits your landscape. Create a circle with the pot centered. Or make it a triangle with the pot either in the center or tucked into one of the corners. For a more relaxed effect, try a crescent shape.

Position this garden in full sun, at least 6 hours of unfiltered, direct light a day. Work compost into the soil at planting time. Also water and fertilize regularly to stimulate good foliar growth and flowering. Remove faded blooms regularly to encourage more flowers.

PLANT LIST

BED:

A.   **36 White sweet alyssums** (*Lobularia maritima*): Annual

B.   **7 Mealycup sages** (*Salvia farinacea*):
Zones 8–11, annual elsewhere

C.   **3 Brazilian vervains** (*Verbena bonariensis*):
Zones 7–11, annual elsewhere

D.   **5 Purple Wave petunias** (*Petunia* 'Purple Wave'): Annual

E.   **13 Zinnias** (*Zinnia* Profusion series hybrids): Annual

F.   **5 Dwarf pink cosmos** (*Cosmos* Sensation series hybrids):
Annual

POT WITH POLE:

G.   **9 White sweet alyssums** (*Lobularia maritima*): Annual

H.   **5 Gazanias** (*Gazania rigens*): Annual

MOSS-LINED BASKET:

I.   **4 Vinca vines** (*Vinca major*): Annual

J.   **1 Purple Wave petunia** (*Petunia* 'Purple Wave'): Annual

BASKET IN A BARREL

Create this nifty double container garden by positioning a sturdy tree limb, gleaned from a pruning project, in a whiskey barrel. Toenail in place with large nails and pack in heavy garden soil halfway up the barrel. (Fill the rest with potting soil.) Secure a wire basket atop the limb by hammering in fence staples. Outfit with a moss liner and plant with trailing flowers.

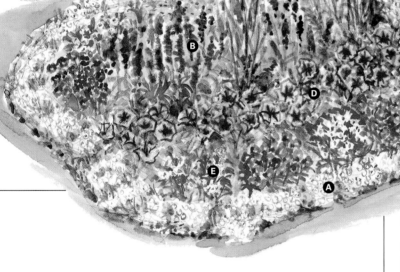

Each square = 1 foot

GARDEN SMARTER

ANNUAL OR PERENNIAL?

Some plants act like perennials or annuals, depending on the region.

Brazilian vervain, shown in this garden, has gained popularity because it attracts butterflies like few other flowers. But it behaves differently in various parts of the country. In Zones 7 to 11 it is a perennial, coming back year after year. In the rest of the country, it's an annual, although it freely self-seeds.

Mealycup sage (*Salvia farinacea*), by way of comparison, is also an annual in most parts of the country, but in Zones 8 to 11 it can be grown as a perennial.

Brighten a Curbside

Banish the streetside blahs with this easy garden of fast-growing flowers that will go from just-planted to profuse in a matter of weeks.

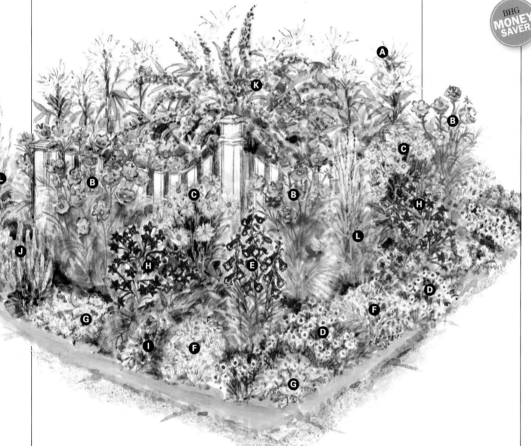

BHG MONEY SAVER

SOW COSMOS FROM SEED

Cosmos are one of the easiest annuals to start from seed, so much so that they're often recommended for children. To save some money—and have fun—try starting them indoors from seed rather than buying transplants.

Plant them in a shallow container filled with seed-starting mix 4 to 6 weeks before your region's last frost date. Keep the soil lightly moist and place the container in bright sunlight indoors. Transplant seedlings into individual pots when they develop two feathery leaves. Transfer seedlings into the garden after all danger of frost has passed.

You can also plant cosmos directly in the garden after the soil has warmed. Direct-sown cosmos mature and bloom a few weeks later than those started indoors.

MAKE A PICKET FENCE THE BACKBONE OF THIS TRIANGULAR GARDEN OF ANNUALS AND PERENNIALS. IT'S A CLEVER WAY TO DRESS UP A VACANT CURBSIDE AND A FRIENDLY WAY TO DETER PEDESTRIANS FROM CUTTING THE CORNER.

The fence is more than just for looks. It also props up the tall annuals, such as the cosmos and spider flowers, which tend to flop late in the season. (You can also loosely stake tall flowers if they begin to topple.)

This sunny garden is jam-packed with plants that attract butterflies and hummingbirds. The tubular flowers of penstemon, flowering tobacco, and petunia are hummingbird magnets. Zinnia and spider flower also draw them in. And the butterfly bush that anchors the corner is irresistible to butterflies. Also nice: The fragrance of flowering tobacco and butterfly bush will delight as you stroll by the garden in the evening.

If you want your garden to include more perennials and fewer annuals, substitute boltonia and purple coneflower for the spider flower behind the fence. But keep the annuals in front of the fence. They'll ensure color all season long.

PLANT LIST

A. **7 White spider flowers**
(*Cleome hassleriana*)
such as 'White Queen': Annual

B. **12 Pink cosmos**
(*Cosmos bipinnatus*): Annual

C. **4 Gloriosa daisies**
(*Rudbeckia hirta*)
such as 'Irish Eyes':
Zones 3–7 (often grown as annual)

D. **9 Narrow-leaf zinnias**
(*Zinnia angustifolia*)
such as 'White Star': Annual

E. **3 Penstemons** (*Penstemon
barbatus*): Zones 4–10, annual
elsewhere.

F. **12 Dusty millers**
(*Senecio cineraria*)
such as 'Silver Dust':
Zones 8–11, annual elsewhere

G. **9 Moss roses**
(*Portulaca grandiflora*):
Zones 9–11, annual elsewhere

H. **6 Flowering tobaccos**
(*Nicotiana alata*): Annual

I. **2 Petunias**
(*Petunia × hybrida*): Annual

J. **1 Speedwell**
(*Veronica* spp.) such as 'Fairytale':
Zones 4–8

K. **1 Butterfly bush**
(*Buddleia davidii*)
such as 'Nanho Blue':
Zones 5–9

L. **2 Feather reed grasses**
(*Calamagrostis × acutiflora*):
Zones 4–9

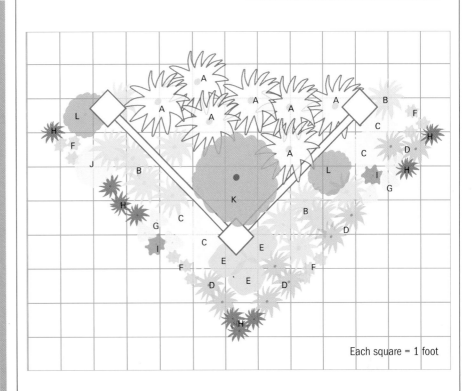

Each square = 1 foot

Ring Around A Fountain

Make splashing water the cooling focal point of a colorful bed for shade.

A LARGE CLAY POT, CONVERTED INTO A WATER FEATURE, IS AN EASY-TO-MAKE CENTERPIECE FOR A SIMPLE BED.

The charming fountain is surrounded with polka-dot plant, an annual that livens up dark parts of the garden with lively splashes of cream and pink.

Impatiens, a shade garden classic available in nearly every hue except blue, add pizzazz. For a splashier look, mix impatiens of various colors in the bed. Or plant a single color, such as pink, for a more subdued effect.

Plant these tender annuals in spring, after all danger of frost has passed. Impatiens and polka-dot plant like rich soil and plenty of moisture, so work plenty of compost into the soil at planting time. Fertilize with a sprinkling of a slow-release fertilizer every 4 to 6 weeks during the growing season to maintain profuse flowering.

Although the fountain is an ideal centerpiece, you can substitute your own water feature or garden art. If you prefer, purchase a fountain, birdbath, or a statue set atop a pedestal of stacked bricks or pavers as an alternate center of interest.

The pink in polka-dot plant foliage plays nicely off pink or red impatiens. But you could substitute any of the other colorful shade loving annuals listed on the page opposite. Adjust the number of plants as needed. Place taller plants closest to the fountain and encircle with shorter plants.

PLANT LIST	
A.	**32 Impatiens** (*Impatiens walleriana*): Annual
B.	**9 Polka-dot plants** (*Hypoestes phyllostachya*): Annual

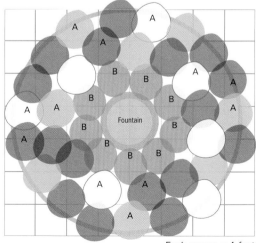

Each square = 1 foot

Wishbone flower

Browallia

Coleus

Scarlet sage

Wax begonia

PLANT SUPERSTARS

FIVE SHOWY ANNUALS FOR SHADE

It can be difficult to find colorful annuals for shady areas. Here are some excellent alternatives to the impatiens and polka-dot plants featured in this garden.

Most of these annuals grow best in part shade to full sun in the northernmost quarter of the U.S. They need more shade farther south. (See page 6 for a more detailed definition of types of shade.) They may require full shade in the southern third of the U.S. All need rich soil with ample water and regular fertilization.

WISHBONE FLOWER *(Torenia fournieri)* This cup-shape flower grows about 12 inches tall and wide with 1-inch-wide bicolor flowers in shades of blue, purple, pink, or white with a splash of yellow in the throat.

BROWALLIA *(Browallia speciosa)* Also called star or sapphire flower, browallia has gorgeous purple-blue or white flowers on plants 12 to 18 inches tall and wide.

COLEUS *(Solenostemon scutellarioides)* This plant produces small flower spikes of pale blue or white in late summer, but the flowers are outdone by gorgeous foliage marked in various combinations of green, white, red, burgundy, and yellow. Leaf shapes vary also. Plants grow 12 to 36 inches tall and 12 to 18 inches wide.

SCARLET SAGE *(Salvia splendens)* Scarlet sage has large, showy flowers in reds, pinks, oranges, creams, or deep purple-red. It does well in full sun or partial shade. This plant likes moisture, and grows up to 2 feet tall and 10 to 15 inches wide.

WAX BEGONIA *(Begonia semperflorens)* Also called bedding or fibrous begonia, wax begonia sports shiny green or bronze leaves on plants 8 to 15 inches tall and wide. Clusters of pink, red, or white flowers dangle above the foliage.

BHG HOW TO

MAKE THIS FOUNTAIN

STEP 1. Choose a pot. A plain clay pot works well, or you can get fancier with a glazed ceramic pot. Also check out fiberglass or resin containers in a variety of shapes.

STEP 2. If using a clay or ceramic pot, seal the inside of the clay pot by brushing it with deck sealant. Allow to cure for three days.

STEP 3. Choose a pump. Fit the nozzle with a short length of copper pipe (cut to fit), making it as high as the surface of the water will be.

STEP 4. Thread the pump cord through the drainage hole in the bottom of the pot (you may need to chip or drill it to make it wider) and seal with an exterior caulk.

STEP 5. Let cure 1 to 2 days, fill with water, plug in, and enjoy!

A Shady Strip Of Annuals

Nearly every garden has one: a long narrow space next to a building that is cloaked in shade most of the day. Lighten it with flowers.

GARDEN SMARTER

GOOD FERNS GONE BAD

Although it's tempting to dig plants of ostrich fern *(Matteuccia struthiopteris)* from your neighbor's yard to save a few bucks, they will quickly overwhelm a small space such as this narrow border. Also, their spreading rhizomes may push up through the brick walkway, creating a maintenance headache. It makes sense to spend a little more at the outset to avoid problems down the road.

IT'S AMAZING HOW MUCH PLEASURE A WELL-LANDSCAPED SMALL SPACE CAN GIVE, ESPECIALLY IF YOU WALK BY IT EVERY DAY.

Side yards are the perfect example. They are the ugly stepsisters of the landscape, too often little more than a neglected spot to stash garbage cans.

This side yard was magically transformed with simple plantings of colorful annuals and easy-care perennials. The tiny shaded strip close to the house limited planting options, but the combination of impatiens, ferns, tuberous begonias, and columbines resulted in a spectacular effect.

A moss-covered brick path keeps the border in bounds. Hanging baskets of fuchsias, tuberous begonias, and variegated vinca contribute to the transformation. Boston ivy (*Parthenocissus tricuspidata*) softens the brick wall with lush green foliage that turns brilliant red in autumn.

In this tiny shaded strip, Christmas ferns are a good choice. They keep their green color nearly year-round, and they won't overwhelm other plantings by spreading. Japanese painted fern (*Athyrium niponicum*), with splashes of silver and maroon, is a showy alternative.

Each square = 1 foot

Wall

PLANT LIST

A. **3 Christmas ferns**
(*Polystichum acrostichoides*):
Zones 3–9

B. **2 Columbines**
(*Aquilegia × hybrida*):
Zones 3–9

C. **11 Impatiens**
(*Impatiens walleriana*): Annual

D. **2 Tuberous begonias**
(*Begonia × tuberhybrida*):
Annual

E. **6 Wishbone flowers**
(*Torenia fournieri*): Annual

SHADE GARDEN

Plant a Circle Of Color

So little sun that grass won't grow? Put in a bright bed of flowers instead!

MATURE TREES ARE A MIXED BLESSING. THEY PROVIDE RESTFUL SHADE, BUT GRASS WON'T GROW WELL UNDER THEIR LEAFY CANOPIES. ONE SOLUTION? BLANKET THE GROUND WITH COLORFUL ANNUALS THAT THRIVE WHERE TURF WON'T.

This garden is filled with brilliant red wax begonias (you could substitute impatiens) close to the tree, where the shade is deepest. The edge of the bed that receives more sun has more subdued color from dusty miller, ageratums, and lobelias.

Boxwoods provide a permanent anchor to the planting. Annual flowers are unequaled at providing season-long color, but if you prefer perennials, consider substituting reblooming fringed bleeding heart *(Dicentra eximia)* for the wax begonias and hardy geraniums for the lobelias and ageratums. Both perennials can provide color all summer. Hostas in various shades of green, white, and gold could substitute for the dusty miller.

GARDEN SMARTER
TIPS FOR PLANTING AROUND TREES

Planting around the base of a tree helps it blend into the overall landscape. Follow these tips when planting flowers next to trees:

Determine how much shade the tree casts. Some trees with high, open canopies and small leaves, such as honeylocust, create little shade, while others with dense, low-hanging branches, such as spruce, create deep shade. (See page 6 for more information on shade in the garden.)

Assess the available soil moisture. Some trees, such as maples, are notorious for sucking moisture from the soil under their boughs. Grow drought-tolerant plants around moisture-hogging trees.

Add no soil over tree roots. Tempting as it may be to build a raised bed around a tree, burying roots with only a few inches of soil can kill a sensitive tree.

Dig with caution. It's okay to slice through a few small roots with a trowel, but avoid cutting roots that are thicker than an inch in diameter.

Play around with pots. An easy way to grow flowers under trees with problematic soil is to tuck in several pots filled with colorful shade-loving annuals.

Get edgy. Install some type of edging around the bed to prevent turf from creeping in. You'll make maintenance even easier.

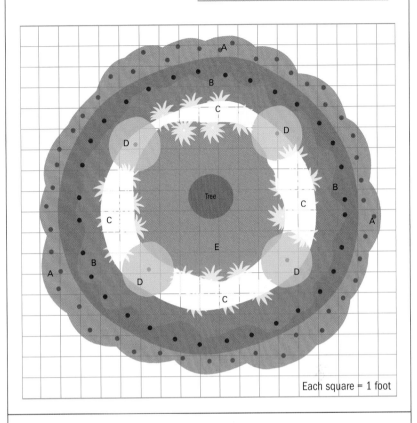

Each square = 1 foot

PLANT LIST

A.	**48 Edging lobelias** (*Lobelia erinus*): Annual	
B.	**32 Ageratums** (*Ageratum houstonianum*): Annual	
C.	**24 Dusty millers** (*Senecio cineraria*): Zones 8–10, annual elsewhere	
D.	**4 Boxwoods** (*Buxus* spp.): Zones 5–7	
E.	**28 Red wax begonias** (*Begonia* × *semperflorens*): Annual	

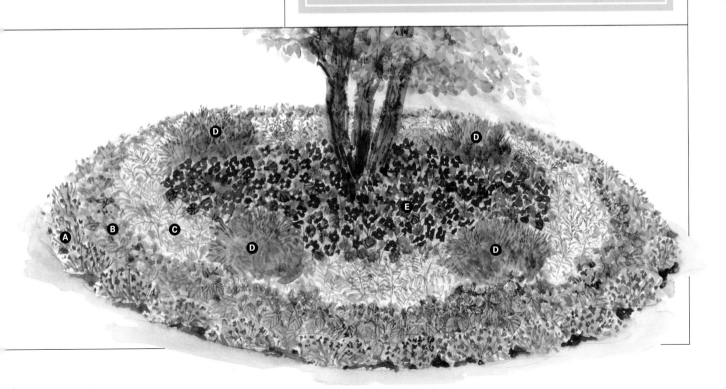

Easy Perennials For Light Shade

Take care of those spots that fall between sun and shade with simple flowers that come back year after year.

HAVE AN AREA WITH PARTIAL SHADE THAT YOU'D LIKE TO FILL WITH MINIMAL-CARE PERENNIALS? THIS IS YOUR GARDEN.

This mix of pretty perennials blooms in purple, pink, and chartreuse. All thrive in light shade—4 to 6 hours of direct, unfiltered morning (or late afternoon) sun a day or dappled shade most of the day. Likely locations for such light conditions are under the canopy of a high tree or next to large shrubs or a building that blocks the afternoon sun. (See page 6 for more information on different types of shade.)

Plant this small garden by itself or extend it with bright pink astilbes planted at one end and pink snapdragons at the other end. The plants featured in this garden need ample moisture. If you plant them under a tree with shallow roots, such as a maple, you'll need to provide supplemental water.

A bonus: All the blooms in this garden are good as cut flowers, ensuring a vase or two of pretty flowers to enjoy indoors for at least a couple of months of the year.

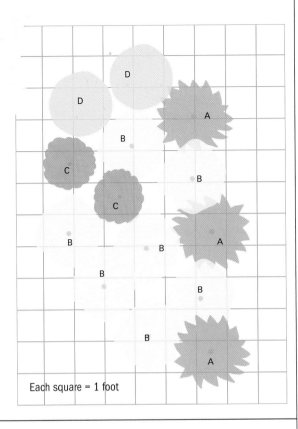

Each square = 1 foot

PLANT LIST

A. **3 Hyssops** (*Hyssopus officinalis*):
   Zones 6–9

B. **7 Lady's mantles** (*Alchemilla mollis*):
   Zones 4–7

C. **2 Hardy geraniums** (*Geranium* 'Rozanne'):
   Zones 4–8

D. **2 Bleeding hearts** (*Dicentra spectabilis*):
   Zones 4–8

Columbine

Coral bells

Daylily

Blue false indigo

Obedient plant

PLANT SUPERSTARS

MORE EASY-CARE PERENNIALS FOR LIGHT SHADE

Here are more tough-as-nails perennials that thrive in partial shade, which is 4 to 6 hours of direct, unfiltered light a day in the South; 6 hours in the northern half of the U.S. where the sun is less intense. Daylily, coral bells, and columbine tolerate even dry shade.

COLUMBINE (*Aquilegia* hybrids) This spring-blooming native with intricate spurred flowers grows 1 to 4 feet tall. Some types reseed freely. Zones 3–9.

CORAL BELLS (*Heuchera* hybrids) Leaves of coral bells earn nearly equal billing as the sprays of pink, coral, or white flowers. Foliage can be medium green, yellow-green, deep purple, silver-streaked, or beautifully variegated. Grows about 12 inches all and wide; flower spikes reach 16 to 30 inches tall. Zones 3–8.

DAYLILY (*Hemerocallis* hybrids) Choose from tall (up to 4 feet) or miniature forms (as short as 1 foot). 'Stella de Oro' is one of the most popular minis. Main bloom is midsummer. Some rebloom several times each year as long as you deadhead diligently. Zones 3–9.

BLUE FALSE INDIGO (*Baptisia australis*) Gorgeous blue flowers appear on spikes in late spring. The attractive blue-green foliage grows 3 to 5 feet tall, depending on light and moisture. Stake to prevent flopping. Zones 3–9.

OBEDIENT PLANT (*Physostegia virginiana*) This spreading moisture-lover grows 1 to 4 feet tall with spikes of white or pink in midsummer to fall. Can be somewhat invasive in ideal conditions. Zones 2–9.

Cool Containers

Container gardens are great garden problem solvers. They can create a welcoming front entry; transform a drab window into a charming vignette; brighten a back doorstep; or turn a porch, deck, or patio into a festive outdoor retreat. *Best of all, nothing is faster and easier than container gardening. Start with a pot, add potting soil and some plants, and you're set. After that, regular watering and a little bit of fertilizing and grooming will keep the container garden in tip-top condition.*

Turn the page for inspired ideas for containers that go beyond the basics.

Fundamentally Foliage

Who needs flowers to create a striking container collection? A varied palette of foliage provides just as much pizzazz as blooms.

THIS COLLECTION OF CONTAINERS IS SPECTACULAR ON STEPS, BUT WOULD BE EQUALLY GORGEOUS FOR A DECK, PATIO, PORCH OR ANY OTHER OUTDOOR ROOM.

Plant these pots as a group, as shown, or plant just one of your favorites. Take care, though, when combining deeply colored foliage. Contrast light colors (such as the lime-green sweet potato vine) or bright shades (such as the rusty orange coleus) with darker ones (such as the purple and burgundy of Persian shield and rex begonia). Otherwise, the color composition can look lost or muddy.

To vary the plan, substitute or mix in other full-sun annuals with interesting foliage, such as variegated geraniums or nasturtiums, purple-leafed perilla or basil, or silvery dusty miller.

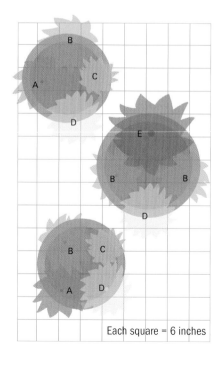

Each square = 6 inches

BHG MONEY SAVER

CREATIVE CONTAINERS

Just about anything can be made into a container garden—from a bucket with holes to an ornate ceramic vessel to the old rubber tire shown here. However, the container must have drainage holes or you risk problems with rotting roots. If a ceramic container has no drainage hole, drill one with a power drill fitted with a diamond-tipped ceramic tile bit.

Containers create opportunities to recycle castoffs. Line an old basket with sheet moss or perforated black plastic. (If the basket's bottom is broken, position it in a flowerbed and bury it slightly in the ground.) Shoes, pots and pans, furniture remnants, bowls, cans, jars, vases, and more can be turned into interesting containers.

Make sure that grouped containers have a unifying element. It may be that they're all made from the same material, such as terra-cotta, or that their shapes are similar, or they fit a particular theme. Remember, too, that a can of spray paint can do wonders, transforming black plastic nursery pots into colorful containers. Or use specialty spray paint to create faux chrome or ersatz stone pots.

GARDEN SMARTER
WISE WATERING

Ample water is critical to keep container plantings healthy and full. Never let them dry out enough to droop. If you do, flowering will be reduced and the plants will become more susceptible to diseases and pests. When potting soil dries completely, it's difficult to wet again because the soil shrinks and water runs down between the pot and the soil. To remedy this situation, soak the pot for an hour or two in a bucket or pan of water filled to reach about one-third up the side of the pot.

When doing regular watering, soak the soil until water runs out the drainage holes. In hot, sunny, or windy weather, be prepared to water twice a day.

PLANT LIST

A. **2 Persian shields** (*Strobilanthes dyerianus*): Zones 10–11, annual elsewhere

B. **4 Coleuses** (*Solenostemon scutellarioides*): Annual

C. **2 Rex begonias** (*Begonia rex-cultorum* hybrids): Zones 10–11, annual elsewhere

D. **3 Lime green sweet potato vines** (*Ipomoea batatas*) such as 'Margarita': Zones 9–11, annual elsewhere

E. **1 Chinese hibiscus** (*Hibiscus rosa-sinensis*): Zones 9–11, annual elsewhere

A Regal Composition

Elegant containers and classic plants combine to create a planting with timeless beauty.

GARDEN SMARTER
SPLURGE ON SOIL

No getting around it: Use top-quality potting soil in your containers. It's tough for plants to grow well in such a tight space for a long time. Treat them to a lightweight, moisture-retentive soil for best plant growth.

PLANT LIST

A. **2 Bigleaf hydrangeas** (*Hydrangea macrophylla*)
such as 'Pia': Zones 6–9

B. **1 Shrub rose** such as 'Anne Boleyn'
or other David Austin Series rose: Zones 5–9

C. **2 Geraniums** (*Pelargonium* spp.):
Zones 10–11, annual elsewhere

D. **2 Wandering Jews** (*Tradescantia zebrina*):
Zones 10–11, annual elsewhere

E. **2 Low-growing sedums** such as *Sedum sieboldii*:
Zones 5–9

F. **2 Rex begonias** (*Begonia rex-cultorum*) such as 'Pink Minx':
Zones 10–11, annual elsewhere

G. **3 Hens-and-chicks** (*Sempervivum tectorum*):
Zones 4–9, annual elsewhere

H. **1 Dichondra** (*Dichondra argentea* 'Silver Falls'):
Zones 9–11, annual elsewhere

I. **1 Silver spear** (*Astelia chathamica*):
Zones 9–11, annual elsewhere

IN THIS DESIGN SOPHISTICATED URNS AND A MUTED PLANTER PLAY STRONG SUPPORTING ROLES. THEY TEAM BEAUTIFULLY WITH THEIR DETAILING OF SWAGS AND GARLANDS, MIMICKING THE LOOK OF CLASSICAL IRON AND LEAD CONTAINERS.

You don't have to pay a king's ransom for such containers. Instead, purchase containers made of fiberglass or other composites that give the look, but not the price tag—or the weight—of heavy stone or metal pots.

These containers are filled with billowy pink hydrangeas, spiky silver spear, mounded succulents, trailing wandering Jews, and purple Rex begonias. A rose bush planted in the ground behind the containers becomes a natural part of the composition. These plants thrive in full sun to light shade.

If you love the plants more than the containers, change the look by substituting two large glazed ceramic pots for the urns and a complementary ceramic trough garden for the long planter. Or grow the hydrangeas in large square wooden planters and pair them with a wooden window box.

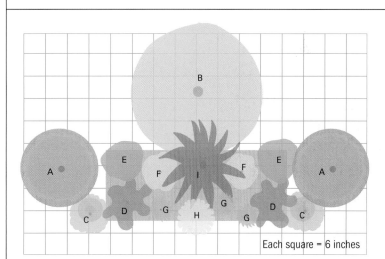

Each square = 6 inches

REGIONAL NOTE

WINTERIZING SHRUBS IN CONTAINERS
You can plant shrubs (such as roses and hydrangeas) and perennials (such as sedum, hens-and-chicks, and silver spear) in containers, but come late fall in colder regions of the country, you'll need to move them to a protected spot to overwinter them.

In Zones 7 and colder (roughly the northern two-thirds of the U.S.), place them in a cool (below 40°F) garage so that the plants go dormant. However, the space should remain warm enough (only occasionally dipping below freezing) so that the soil doesn't freeze solid.

In Zones 8 and warmer (roughly the southern third of the U.S. as well as coastal Pacific Northwest), you can leave the containers outdoors unprotected.

Really Red

Give your container plantings punch with one of these knockout combinations in brilliant red.

A MAJOR ROLE FOR CONTAINER GARDENS IS TO ADD COLOR. THESE TWO DESIGNS PLAY IT TO THE HILT.

Containers are portable splashes of color. No matter how barren, baked, or shady the spot, you can concoct a container garden that will thrive there.

Get the biggest bang for your buck by sticking with a color that stands out—like red! Cheerful yellow, serene white, and perky pink also jump out, but none have quite the same impact as red. These two designs for containers with red color schemes are excellent starting points. But let your imagination—and your trowel—run free, and mix in other red plants that you particularly like.

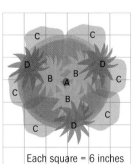

Each square = 6 inches

PLANT LIST

A. **1 Red Chinese hibiscus standard**
(*Hibiscus rosa-sinensis*):
Zones 9–10, annual elsewhere

B. **3 Japanese blood grasses**
(*Imperata cylindrica* 'Red Baron'):
Zones 4–9

C. **6 Red New Guinea impatiens**
(*Impatiens hawkeri*): Annual

D. **3 Scarlet sages** (*Salvia splendens*): Annual

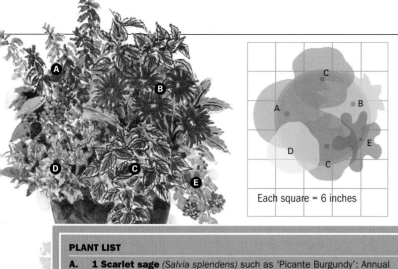

Each square = 6 inches

PLANT LIST

A.	**1 Scarlet sage** *(Salvia splendens)* such as 'Picante Burgundy': Annual
B.	**1 Red gerbera** *(Gerbera jamesonii)*: Zones 8–10, annual elsewhere
C.	**2 Burgundy coleuses** *(Solenostemon scutellarioides)* such as 'Wizard Velvet Red': Zones 10–11, annual elsewhere
D.	**1 Stellar zonal geranium** *(Pelargonium × hortorum)* such as 'Vancouver Centennial': Zones 10–11, annual elsewhere
E.	**1 Red annual verbena** *(Verbena × hybrida)* such as 'Quartz Scarlet': Annual

PLANT SUPERSTARS

UNBEATABLE CONTAINER PLANT COMBINATIONS

When mixing plants in a pot or planter, a good rule of thumb is to combine these three different plant forms:

THRILLER: A TALL, SPIKY PLANT THAT SERVES AS A VERTICAL ELEMENT. EXAMPLES INCLUDE:

ANNUAL SALVIA
Sun-loving mealycup sage *(Salvia farinacea)* is a beautiful blue upright accent. *Salvia splendens* takes some shade and comes in reds, whites, purples, and more.

ORNAMENTAL GRASSES
Ornamental grasses, such as maidengrass, offer graceful shape and interest from spring through fall.

SPILLER: A TRAILING PLANT TO SOFTEN THE EDGES OF THE CONTAINER. EXAMPLES INCLUDE:

ENGLISH IVY
A vigorous trailing plant for shade, English ivy *(Hedera helix)* has hundreds of forms and color variegations of green, white, and gold.

LOBELIA
Best suited to spring's cool weather, annual lobelia *(Lobelia erinus)* comes in either trailing types or edging types, which mound nicely. In hot climates, substitute a trailing verbena, such as 'Imagination'.

FILLER: A MOUNDED PLANT THAT WILL FILL THE GAPS BETWEEN THE SPIKY AND TRAILING PLANTS. EXAMPLES INCLUDE:

FRENCH MARIGOLD
Cheery, colorful French marigold *(Tagetes patula)* is a classic annual flower that loves sun and heat. It teams nicely with terra-cotta.

VINCA
Vinca *(Catharanthus roseus)* stays fresh looking all summer long with lustrous green foliage and inch-wide blooms in pink, white, rose, lavender, red, or blends.

Annual salvia

Maidengrass

English Ivy

Lobelia

French marigold

Vinca

Plant a Deck With Color

Add a burst of color to a deck with a tumble of brilliant annuals tucked into a large planter box.

A DECK IS A WONDERFUL PLACE TO TAKE IN THE GREAT OUTDOORS. AND IT'S EVEN BETTER WHEN YOU EMBELLISH IT WITH LOTS OF COLORFUL FLOWERS, BRINGING THE GARDEN UP CLOSE AND PERSONAL.

Fill your planters with rambling annuals that scramble and sprawl as they grow, creating a casual intertwining mass of flowers that's sure to delight. This design is perfect for an urban rooftop or balcony to soften hard architectural features, or for a deck with a backdrop of woods or fields to blend with the natural surroundings.

Raised planters are especially useful on a deck, where they serve as a half-wall, creating privacy from views below. For additional seclusion, include a built-in trellis, small trees, or a hedge of shrubs.

A raised planter is also helpful for gardeners who have difficulty getting out in a yard, where footing can be uneven and unsure. It also reduces bending to water and maintain flowers. Add a ledge to the planter or build it from landscape timbers to make the walls comfortable enough to sit on while tending the garden.

PLANT LIST

A. **5 Nasturtiums**
(Tropaeolum majus):
Annual

B. **8 Bidens**
(Bidens ferulifolia) such as
'Golden Goddess':
Zones 8–11, annual elsewhere

C. **4 Annual verbenas**
(Verbena × hybrida) such as
'Quartz Rose':
Annual

D. **1 Parrot's beak**
(Lotus berthelotii):
Zones 9–11, annual elsewhere*

E. **7 Snapdragons**
(Antirrhinum majus):
Zones 6–9, annual elsewhere

F. **3 Marguerite daisies**
(Argyranthemum frutescens)
such as 'Butterfly':
Zones 10–11, annual elsewhere

*   Can substitute another sun-
    loving trailer with silver foliage
    such as dichondra (Dichondra
    argentea 'Silver Falls') or licorice
    plant (Helichrysum petiolare
    'Silver Mist').

Each square = 6 inches

DECK GARDENING MADE BETTER

Slightly elevate containers. Set small stones, blocks of scrap wood, or clay or metal pot feet sold in garden centers to set underneath pots and planters to raise them off the wood. This prevents mildew and rot.

Minimize weight. Some decks can't handle large planters. You may be able to minimize the amount of soil (and added weight) by placing a false bottom in the planter. Most flowers do well in 12 to 18 inches of soil. Small

trees and large shrubs need up to 3 feet of soil. Add extra support under the deck to handle the extra weight if necessary.

Erect a screen. This is an easy privacy solution. Erect a large trellis at the back of a planter and plant the base with medium-size vines, such as clematis or climbing roses.

Add shade. A pergola or lattice overhead will cool things down considerably. Plant with trumpet vine, grapes, or wisteria to sprawl over the pergola for denser shade.

Wonderful With White

Use white flowers generously to keep containers looking as fresh as, well, a daisy!

WHITE FLOWERS ADD A CLEAN, BREEZY NOTE TO ANY PLANTING. WHITE ALSO MAKES OTHER FLOWER COLORS POP. REDS ARE REDDER, BLUES ARE BLUER, AND YELLOWS APPEAR EVEN SUNNIER. WHITE CAN BE AN EFFECTIVE VISUAL UNIFIER, TOO, WHEN USED AMONG VARIOUS POTS AND PLANTERS.

White marguerite daisies and white sweet alyssum dominate the plantings shown here. Pink and red primroses contribute vibrant spring color.

When daytime temperatures top 80°F, primroses start to fade and die back. Replant with more heat-tolerant annuals, such as vinca or celosia, for summer color. After fall frost nips these heat-loving annuals swap them out with pansies, chrysanthemums, or ornamental kale or cabbage.

This planting also shows how you can create a garden even where there's no soil. It's a clever strategy to brighten a bleak spot, or soften a fenceline or wall. Use this trick to create a portable flowerbed any place you want flowers and greenery but don't have soil.

GARDEN SMARTER
FERTILIZING CONTAINER GARDENS

Even if your potting soil includes a slow-release fertilizer, constant watering of containers flushes out nutrients rapidly. After a few weeks or a few months of watering, most of the fertilizer will be gone. For lush plantings and continuous bloom, supplement with a liquid fertilizer or time-released product according to the instructions on the fertilizer label.

PLANT LIST

A. **2 Marguerite daisies**
(*Argyranthemum frutescens*):
Zones 10–11, annual elsewhere

B. **2 White sweet alyssums**
(*Lobularia maritima*):
Annual

C. **7 Polyanthus primroses**
(*Primula × polyantha*):
Treat as an annual

D. **9 Japanese primroses**
(*Primula japonica*):
Treat as an annual

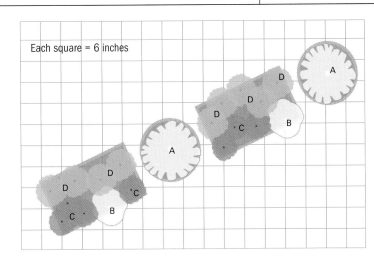

Each square = 6 inches

Polyanthus primrose

German primrose

PLANT SUPERSTAR
PRIMROSES

Walking down the primrose path can be made delightful reality when you plant colorful primroses. Available in an amazing array of colors, they're charming spring bloomers that bloom and thrive in cool temperatures (50° to 60°F). In the southern U.S. and in regions where springs are long, cool, and moist, they provide long-lasting color.

Because primroses need moist but well-drained, rich soil, they're a natural for containers. Most are relatively low growers so raising them up in containers where you can see them better is an added benefit. If you plant primroses in containers, it's best to treat them as annuals. Many delightful species of primroses are available:

POLYANTHUS PRIMROSE (*Primula × polyantha*), a complex cross of several species, is one of the most popular. Its low-growing rosette of leaves bears clusters of brightly colored blooms in a wide range of colors on a 6-inch-tall stalk. It is hardy in Zones 6 to 8, but is often grown as an annual bedding plant.

ENGLISH PRIMROSE (*Primula vulgaris*), also a low grower, is hardy in Zones 4 to 8 and matches polyanthus primrose for color diversity.

JAPANESE PRIMROSE (*Primula japonica*) has reddish purple, pink, or white flowers that bloom on stalks up to 18 inches tall. It is hardy in Zones 3 to 8.

GERMAN PRIMROSE (*Primula obconica*) grows up to 1 foot tall and bears flowers in shades of red, pink, lavender, blue, or white. It is hardy in Zones 10 to 11. Its foliage can cause skin irritation, so handle it with caution.

One Pot, Three Seasons

Keep the plants in a container looking their best from early spring through fall by following this clever switch-out scheme.

NO MORE EMPTY POTS! PLAN FOR SEASONAL CHANGES AND KEEP YOUR CONTAINER GARDEN GLORIOUS SPRING, SUMMER, AND FALL. JUST REMOVE AND REPLACE A FEW KEY PLANTS.

It's tough to keep container plantings at their prime for months on end because a pot or planter is a challenging environment. Plants must endure limited root space, limited nutrients, and erratic soil moisture. The key to maintaining a lush, healthy look all season long is to change out a few of the plants with the seasons. (Public gardens routinely replant containers with the change of seasons so that the plantings always look their best.)

Rather than starting from scratch each spring, this container garden cleverly recycles four framework plants throughout the year. On their own, these four foliage permanent plantings would be drab, so each season add bright, colorful, blooming plants alongside them to give the pot pizzazz.

Use this change-out strategy with patio planters, window boxes, or any other site where you want a seasonal boost of color. In cold winter regions, leave the container in place, and tuck in branches of cut evergreens or woody stems with colorful bark or berries that won't mind the snow and ice.

SPRING

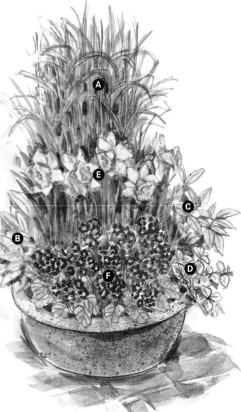

BHG REGIONAL NOTE

PERENNIAL OR NOT?
Hardy perennials can be left in the container year-round in Zones 8 and warmer (see page 216). In Zones 7, mulch well with a mound of straw or wood chips. In Zones 6 and colder, move the container to a cool garage. (If the soil freezes solid in a container, plants often will be killed. Plants growing directly in the ground are more protected from extreme temperatures.)

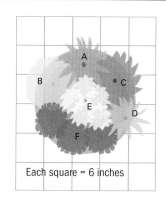

Each square = 6 inches

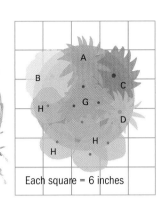

Each square = 6 inches

SUMMER

FALL

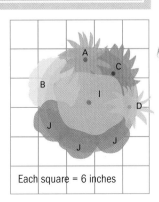

Each square = 6 inches

PLANT LIST

PERMANENT PLANTINGS:

A. **1 Feather reed grass** (*Calamagrostis* × *acutiflora* 'Karl Foerster'): Zones 5–9*

B. **1 Lamb's ears** (*Stachys byzantina*): Zones 4–8*

C. **1 Heavenly bamboo** (*Nandina domestica*): Zones 6–9*

D. **1 Variegated wintercreeper** (*Euonymus fortunei* 'Emerald Gaiety'): Zones 5–9*

SPRING TEMPORARY PLANTS:

E. **5 Daffodils** (*Narcissus* spp.) planted as established plants from pots: Zones 2–10, treat as annual*

F. **3 German primroses** (*Primula obconica*): Zones 10–11, treat as annual

SUMMER TEMPORARY PLANTS:

G. **3 Dwarf Asiatic lilies** (*Lilium* Pixie series): Zones 3–8, treat as annual

H. **5 China pinks** (*Dianthus chinensis*): Annual

FALL TEMPORARY PLANTS:

I. **1 Florists' chrysanthemum** (*Chrysanthemum* × *grandiflorum*): Treat as annual

J. **3 Flowering kales** (*Brassica oleracea*): Treat as annual

Hardiness zones given are for plants growing in the ground. Plants will need special care if overwintered in containers in cold climates.

An Overflowing Window Box

Everyone loves a lush window box, spilling over with gorgeous plants. It starts with intensive planting.

THIS PLANTING EXPLODES WITH COLOR AND TEXTURE. THE RESULT MAY LOOK CASUAL, BUT THE EFFECT IS DELIBERATE.

For a gloriously overflowing container of any sort, it's important to choose plant overachievers that will grow up or out, such as the spiky scarlet sage, trailing petunias, and purple-black sweet potato vine shown here. With intense competition for space there's no room for plants that fail to grow vigorously. (Good news: "Vigorous" translates into "easy.")

To achieve a window box this full, start with top-quality potting soil. Work in a slow-release granular fertilizer at planting time (unless the potting soil already has it), and then use a liquid flowering plant fertilizer throughout the growing season to encourage fast growth and big blooms.

In most regions this window box planting will thrive in full sun. But in the South and Southwest provide afternoon shade or dappled sunlight.

PLANT LIST

A. **5 Petunias** *(Petunia × hybrida)*: Annual

B. **1 Texas sage** *(Salvia coccinea)*: Annual

C. **3 Licorice plants** *(Helichrysum petiolare)*: Zones 10-11, annual elsewhere

D. **2 Annual verbenas** *(Verbena × hybrida)*: Annual

E. **2 Wishbone flowers** *(Torenia fournieri)*: Annual

F. **1 Sweet potato vine** *(Ipomoea batatas* 'Blackie'): Annual

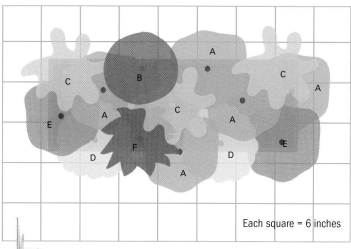

Each square = 6 inches

GARDEN SMARTER

GROOMING CONTAINERS

At each watering, do a little plant primping. Use a scissors, hand shears, or just your fingers to remove dead or damaged stems or foliage and pinch or trim off spent blooms to encourage more flowers.

In midsummer, give sprawling, leggy plants a haircut, cutting them back by about two-thirds to encourage branching near the plant's base and fuller growth for the rest of the growing season.

Site Solutions

Whether the problem area in your garden stems from too much shade, an extreme slope, or a sun-drenched spot that receives minimal water, you'll find a plan in this chapter that will solve it. *In the following pages, enjoy beautiful shade plantings, landscaping plans for slopes, and drought-tolerant gardens that look lush with minimal moisture. Also check out planting plans for troublesome areas around water gardens and a seaside garden that defies salt and wind—solutions for whatever challenges your landscape dishes out!*

A Soothing Shady Border

Cool, green, and refreshing, this low-key planting for full shade is restful and elegant.

LEARN TO APPRECIATE THE SUBTLE GRADATIONS OF FOLIAGE COLORS, TEXTURES, AND SHAPES BY TENDING A PEACEFUL SHADE GARDEN.

Gardeners with limited sun often are frustrated because they can't grow the wide variety of plants with showy flowers that is possible with more light. However, over time most shade gardeners readjust their expectations to appreciate the beautiful foliage, distinctive plant shapes, subtle colors, softly colored flowers, and textural differences among shade-tolerant plants.

This plan is a delightful place to start appreciating shade. It features a variety of plant highlights, from the beautiful, fragrant spring flowers of an azalea to the delicate foliage of fringed bleeding heart to the bold, architectural foliage of hostas. You can follow the plan exactly or take liberties and substitute with shade plants featured in Top Perennial Picks for Shade on the opposite page.

The plants in this shade garden grow best in moist, loamy soil. If your garden's soil is less desirable, work in compost at planting time to help retain moisture and nutrients.

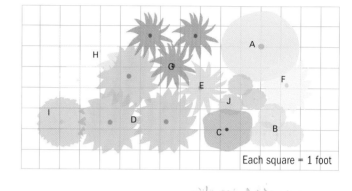

Each square = 1 foot

Mulch is especially important in a moisture-loving shade garden such as this one. Apply 1 to 3 inches, refreshing each spring.

PLANT LIST

A. **1 Azalea** (*Rhododendron* spp.) Zones 4–9

B. **3 Fringed bleeding hearts** (*Dicentra exima*): Zones 4–8

C. **1 Virginia knotweed** (*Persicaria virginiana*): Zones 5–9

D. **3 Fragrant hostas** (*Hosta plantaginea*) or other medium-large hostas: Zones 3–8

E. **1 Variegated hybrid hosta** (*Hosta* spp.) such as 'Patriot': Zones 3–8

F. **1 Narrow-spiked ligularia** (*Ligularia stenocephala* 'The Rocket'): Zones 4–8

G. **3 Solomon's seals** (*Polygonatum commutatum*): Zones 3–8

H. **3 Yellow foxgloves** (*Digitalis grandiflora*): Zones 3–8

I. **1 Old-fashioned bleeding heart** (*Dicentra spectabilis*): Zones 3–9

J. **3 Hybrid anemones** (*Anemone* × *hybrida*): Zones 4–8

PLANT SUPERSTARS

TOP PERENNIAL PICKS FOR SHADE

Even if sunlight is in short supply, don't despair. You can still have a flowerbed that really shines. Below are some excellent picks for perennial plants that thrive in partial to full shade, as long as they also get ample moisture.

AJUGA *(Ajuga reptans)* With dozens of cultivars now available, this pretty groundcover makes a striking show with variegated foliage in tones of green, white, pink, burgundy, and silver. It also produces blue or pink flowers; grows 6 inches tall. Zones 3–9.

ASTILBE *(Astilbe* spp.) This plant's ferny foliage and feathery plumes have made it a favorite. Many types are available ranging in color from pink to white, red, lavender, or peach. Grows 6 inches to 3 feet tall, depending on species. Zones 4–9.

YELLOW CORYDALIS *(Corydalis lutea)* One of the longest bloomers among shade-loving plants, this plant produces yellow flowers starting in spring and continuing through fall. Needs ample moisture but also good drainage. Grows to 16 inches tall. Zones 5–8.

BLEEDING HEART Choose from either fringed bleeding heart *(Dicentra exima)* or old-fashioned bleeding heart *(Dicentra spectablis)*. Fringed bleeding heart grows less than a foot tall, with feathery foliage and white or pink flowers all season long except in the heat of summer. Old-fashioned bleeding heart sends forth spectacular arches of heart-shape blooms in pink and white in spring and then its foilage dies back. Both types thrive in Zones 3–9.

AZURE MONKSHOOD *(Aconitum carmichaelii)* Resembling delphinium, this perennial produces spikes of beautiful deep blue flowers in early fall. It grows 4 to 6 feet tall. Zones 3–7.

SPIDERWORT *(Tradescantia* spp.) This plant with grassy foliage produces clusters of blue, purple, or white flowers on stems that grow up to 3 feet tall. Zones 4–9.

Azure monkshood

Ajuga

Spiderwort

Bleeding heart

Yellow corydalis

Astilbe

Hostas By A Fountain

What could be more cooling—or cooler—than a water feature surrounded by moisture-loving hostas?

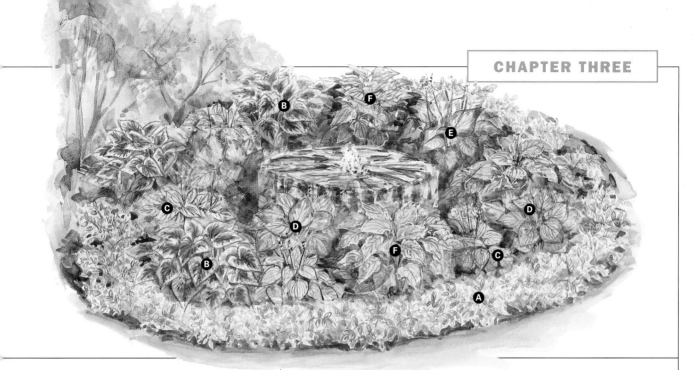

WATER AND SHADE ARE A NATURAL PAIRING. THEY BRING TO MIND BABBLING BROOKS AND LEAFY RIVERSIDES. RECREATE THAT FEELING IN YOUR OWN BACKYARD.

The centerpiece of this evocative garden is a millstone fountain. Millstone replica versions are readily available at many garden centers. Or you can substitute a different ready-made fountain kit. Just set it up, fill with water, plug it in, and enjoy! (Note: You'll need a GFCI outdoor electrical source for the fountain. Have an electrician install a GFCI outlet near the desired fountain location. As the plants grow they will hide the electrical source.)

Surround the fountain with a variety of hostas. The plan suggests specific cultivars, but you can mix and match with your favorite types. The key is to include a range of colors (yellow-green, variegated green and white, blue-green) and textures (smooth, crinkled, and curled leaves).

Smaller, variegated types of wintercreeper make an excellent, low-maintenance edging. However, be sure to seek out a cultivar that grows no more than 2 feet high and 2 feet wide, such as 'Emerald 'n' Gold' and some types of 'Green 'n' Gold' (check the label to be certain on size). Other types of wintercreeper can get 5 or 6 feet high and wide.

Alternative shade-tolerant edging plants include impatiens, lady's mantle, bergenia, and fringed bleeding heart.

PLANT LIST

A. **30 Small-growing wintercreepers** *(Euonymous fortunei)*: Zones 5–9

B. **3 Green and white variegated hostas** such as 'Night Before Christmas': Zones 3–8

C. **4 Blue-green hostas,** such as 'Halcyon': Zones 3–8

D. **2 Yellow-green hostas with blue-green splashes** such as 'Tokudama Aureonebulosa': Zones 3–8

E. **2 Gold hostas with blue-green edging** such as 'Paul's Glory': Zones 3–8

F. **3 Fragrant hostas** *(Hosta plantaginea)*: Zones 3–8

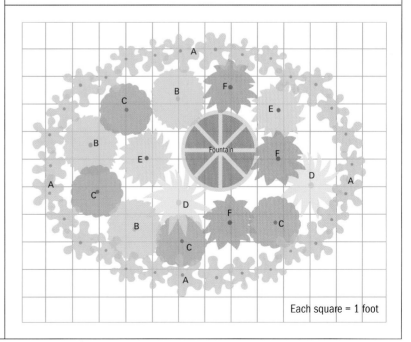

Each square = 1 foot

A Garden By The Woods

This shade-loving bed makes a perfect transition from lawn to woods. In fact, it's ideal for just about any low-light location.

SEAMLESSLY BLEND A MANICURED LAWN WITH TOWERING TREES BY PLANTING A PLEASANT, CURVING STRIP OF PERENNIALS.

The boundary between a wooded area and a lawn can be tricky to landscape. A formal flowerbed looks artificial juxtaposed with the wild of the woods. And a more casual planting can look like an unkempt extension of the wooded area.

This border is a perfect solution. It's filled with plants that naturally do well in the partial shade found near mature trees.

Birdhouses on posts add vertical accents to the bed and mimic the tree trunks that form a backdrop to the garden. The bird abodes help further tame the planting, indicating the touch of humans on the border. Boulders dug up from elsewhere on the property are positioned to serve as natural sculptures. If your property is stone-free, you could use rocks from another local source, or substitute additional plants or garden ornaments.

You could also plant this border next to a tall fence or alongside a building that casts light shade.

PLANT LIST

A. 5 **Yellow-green hybrid hostas** such as 'Piedmont Gold': Zones 3–8

B. 1 **Blue-green hosta** such as 'Hadspen Blue': Zones 3–8

C. 1 **Green with gold edge hosta** such as 'Golden Tiara': Zones 3–8

D. 3 **Caladiums** (Caladium bicolor): Zones 8–11, annual elsewhere

E. 2 **Yellow-green hostas with blue-green edge** such as 'Captain Kirk': Zones 3–8

F. 1 **Siebold hosta** (Hosta sieboldiana): Zones 3–8

G. 1 **Blue-green hosta with gold edges** such as 'Tokudama Flavocircinalis': Zones 3–8

H. 6 **Lungworts** (Pulmonaria saccharata) such as 'Mrs. Moon': Zones 4–8

I. 9 **Woodland phloxes** (Phlox divaricata): Zones 4–9

J. 1 **Cutleaf Japanese maple** (Acer palmatum 'Dissectum Rubrifolium'): Zones 6–8

K. 5 **Impatiens** (Impatiens walleriana): Annual

L. 2 **Large yellow-green hostas** such as 'Sum and Substance': Zones 3–8

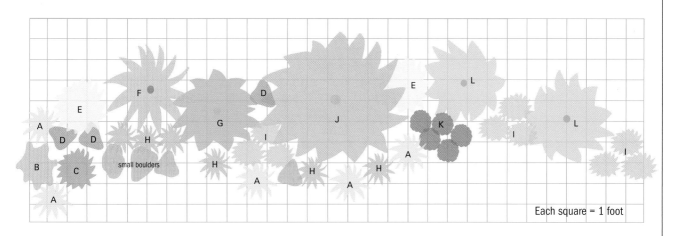

A
B
E
D D
C
small boulders
H
F
G
H
A
D
I
A
H
J
A
H
E
A
K
L
I
L
I
I

Each square = 1 foot

TIPS FOR LANDSCAPING NEAR WOODLANDS

Step up with shrubs. Shrubs and small landscape trees help the eye to visually adjust to taller woodland trees. A border of shrubs is extremely effective in blending cultivated areas with woodland.

Go natural. Accent the garden with nature-themed accessories. The birdhouses and stones in this garden are excellent examples. Also consider bee skeps, decorative bird feeders, driftwood, or small statues of woodland animals.

Outsmart the animals. Rather than fighting the deer and rabbits, seek out and plant flowers and shrubs that they find less tasty and are more likely to leave alone.

Shade Pocket Garden

Illuminate a small low-light nook with colorful plants that don't need much sun.

NEARLY EVERY YARD HAS ONE—A DARK CORNER TUCKED AWAY WHERE NOTHING BUT WEEDS SEEM TO GROW. FIX IT!

It could be a spot by your back door, a niche between your garage and house, or a forlorn corner of your yard that cries out for sprucing up. Fill it will colorful shade-loving plants that are easy to grow.

Two large hostas dominate the back of this planting. Even when the hostas lack flowers, their foliage is attractive. If you choose hostas that have leaf edges variegated in yellow, cream, or white, the planting will pop even more.

Caladiums also play a key role in this bed. Few plants adapted to shade are wildly colorful, but caladiums fit the bill. They thrive in summer's heat and humidity. Although they are perennial only in Zones 10 and 11, gardeners in colder areas can save the cost of replacing them annually by digging up tubers in the fall and storing them over winter. Another cost-saving idea: Substitute coleus for the caladiums. They provide color at a fraction of the cost.

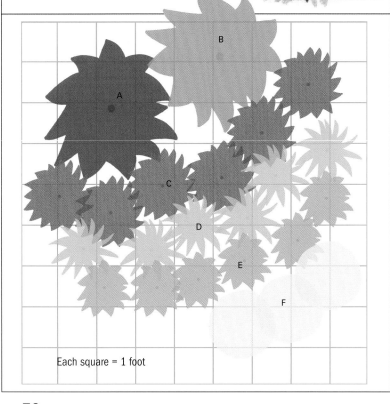

Each square = 1 foot

PLANT LIST	
A.	**1 Green hosta with white edge** such as 'Regal Splendor': Zones 3–8
B.	**1 Green hosta with gold edge** such as 'Yellow River': Zones 3–8
C.	**6 Red caladiums** (*Caladium bicolor*) such as 'Florida Cardinal': Zones 10–11, annual elsewhere
D.	**6 Chartreuse caladiums with red flecks** (*Caladium bicolor*) such as 'Miss Muffet': Zones 10–11, annual elsewhere
E.	**6 Lungworts** (*Pulmonaria saccharata*): Zones 4–8
F.	**3 Impatiens** (*Impatiens walleriana*): Zones 10–11, annual elsewhere

Caladium
'Florida Cardinal'

PLANT SUPERSTAR
CALADIUM

Caladiums look like the exotic tropical plants they are. In their native Central and South America, they grow on the banks of streams of rain forests in gorgeous swaths of color. Their big, arrow-shape leaves have vivid markings, often speckled or veined, in pinks, greens, reds, silvers, and whites. Dwarf types grow just a foot tall while taller types can reach 3 feet. Leaves can be as small as 6 inches or as long as 2 feet.

Caladiums are available in the spring either as established plants in pots or as tubers. Most varieties prefer at least afternoon shade, though some newer types tolerate sun. Provide plenty of water (1 inch or more per week) to actively growing plants. Caladiums prefer loose, moist soil, so work in plenty of compost at planting time.

Caladiums will come back year after year in subtropical regions (Zones 10 to 11). They won't tolerate frost. In colder regions you can treat them as annuals and let them die out in fall. Or to save the cost of replacing them next year, dig the caladium tubers after the first frost. Remove soil from the tubers, and store them indoors in sawdust or dry peat moss in a cool (60°F) location. Pot up the tubers in late winter to get a head start on spring planting.

Minimum H₂O, Maximum Show

This drought-tolerant garden is filled with plants that are at their prime in the heat of late summer.

BY AUGUST AND SEPTEMBER, MANY LANDSCAPES LOOK WORN OUT. BUT WITH SMART PLANT SELECTION, YOU CAN HAVE A GARDEN THAT COMES INTO ITS OWN AS SUMMER WANES, LIGHTING UP YOUR YARD JUST WHEN IT NEEDS IT MOST.

This easy-care garden is designed with plants that peak in late summer and early autumn. They're also drought-tolerant, requiring little water to thrive, saving you time, money, and effort.

The plan includes two types of ornamental grasses, which, with their graceful foliage and beautiful seed heads, are showy enough to star in the late summer garden. This design also delivers blasts of color from torch lilies and golden black-eyed susans.

The birdbath serves as a focal point. For a shallower planting, better suited for lining against a fence or building, omit the Matilija poppy in the back. If you have a long, narrow space to fill, simply repeat the garden a time or two to extend the length of the bed.

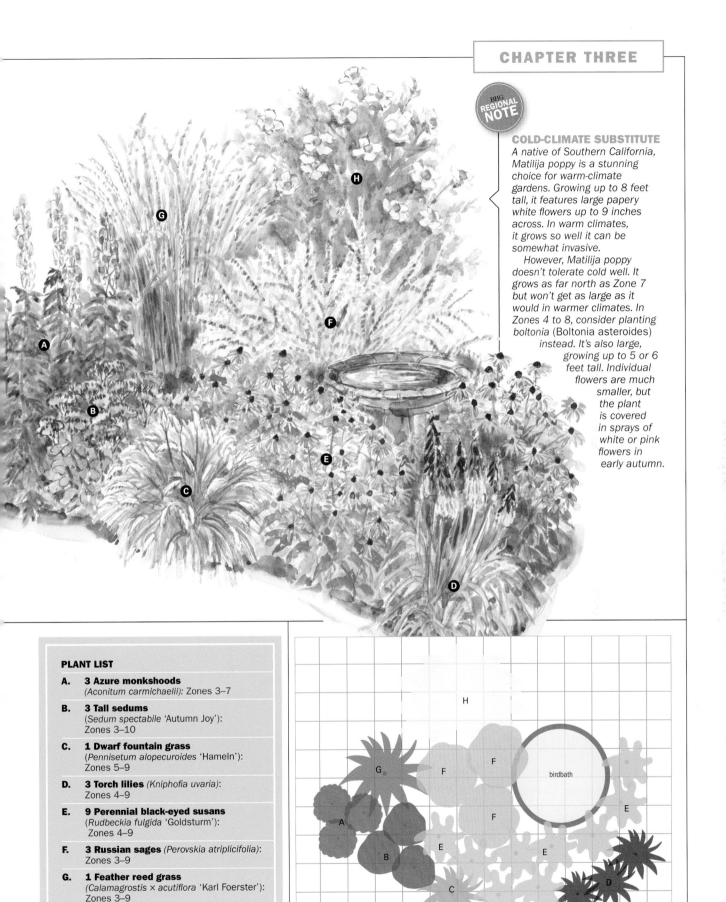

REGIONAL NOTE

COLD-CLIMATE SUBSTITUTE

A native of Southern California, Matilija poppy is a stunning choice for warm-climate gardens. Growing up to 8 feet tall, it features large papery white flowers up to 9 inches across. In warm climates, it grows so well it can be somewhat invasive.

However, Matilija poppy doesn't tolerate cold well. It grows as far north as Zone 7 but won't get as large as it would in warmer climates. In Zones 4 to 8, consider planting boltonia (Boltonia asteroides) instead. It's also large, growing up to 5 or 6 feet tall. Individual flowers are much smaller, but the plant is covered in sprays of white or pink flowers in early autumn.

PLANT LIST

A. **3 Azure monkshoods**
(*Aconitum carmichaelii*): Zones 3–7

B. **3 Tall sedums**
(*Sedum spectabile* 'Autumn Joy'):
Zones 3–10

C. **1 Dwarf fountain grass**
(*Pennisetum alopecuroides* 'Hameln'):
Zones 5–9

D. **3 Torch lilies** (*Kniphofia uvaria*):
Zones 4–9

E. **9 Perennial black-eyed susans**
(*Rudbeckia fulgida* 'Goldsturm'):
Zones 4–9

F. **3 Russian sages** (*Perovskia atriplicifolia*):
Zones 3–9

G. **1 Feather reed grass**
(*Calamagrostis* × *acutiflora* 'Karl Foerster'):
Zones 3–9

H. **1 Matilija poppy** (*Romneya coulteri*):
Zones 7–11, annual elsewhere

Each square = 1 foot

Curb Your Water Use

Give up the grass! Instead plant water-wise native flowers and grasses.

SOME GARDENERS CALL IT THE HELL STRIP—THAT BIT OF GROUND BETWEEN THE STREET AND SIDEWALK THAT'S TOUGH TO MAINTAIN. BUT YOU CAN TURN IT INTO A HEAVENLY OASIS OF COLOR AND BLOOM.

Surrounded by concrete and filled with compacted clay, sand, and gravel, the hell strip often becomes a hot, dry wasteland ill-suited to growing cool-season turf. The shallow roots of lawn grasses are not adapted to such difficult locations.

Instead, plant an assortment of street-smart perennials that thrive with minimal supplemental water and don't mind the hot spot between two strips of pavement. The plants in the plan are native to sun-drenched prairies so they scoff at the extremes found curbside. And since they're survivors, they're easy to care for, with few pest problems and little need for staking, pruning, or fertilizing.

You can adapt this plan to a variety of sizes, depending on the width of your planting area. The plan would also work well along a driveway or front walk.

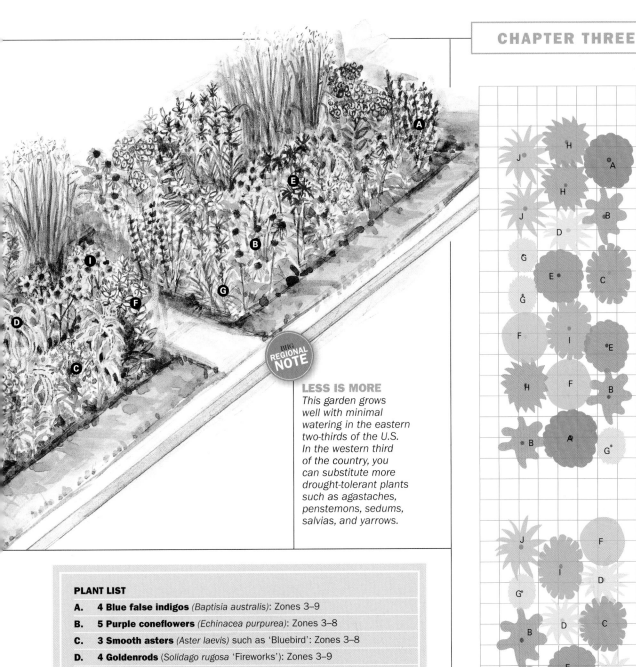

REGIONAL NOTE

LESS IS MORE
This garden grows well with minimal watering in the eastern two-thirds of the U.S. In the western third of the country, you can substitute more drought-tolerant plants such as agastaches, penstemons, sedums, salvias, and yarrows.

PLANT LIST

A. **4 Blue false indigos** (*Baptisia australis*): Zones 3–9

B. **5 Purple coneflowers** (*Echinacea purpurea*): Zones 3–8

C. **3 Smooth asters** (*Aster laevis*) such as 'Bluebird': Zones 3–8

D. **4 Goldenrods** (*Solidago rugosa* 'Fireworks'): Zones 3–9

E. **4 Bee balms** (*Monarda didyma*) such as 'Jacob Kline': Zones 4–9

F. **3 Turtleheads** (*Chelone lyonii*): Zones 3–8

G. **4 Tall gayfeathers** (*Liatris scariosa*): Zones 4–8

H. **6 Garden phloxes** (*Phlox paniculata*) such as 'Shortwood': Zones 4–8

I. **2 False sunflowers** (*Heliopsis helianthoides*): Zones 3–9

J. **5 Switchgrasses** (*Panicum virgatum*): Zones 2–9

WORK SAVER

For easier care, eliminate the strip of turf around the garden. While trimmed turf makes an attractive carpet around the garden, it requires frequent mowing and edging to prevent grass from creeping into the bed. If you plant the entire swath between the curb and sidewalk with native perennials, you can eliminate the weekly chore of mowing.

Each square = 1 foot

No Water, No Fuss

This drought-tolerant garden is filled with easy-to-grow perennials that need minimal care.

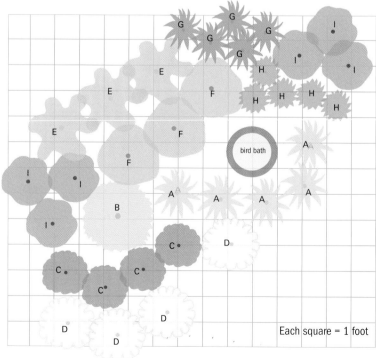

Each square = 1 foot

PLANT IT AND (ALMOST) FORGET IT! THIS GARDEN IS FILLED WITH TOUGH-AS-NAILS PERENNIALS THAT COME BACK EACH YEAR.

Even then, they need little more than the occasional tidying up.

Silvery gray-green foliage is a common thread tying together drought-tolerant perennials such as santolina, lavender, yarrow, Russian sage, and catmint. It coordinates well with the centerpiece blue birdbath, which adds a touch of cooling moisture to the dry garden and draws in feathered visitors.

Most dry-climate plants demand excellent drainage, so where soils are heavy, work in plenty of compost or grit, such as sharp sand, to improve drainage. Gravel is the mulch of choice for plants that like good drainage. It quickly drains excess water away from the plants' crowns—where stems meet the roots—to thwart fungal rot problems.

PLANT LIST

A. **5 Catmints**
(Nepeta × faassenii):
Zones 3–8

B. **1 Yarrow**
(Achillea 'Moonshine'):
Zones 3–9

C. **4 English lavenders**
(Lavandula angustifolia),
such as 'Hidcote' or 'Munstead':
Zones 5–8

D. **4 Santolinas**
(Santolina chamaecyparissus):
Zones 5–10

E. **3 Russian sages**
(Perovskia atriplicifolia):
Zones 5–9

F. **3 Purple coneflowers**
(Echinacea purpurea):
Zones 3–8

G. **5 Firecracker pentstemons**
(Penstemon eatonii):
Zones 4–9

H. **5 Pineleaf pentstemons**
(Penstemon pinifolius):
Zones 4–10

I. **6 Garden phloxes**
(Phlox paniculata):
Zones 4–8

Penstemon serratus

Agastache

Yucca

Artemisia 'Powis Castle'

Salvia greggii

PLANT SUPERSTARS
PERENNIALS THAT NEED MINIMAL WATER

In addition to the plants featured in this garden, many other excellent perennials thrive in low-water sites. Here are five of the best. All plants listed need full sun.

PENSTEMON (*Penstemon* spp.) Beyond the two species included in this plan, dozens of cold-hardy and drought-tolerant penstemons are available. *P. barbatus* 'Elfin Pink' (Zones 4–8) has pink tubular blooms on 2-foot stems. 'Red Rocks' and 'Pike's Peak Purple' (Zones 5–9) grow only 18 inches tall.

AGASTACHE (*Agastache* spp.) The tubular flowers of this perennial are a favorite of hummingbirds. Grows up to 3 feet tall. 'Desert Sunrise', a cross between *A. cana* and *A. rupestris*, is a particularly beautiful and water-thrifty cultivar with peachy pink blooms. Zones 5–10.

YUCCA (*Yucca* spp.) The sword-like foliage of yucca is impressive. Dramatic creamy white flowers appear on tall stalks each year. Adam's needle (*Y. filamentosa*, Zones 5–10), is common in the east. Beaked yucca (*Y. rostrata*, Zones 6–9) has a finer texture and is better adapted in drier climates.

ARTEMISIA (*Artemisia* spp.) Flowers are secondary to the silvery foliage of artemisia. 'Powis Castle' is 3 feet tall and nearly as wide, Zones 4–9. *Artemisia* 'Sea Foam', just 8 inches tall, has frothy curled silver foliage, but is best adapted to areas with low humidity. Zones 4–10.

SALVIA (*Salvia* spp.) Also known as sage, perennial salvias range in color from blue to purple, scarlet, or pink. *S. nemorosa* 'May Night', Zones 4–9, is a popular deep-blue spring and summer bloomer. Autumn sage (*S. greggii*, Zones 6–10) blooms later in the season.

A Splash of Color

Surround a cooling fountain with drought-tolerant plants, the perfect combo of refreshing flowers and foliage for a parched site.

DROUGHT-TOLERANT BY DESIGN

With some clever design tricks, you can reduce the amount of water you need to pour onto your landscape.

Group plants according to water needs. Create an oasis zone close to the house (and water source) for thirsty plants. Group plants that need only occasional watering farther out. Place the most self-sufficient plants at the perimeter of the property.

Reduce lawn. Replace thirsty lawn grasses with beds and borders of ornamental grasses, low-water groundcovers, and drought-tolerant perennials and shrubs.

Create shade. Afternoon shade is especially helpful to plants that wilt under intense sun. Plant trees that have a high canopy and cast dappled shade. Or construct a lattice house, a pergola, or other structure that casts shade.

EVEN IN THE DRIEST CLIMATES, THIS GARDEN WILL THRIVE. IT'S FILLED WITH PLANTS THAT NEED LITTLE SUPPLEMENTAL WATER AND YET OVERFLOWS WITH COLOR AND FRAGRANCE.

Forget the water-guzzling landscape. In this earth-friendly plan, lavender, sweet alyssum, Russian sage, thyme, iris, cosmos, and sedum offer up a garden filled with lush aromas and gorgeous flowers but require little supplemental moisture.

A footpath meanders through the garden to bring visitors up close to enjoy the sweet perfume of alyssum and the pungent scents of the herbs.

These plants adapt to the thin, dry soils of arid regions. However, they'll grow much better if you work compost into the soil at planting time.

The three-tiered formal fountain provides a pleasant contrast to the low, informal plantings surrounding it. At the same time, it balances the taller plantings at the opposite end of the garden and brings the element of sound to the garden with its splashing water.

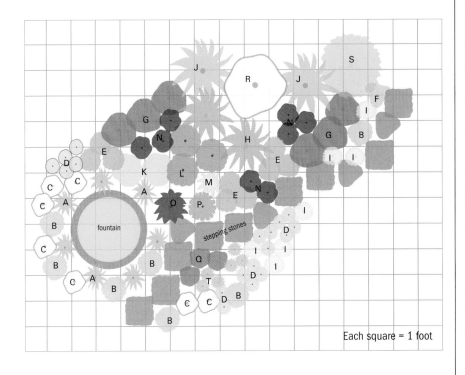

Each square = 1 foot

PLANT LIST

A. 7 Blue fescues
(*Festuca glauca*):
Zones 4–8

B. 7 Thymes
(*Thymus* spp.):
Zones 4–9

C. 7 Snow-in-summer
(*Cerastium tomentosum*):
Zones 2–8

D. 18 Johnny-jump-ups
(*Viola tricolor*):
Annual, reseeding

E. 9 Yellow cosmoses
(*Cosmos sulphureus*):
Annual

F. 1 Foothill penstemon
(*Penstemon heterophyllus*):
Zones 6–10

G. 6 English lavenders
(*Lavandula angustifolia*)
such as 'Munstead':
Zones 5–9

H. 2 Russian sages
(*Perovskia atriplicifolia*):
Zones 6–9

I. 7 Sweet alyssums
(*Lobularia maritima*):
Annual

**J. 2 Silver Feather
maiden grasses**
(*Miscanthus sinensis*
'Silver Feather'):
Zones 4–9

K. 2 Torch lilies
(*Kniphofia uvaria*):
Zones 6–9

L. 3 Showy sedums
(*Sedum spectabile*
'Autumn Joy'):
Zones 3–10

M. 1 Asiatic lily
(*Lilium* hybrids):
Zones 3–9

N. 8 Ice plants
(*Delosperma cooperi*):
Zones 5–9

O. 1 Siberian iris
(*Iris sibirica*):
Zones 3–9

P. 1 Pincushion flower
(*Scabiosa columbaria*):
Zones 3–8

Q. 3 Turkish speedwells
(*Veronica liwanensis*):
Zones 4–9

R. 1 Brugmansia
(*Brugmansia* hybrids):
Zones 10–11, annual elsewhere

S. 1 Rocky Mountain juniper
(*Juniperus scopulorum*):
Zones 4–7

T. 6 Dwarf hairy penstemons
(*Penstemon hirsutus* 'Pygmaeus'):
Zones 3–9

Fill a Slope With Fragrant Flowers

Tame a slope with roses and other fragrant beauties for a garden that's spectacular from top to bottom.

LANDSCAPING A HILLSIDE CAN BE A DAUNTING TASK, BUT THIS PLAN BREAKS IT DOWN AND MAKES IT EASY.

This landscape plan delivers. It will turn even the most forlorn slope into a showstopper with an array of beautiful low-maintenance roses combined with fragrant annual and perennial flowers. Partnering reblooming roses with nonstop bloomers such as pincushion flower and alyssum ensures a dramatic show. Anchoring the base of the slope with railroad ties raises the garden for better viewing and creates a strong contrast to billowy mounds of flowers.

The plan lists specific easy-care shrub roses in pink and white, but you can substitute your favorites or what your local garden center has in stock. Choose low-maintenance landscape roses, such as those in the Knock Out, Flower Carpet, or Easy Elegance series. This is especially important in Zones 5 and colder, where winter protection is an issue. 'Polar Joy' is a good substitute for the 'Iceberg' tree rose in these colder regions.

DESIGN TIPS FOR SLOPES

Control erosion. Avoid working the soil excessively. Make narrow, deep planting holes to minimize disturbing the surface soil.

Terrace to tame a slope. In addition to landscape timbers, you can use flagstones or paving stones stacked two or three high to create a short wall. Make a solid base for the wall and bury the first layer in soil.

Opt for shrubs and perennials. Their extensive root systems better anchor the soil. Also, you don't have to dig up the soil each year as you would with annual flowers.

Choose heavy mulch. Mulch prevents erosion, but light mulches, such as pine needles or cocoa hulls, wash away easily. Choose nugget-size chunks of bark that are more likely to remain in place.

Consider containers. Potted plants add interest. Slightly bury the base into a slope for stability. Fill each with brilliant annuals for bright spots of color.

GARDEN SMARTER
DO IT YOURSELF?

When landscaping a slope, it can be tricky to figure out whether you should create the terraces or low retaining walls yourself or have a pro do it. If the walls will be no more than a foot high, you're probably safe. Otherwise, hire a professional to prevent frustrating erosion or a potentially dangerous collapse.

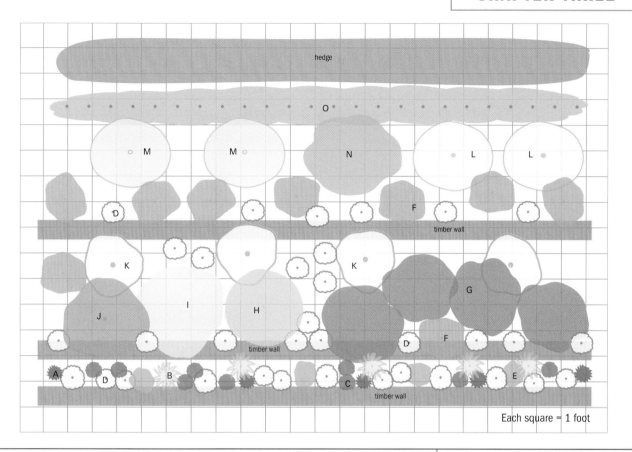

hedge

O

M M N L L

D F

timber wall

K K G

J I H

D F

timber wall

A D B C E

timber wall

Each square = 1 foot

PLANT LIST

A. **5 Pink or red annual phloxes**
(Phlox drummondii): Annual

B. **5 Flowering tobaccos**
(Nicotiana × sanderae): Annual

C. **9 Blue or purple violas**
(Viola tricolor): Annual

D. **34 Sweet alyssums**
(Lobularia maritima): Annual

E. **4 Edging lobelias**
(Lobelia erinus): Annual

F. **9 Pink or blue pincushion flowers**
(Scabiosa columbaria): Zones 3–9

G. **4 Pink shrub roses** such as 'Gertrude
Jekyll': Zones 5–9

H. **1 Pink shrub rose** such as 'Heritage':
Zones 5—9

I. **1 Soft pink shrub rose** such as
Katherine Morely: Zones 5–9

J. **1 Apricot-color shrub rose** such as
'Abraham Darby': Zones 4–9

K. **4 'Iceberg' or other white tree roses**:
Zones 6–9

L. **2 White floribunda roses** such as
'Margaret Merril': Zones 5–10

M. **2 Soft pink shrub roses** such as
'Sheer Bliss': Zones 6–10

N. **1 Pink shrub rose** such as 'Hero':
Zones 4–9

O. **24 Foxgloves**
(Digitalis purpurea): Zones 4–8

Tough Flowers To Tame a Slope

These cold-climate perennials and colorful annuals are a resourceful solution for a problem incline.

A BEAUTIFUL TUMBLE OF PERENNIALS AND ANNUALS SOFTENS THE LOOK OF STONES USED TO HOLD BACK THE HILL WHILE ROOTS PREVENT EROSION.

A fence and hedge provide protection from drying, chilling winds for this garden. Several boulders allow convenient access for tending the garden without compacting the soil. A low stone terrace wall (concealed by the plantings), installed at the same time as the cut stone and brick stairway, unifies the planting with the hardscape materials, prevents erosion, and provides a good spot to stand while weeding and watering.

The perennials selected for this sloped garden are especially cold-hardy. There are also a few annuals tucked in for continuous color from spring through frost.

retaining wall

rock

Each square = 1 foot

Basket-of-gold

Candytuft

Ice plant

Rock soapwort

Snow-in-summer

Stonecrop

PLANT SUPERSTARS

CASCADING PERENNIALS FOR SLOPES

Some of the best plants for slopes are those that tumble and spread, growing no more than a foot high. Substitute some of these for plants in the planting plan, or use them to create a beautiful slope garden all your own.

BASKET-OF-GOLD (*Aurinia saxatilis*) This short-lived perennial thrives in poor, dry soil. It creates a carpet of beautiful golden yellow flowers in spring. Give it full sun. Zones 4–10.

CANDYTUFT (*Iberis sempervirens*) The perennial version of the annual candytuft featured in the garden plan bears pure white flowers atop evergreen foliage in spring. Full sun. Zones 5–9.

ICE PLANT (*Delosperma cooperi*) The magenta flowers of ice plant cover succulent evergreen foliage in summer. It needs excellent drainage and full zun. Zones 5–9.

ROCK SOAPWORT (*Saponaria ocymoides*) Soapwort has spreading lustrous green foliage topped with pink flowers in late spring to early summer. Cut it back after the first flush of bloom for a repeat cycle. It prefers full sun but tolerates partial shade. Zones 2–7.

SNOW-IN-SUMMER (*Cerastium tomentosum*) Snow-white flowers atop of gray foliage give the plant its common name. It needs excellent drainage and full sun. Zones 3–7.

STONECROP (*Sedum* spp.) Tough succulents that love full sun and hot, dry conditions, the various stonecrops pair beautifully with rocks. Goldmoss stonecrop (*S. acre*) bears yellow flowers. Two-row stonecrop (*S. spurium*) has white or pink blooms. Zones 3–9.

PLANT LIST

A. **5 Gazanias** (*Gazania rigens*): Zones 8–10, annual elsewhere

B. **1 Petunia** (*Petunia* × *hybrida*): Annual

C. **10 Globe candytufts** (*Iberis umbellata*): Annual

D. **2 Tufted hair grasses** (*Deschampsia cespitosa*): Zones 4–9

E. **6 Pinks** (*Dianthus* spp.): Annual

F. **1 Showy sedum** (*Sedum spectabile*): Zones 4–9

G. **3 Shasta daisies** (*Leucanthemum* × *superbum*): Zones 4–8

H. **2 Oriental poppies** (*Papaver orientale*): Zones 3–8

I. **3 Lupines** (*Lupinus perennis*): Zones 4–9

J. **1 Lychnis** (*Lychnis* × *arkwrightii*): Zones 4–8

K. **5 Tickseeds** (*Coreopsis grandiflora*): Zones 4–9

L. **4 Hollyhocks** (*Alcea rosea*): Biennial

M. **1 Black-eyed susan** (*Rudbeckia fulgida*): Zones 4–9

Sky High Gardening

Mountain climates mean rapid temperature changes, short growing seasons, and problem soils. This garden defies them all.

HIGH-ALTITUDE GARDENERS ARE BLESSED WITH GORGEOUS MOUNTAIN VIEWS BUT HERE'S A GARDEN SO SPECTACULAR IT WILL RIVAL EVEN THE MOST MAGNIFICENT BACKDROP.

The key to this garden is a raised bed. It not only creates a level planting surface that prevents erosion but also makes soil amendment easy. Simply fill the bed with best-quality topsoil or a blend of compost and soil. On a more sloping site, you might need timbers on only three sides of the bed, snugging it into the hillside.

This bed is filled with tough annuals and perennials that withstand the vagaries of mountain weather— warm temperatures one day, cold winds the next.

TIPS FOR SUCCESS AT HIGH ALTITUDES

Add organic matter. Rocky, gravelly soils drain well but hold few nutrients. Mix in up to one-third by volume of compost to the existing soil.

Choose native plants. Seek out plants that tolerate the temperature extremes found at high altitudes. Plants native to mountainous areas have evolved over centuries to deal with this very problem.

Protect from winds. Position beds and borders in sheltered areas, especially from west and north winds. Plant evergreens such as pines, spruces, and junipers to buffer plantings.

PLANT LIST

A. **1 Showy sedum** (*Sedum spectabile*): Zones 4–9

B. **1 German statice** (*Goniolimon tataricum*): Zones 4–9

C. **2 Black-eyed susans** (*Rudbeckia fulgida*): Zones 4–9

D. **7 Zinnias** (*Zinnia elegans*): Annual

E. **8 Bachelor's buttons** (*Centaurea cyanus*): Annual

F. **2 Ornamental kales** (*Brassica oleracea*): Annual

G. **9 Tall cosmoses** (*Cosmos bipinnatus*): Annual

H. **6 Snapdragons** (*Antirrhinum majus*): Zones 5–9

I. **9 Ageratums** (*Ageratum houstonianum*): Annual

J. **3 Edging lobelias** (*Lobelia erinus*): Annual

K. **5 Corn poppies** (*Papaver rhoeas*): Annual

L. **1 African daisy** (*Osteospermum* spp.): Zones 10–11, annual elsewhere

M. **2 Calendulas** (*Calendula officinalis*): Annual

REGIONAL NOTE

THE LOW DOWN ON DIRT

So what soil to use for filling raised beds? The top 18 inches of the bed should be excellent quality topsoil with ample amounts of compost worked in. If the bed is deeper, soil underneath can be ordinary low-quality "fill dirt."

Each square = 1 foot

Pondside Planting

Take your water feature to the next level by surrounding it with luxurious plantings.

TOO OFTEN, WATER GARDENS ARE PLUNKED DOWN INTO LANDSCAPES WITHOUT ANY PLANTINGS AROUND THEM TO HELP BLEND IN. THIS PLAN SOLVES THAT PROBLEM, ADDING TEXTURE, COLOR, AND INTEREST WHILE INTEGRATING THE POOL INTO ITS SURROUNDINGS.

A water garden is beautiful in its own right, but adding plants around the edge anchors the pond to the landscape, creating the illusion that it's always been in place, and softens harsh edges.

This garden is lightly shaded from a large tree nearby, so part of it is surrounded with plants adapted to light shade—hostas, astilbes, lungworts, bleeding hearts, and ferns. Other less shady portions are filled with plants that need more sun—lamb's ears, catmint, ageratums, and speedwell.

Almost all the plants in this design need a uniform supply of moisture. But the pond does not supply water to the plants (except for anything growing directly in the water). Because the pond is lined, no water escapes, and the soil next to a water garden is no wetter than other areas of your yard. Water plants as necessary to avoid stress brought on by dry conditions.

And, of course, as with all the plans in this book, you can adapt the scheme to fit with your particular size and shape of water feature. Simply add, subtract, expand, or repeat plantings as desired!

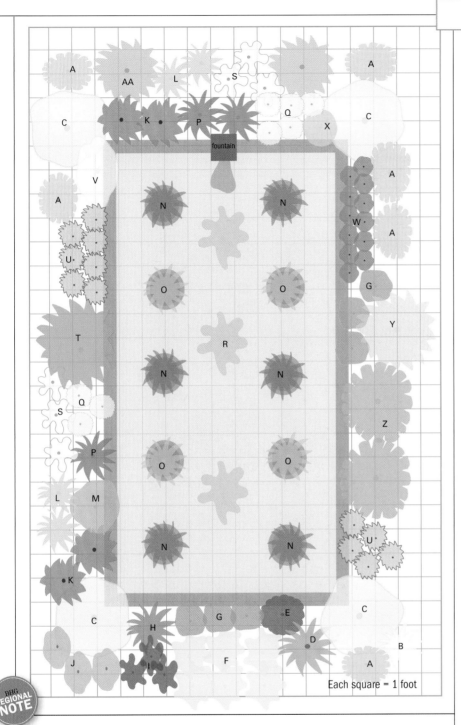

Each square = 1 foot

PLANT LIST

A. **6 Lamb's ears** *(Stachys byzantina)*: Zones 4–8

B. **1 White speedwell** *(Veronica spicata 'Icicle')*: Zones 3–8

C. **4 Azaleas** *(Rhododendron)* such as 'Delaware Valley White'): Zones 6–8

D. **1 Spiderwort** *(Tradescantia spp.)*: Zones 4–9

E. **1 Hardy geranium** *(Geranium spp.)*: Zones 4–9

F. **6 Lady's mantles** *(Alchemilla mollis)*: Zones 4-7

G. **6 Moss phlox** *(Phlox subulata)*: Zones 3–8

H. **1 Japanese painted fern** *(Athyrium niponicum var. pictum)*: Zones 4–8

I. **3 New Guinea impatiens** *(Impatiens hawkeri)*: Annual

J. **3 Fringed bleeding hearts** *(Dicentra eximia)*: Zones 4–8

K. **4 Lungworts** *(Pulmonaria saccharata)*: Zones 4–8

L. **4 Variegated Japanese sedges** *(Carex morrowii)*: Zones 5–9

M. **1 Ladybells** *(Adenophora confusa)*: Zones 3–8

N. **6 Japanese irises** *(Iris ensata)*: Zones 5–8

O. **4 Ribbon grasses** *(Phalaris arundinacea picta)*: Zones 4–9

P. **3 Wood ferns** *(Dryopteris spp.)*: Zones 4–8

Q. **8 Ageratums** *(Ageratum houstonianum 'Hawaii Shell Pink')*: Annual

R. **3 Waterlilies** *(Nymphea spp.)*

S. **6 Creeping lilyturfs** *(Liriope spicata)*: Zones 5–10

T. **1 Siebold hosta** *(Hosta sieboldiana 'Elegans')*: Zones 3–8

U. **12 Astilbes** *(Astilbe × arendsii 'Bridal Veil')*: Zones 4–9

V. **1 Tube clematis** *(Clematis heracleifolia)*: Zones 3–8

W. **12 Pansies** *(Viola × wittrockiana)*: Zones 4–8

X. **1 Licorice plant** *(Helichrysum petiolare)*: Annual

Y. **1 Wormwood** *(Artemisia absinthium)*: Zones 4–8

Z. **2 Catmints** *(Nepeta 'Six Hills Giant')*: Zones 4–8

AA. **2 Junipers** *(Juniperus scopulorum 'Skyrocket')*: Zones 4–7

POND PLANTS IN POTS

Plants that love wet, boggy soil will do well in a pot set into a pond.

In addition to the Japanese iris and ribbon grass shown in the plan, numerous other "marginal" water garden plants adapt well to container culture in water. Arrowhead (Sagittaria spp.), canna (Canna × generalis), elephant's ear (Colocasia esculenta), yellow flag iris (Iris pseudacorus), cattail (Typha spp.), sweet flag (Acorus spp.), and papyrus (Cyperus spp.) are a few of the choices.

True to their name, these plants thrive in the shallow margins of water gardens. Many water gardens are designed with a shelf for holding containers of marginal plants. In deeper sections of the pond, you can place them on stacked stones, bricks, or concrete blocks to raise the pot to the correct height.

You can purchase special water garden potting soil or use ordinary garden soil in the pots. Be sure to mulch the surface with gravel or pebbles to prevent the soil from floating out.

Splash Of Color

A simple planting of perennials and annuals around the rim of a pond makes a colorful transition.

THIS PONDSIDE PLANTING HAS ONE END IN SHADE AND THE OTHER IN SUN. THIS DESIGN IS TAILORED TO A GRADATION IN LIGHT. THE END RESULT SOFTENS THE EDGES OF THE POND AND ADDS COLOR AND FRAGRANCE.

This water garden cried out for plantings around its perimeter, but the homeowners had to take care in plant selection because light levels change dramatically from one end of the pool to the other. Deep shade exists near the statuary fountain, perfect for fragrant hostas and English ivy cascading to the water's edge. At the other end of the pond, where more sunlight falls, a collection of colorful blooms beckons. Pinks, sedums, verbenas, spider flowers, and pentas flourish here.

Japanese irises in containers (shown in the photo but not the illustrations) mimic the natural growth of irises in the shallow portions of ponds in the wild, and create a transition with the plantings outside of the pool. To grow Japanese irises partially submerged in water, plant them in garden soil in a pot. Place the rim of the container just below the surface of the water. If your pond has no shallow shelf, place the pot on bricks or concrete blocks to adjust the depth to the correct level.

PLANT LIST

A. **3 Fragrant hostas** *(Hosta plantaginea)*: Zones 3–8

B. **8 English ivies** *(Hedera helix)*: Zones 5–10

C. **2 Fan flowers** *(Scaevola aemula)*: Annual

D. **8 Pinks** *(Dianthus hybrids)*: Annual

E. **5 Low-growing sedums** *(Sedum rupestre)* such as 'Angelina': Zones 6–9

F. **8 Verbenas** *(Verbena × hybrida)*: Annual

G. **5 Ajugas** *(Ajuga reptans)*: Zones 3–8

H. **5 Pentases** *(Pentas lanceolata)*: Annual

I. **3 Golden moneyworts** *(Lysimachia nummularia* 'Aurea'): Zones 4–8

J. **4 Japanese irises** *(Iris ensata)*: Zones 4–8

K. **1 Dwarf Virginia sweetspire** *(Itea virginica* 'Little Henry'): Zones 5–9

L. **3 Spider flowers** *(Cleome hassleriana)*: Annual

GARDEN SMARTER

TIPS FOR SUCCESSFUL PONDSIDE PLANTINGS

CONSIDER THE VANTAGE POINT. If the pond will be viewed from all sides, keep plantings low all around. However, if it will be viewed from only two or three sides, consider planting taller plants at the far side to create a backdrop for the pond.

PROVIDE CLOSE-UP VIEWING. Ponds attract people. Incorporate stepping stones or other access spots that allow one or two people to stand close and look down into the water.

CHOOSE ADAPTED PLANTS. Although the soil next to a pond is no wetter than other soil in the yard, place plants that love moisture, such as ferns, sedges, irises, ivies, and hostas, next to the pond. They'll look more natural adjacent to water than would drought-tolerant plants.

CONSIDER A BOG. Dig out an area 18 inches deep and fill with liner. Make a few slashes to create very slow drainage. Fill with rich topsoil and/ or compost. You'll have the perfect spot to nurture cattails, ligularia, astilbe, arrowhead, cannas, swamp iris, and other plants that love wet feet.

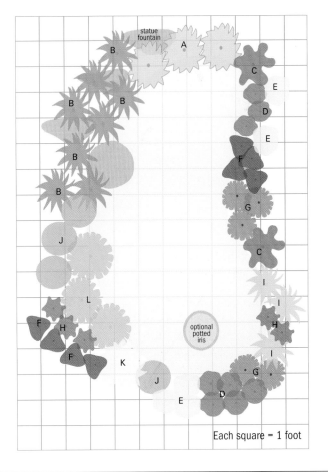

Each square = 1 foot

Seaside Solution

Don't let sweeping winds, sandy soils, and salt spray get your garden down. Work with nature rather than battling with it.

SMART PLANT SELECTION AND CLEVER GARDENING TRICKS TURN A SANDY, BARREN SITE INTO A SPECTACULAR GARDEN SETTING.

If you're lucky enough to live close to the sea, you may wish for it all: the beauty and pleasures of the nearby ocean *and* a flourishing garden.

The two need not be mutually exclusive. This plan highlights perennials that grow well in sandy soil and tolerate salty sites. They're best suited to cool conditions, capable of withstanding harsh New England winters.

A major challenge of gardening near the ocean is salt, both in the soil and in the air. (Winds can carry salt spray dozens of miles inland.) Salt burns leaves and stunts plant growth.

Winds pose another challenge. Those beach winds that make flying kites and sailing so wonderful tend to dry out soil and leaves, and can topple tall plants.

Sandy soil is problematic because it retains little water, so plants dry out quickly. In addition, its nutrient-poor nature starves plants unless you add supplemental organic matter and fertilizer.

However, you can overcome these elements by selecting adapted plants to create an oceanside garden that is nothing short of gorgeous.

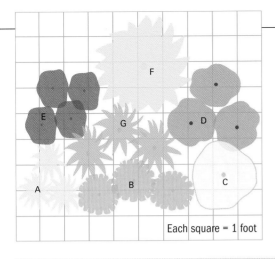

Each square = 1 foot

PLANT LIST

A. **3 Miniature daylilies** (*Hemerocallis* hybrid) such as 'Stella de Oro': Zones 3–10

B. **3 Lamb's ears** (*Stachys byzantina*): Zones 4–8

C. **1 Gooseneck loosestrife** (*Lysimachia clethroides*): Zones 4–9

D. **3 Rose campions** (*Lychnis coronaria*): Zones 4–8

E. **4 Maltese crosses** (*Lychnis chalcedonica*): Zones 4–8

F. **1 False sunflower** (*Heliopsis helianthoides*): Zones 4–9

G. **3 Large daylilies** (*Hemerocallis* hybrid) such as 'Lady Lucille': Zones 3–10

GARDEN SMARTER
GROW A BEAUTIFUL SEASIDE GARDEN

Wind, salt, and sandy soils all conspire to make gardening by the sea a challenge. But you can help nature along by selecting plants well suited to the conditions as well as by making some small changes to the environment.

PREPARE THE SOIL WELL. Add lots of compost to sandy and rocky soils to improve their ability to absorb water and to hold nutrients. Make a habit of spreading at least 1 inch of compost on top of the soil each spring.

SLOW THE WIND. Find a sheltered spot or plant fast-growing evergreens, such as pines or junipers, to use as a windbreak. In cold regions, this protects plants from drying, killing winter winds, and in all regions it makes plants dry out less in warm weather. It also screens salt spray.

START SMALL. Small plants acclimate more readily to difficult conditions than do larger plants moved from a favorable site.

Thrift

Caryopteris

Rugosa rose 'Hansa'

Catmint

Russian sage

PLANT SUPERSTARS
FIVE GREAT SEASIDE PLANTS

Plants that thrive in coastal conditions often possess waxy leaves or gray or silver foliage—sedum, artemisia, sea holly, and lavender are a few examples. Here are five additional outstanding blooming perennial plants to consider planting if you garden by the sea.

THRIFT (*Armeria maritima*) Sometimes called sea thrift, this low-growing plant with grassy foliage bears orbs of pink blooms on slender stalks up to 1 foot tall. Heaviest bloom is in spring, but it will bloom sporadically throughout the summer, especially if spent flowers are removed. Zones 3–8.

CARYOPTERIS (*Caryopteris* × *clandonensis*) Also known as blue-mist spirea, this shrub is best treated as a perennial that is cut back in fall after frost fells it. Tufts of blue blooms that attract bees line the silvery stems through late summer. Zones 5–8.

RUGOSA ROSE (*Rosa rugosa* hybrids) Deeply textured green foliage sets off the single blooms of rugosa rose, also called beach rose. Leaves can be glossy or rough. Dozens of different cultivars are available growing as low as 3 feet and as tall as 6 feet. Zones 2–7.

CATMINT (*Nepeta* spp.) Catmint—not the same thing as catnip—is a lovely mounded plant with scalloped silver foliage and short spikes of purple-blue flowers. Heaviest bloom occurs in late spring to early summer, but if you cut back the plant as blooms begin to fade it will reward you with an additional flush of blooms. Many different cultivars are available, some growing just a foot or two high with the largest, 'Six Hill's Giant', spreading 4 feet. Zones 4–9.

RUSSIAN SAGE (*Perovskia* × *atriplicifolia*) With light staking, shrubby Russian sage holds up well to gale-force winds. In mid- to late summer, it produces lavender-purple flowers on silvery gray stems up to 4 feet tall. Zones 4–10.

Creative Color Combos

Nature supplies a wide-ranging palette of colors that makes it easy for you to have fun playing around with all those shades and hues—just like a kid with a paint box.

A bed or border designed with thoughtful attention to color can make the difference between a planting that's simply pleasant to look at or one that's a knockout.

On the next few pages, you'll learn more about using color in the garden and find plans that will help you create beds and borders that will dazzle.

Working with Color

Do you love blue? Are you passionate about red? Does yellow make you feel happy just looking at it? Learn how to mix and match colors for glorious gardens that give you pleasure.

The orange of Oriental poppies pumps some excitement into an otherwise serene blue and purple garden of iris, salvia, gasplant, and penstemon.

No matter what colors you love, you'll have fun incorporating favorites into your garden. On the following pages, you'll see plans for beds and borders with specific color combinations. Use them exactly as they are for a tried-and-true showstopper or modify them to create a color-themed garden that is uniquely your own.

As with all things artistic, basic guidelines will help you achieve the best results:

Keep it simple. "Rainbow" is not a color scheme. Plant a hodge-podge of colors and guess what? The results look like, well, a hodge-podge. Decide on a limited combination of colors.

Get inspired. Gardening magazines, public gardens, and the Internet are good places to get ideas for bed and border color schemes. See a color combo you love? Tear it out or print it and refer to it while shopping for plants.

Focus on one color. This is an easy way to get started planting a color-themed garden. Check out the blue, yellow, red, all-white, and other single-color themed plantings on the following pages.

Combine two or three colors. Mix colors in your garden the way you would in your wardrobe. Unless you're a bold dresser, you'd never wear bright orange and magenta together in an outfit. But blues, purples, and pinks blend together well. Or try a combination of yellow, blue, and white.

Consider the effect of foliage. Leaf color may range from medium green to deep green, lime green, yellow-green, or gray-green. Other plants have deep purple foliage and still others are variegated with splashes, splotches, stripes, and other colorful patterns. Keep foliage in mind as you create your garden's color scheme. (Blue and white with touches of gray foliage, for example, is a beautiful classic color scheme.)

Lavender ageratum, deep purple heliotrope, feathery blue nigella (love-in-a-mist), wishbone flower, and nemesia make this combination an appealing raised bed border.

GARDEN SMARTER
NOT ALL COLORS ARE EQUAL

Take note of the intensity of colors. Yellow, for example, can be a soft, pastel buttery yellow; or a bright, clear yield-sign yellow; or a muted gold; or nearly fluorescent. Group flowers with similar color intensities next to one another, mixing pastels with pastels, clear bright hues with other clear bright tones, muted colors with less-intense shades, and so forth. Doing so creates striking cohesion in a design.

'Licktkonigen Lucia' rose

Potentilla

'Turner's Shari' oleander

GARDEN SMARTER
EVER-CHANGING COLOR

Think of the color schemes in your garden as moving targets. After all, gardens are ever-changing. Some colors are easier to find at certain times of the year than others—pastels in the spring, rich jewel tones in the fall.

Experienced gardeners often create perennial beds that start out with the soothing pinks, soft yellows, and blues of spring. In late summer and fall as russets, reds, oranges, and golds predominate, plants that bloom in those colors take center stage in their gardens.

If creating color combinations is new to you, experiment with annuals first. Annual flowers provide constant, consistent color through the growing season and are easier to redo next year if you're not pleased with the results. Move, tweak, and play around with the arrangement and colors until you're satisfied with the result.

Pink and magenta roses clamber over this front yard arbor. They pick up on color cues from hardy geranium flowers and Japanese maple foliage.

Build a Bed In Purple and Red

This bold color combo stands out with a tropical look and flamboyant colors.

YOU'LL SELDOM SEE PURPLE AND RED COMBINED IN ROOM DECOR, BUT THEY'RE A KNOCKOUT IN A FLOWER BED. THESE NEIGHBORS ON THE COLOR WHEEL PLAY OFF EACH OTHER SPECTACULARLY.

If your garden's plantings are ho-hum, design a bed with red and purple flowers to liven it up.

You might expect cool, rich purple to calm down vibrant red. But instead, it revs up red even more.

The planting here is lively, but not excessively exuberant. Purple rose verbena sprawls next to magenta hardy geranium flowers. Cannas at the back of the planting echo the rosy bougainvillea blossoms. The variegated bougainvillea leaves, deep green verbena foliage, and yellowish green geranium leaves provide visual relief from the intense floral display. The fountain grass in the middle of the bed adds a beautiful fine-textured spray to the composition and tones it down with creamy pink seed heads.

You can vary this planting by including purple foliage. Heuchera, purple fountain grass, red barberry, and purple smokebush are good candidates to add.

PLANT LIST

A. **1 Magenta hardy geranium** (*Geranium* spp.) such as 'Ann Folkard': Zones 5–9

B. **3 Purple rose verbenas** (*Verbena canadensis*) such as 'Homestead Purple': Zones 6–9, annual elsewhere

C. **1 Dwarf fountain grass** (*Pennisetum alopecuroides*) such as 'Hameln': Zones 5–9

D. **1 Compact bougainvillea** (*Bougainvillea glabra*) such as 'Raspberry Ice': Zones 9–11, annual elsewhere

E. **4 Rose-flowered cannas** (*Canna* × *generalis*) such as 'Pfitzer's Chinese Coral': Zones 8–11, annual elsewhere

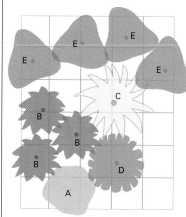

Each square = 1 foot

PASTELS

With so many pink, blue, and purple spring bloomers to choose from, creating a flower bed with these calming colors is a snap.

Pretty In Pink, Purple, and Blue

ONE OF THE EASIEST COORDINATED COLOR SCHEMES IS PINK AND PURPLE WITH TOUCHES OF BLUE. YOUR CHOICES OF FLOWERS IN THESE COLORS ARE NEARLY ENDLESS.

Pink, purple, and blue are forgiving colors. Unlike reds, nearly all tints and shades of these colors work well together. It's nearly impossible to create a mix of these three hues that clash (with the possible exception of certain salmon pinks or bold magentas).

This sun-loving small garden is a classic combination of purple bearded iris surrounded by pink carnations and moss phlox interspersed with blue forget-me-nots, violets, and Johnny-jump-ups. It's a garden that will come back year after year. Although Johnny-jump-ups are annuals, they reseed themselves prolifically from year to year.

All the flowers in this garden bloom late spring through early summer. To extend the bloom time and the color scheme through fall, add purple coneflowers, pink Asiatic lilies, and blue and purple asters behind this planting.

PLANT LIST

A. **3 German bearded irises** *(Iris germanica)*: Zones 3–10

B. **5 Maiden pinks** *(Dianthus deltoides)*: Zones 3–10

C. **1 Pink moss phlox** *(Phlox subulata)*: Zones 2–8

D. **3 Woodland forget-me-nots** *(Myosotis sylvatica)*: Zones 5–8

E. **5 Johnny-jump-ups** *(Viola tricolor* hybrid): Annual

F. **3 Labrador violets** *(Viola labradorica)*: Zones 3–8

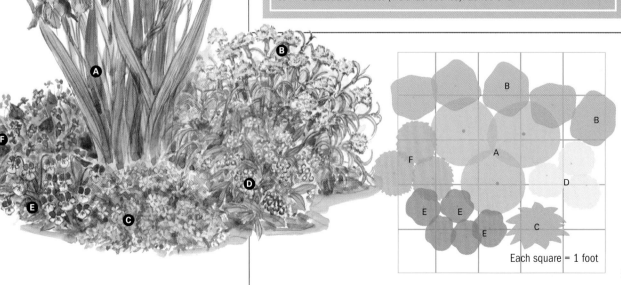

Each square = 1 foot

Springtime Splendor

Cool colors create a flower bed that's soothing and full of sweet romance.

Plan for visual interest beyond peak bloom. Once flowers fade on the peonies, irises, and false indigo, this bed becomes more subtle, but foliage remains attractive the rest of the summer. By midsummer Russian sage takes center stage. The sundial draws attention no matter what the season.

WHETHER YOU'RE SINGING THE BLUES OR ARE IN THE PINK, SOFT COLORS ARE THE WAY TO GO WHEN YOU'RE LOOKING TO SET A RESTFUL MOOD.

This sun-loving garden, which is at its peak in late spring, is filled with purple and white Siberian irises, soft pink peonies, and subdued cream and maroon from white false indigo. Later in the season, Russian sage adds another touch of light purple.

Variegated hosta leaves add volume and a refreshing touch of green that prevents the color scheme from becoming too precious. After early summer plants have finished blooming, the garden will continue to look fresh and attractive until frost. A sundial provides a sculptural focal point, though the grouping of plants could stand on its own. Or substitute another focal point, such as a birdbath or garden art.

HOW COOL IS THIS?

Cool colors—blues, purples, lavenders, blue-grays, greens, and soft pinks— are perfect to use anywhere you want a calming, romantic effect. Unlike hot colors (see pages 80-81), cool colors never scream: They whisper.

Nearly all cool colors work together. Mix them freely.

Green foliage works well with cool-color flowers, but plants with gray foliage such as artemisia, dusty miller, lambs' ears, and lavender really excel at setting off those soft colors most strikingly. Add a few white plants here and there to make the soft hues stand out a bit more.

Each square = 1 foot

PLANT LIST

A. **1 Variegated hosta**
such as *Hosta albomarginata*:
Zones 3–8

B. **1 Dwarf Russian sage**
(*Perovskia atriplicifolia* 'Little Spire'):
Zones 5–9

C. **1 White false indigo**
(*Baptisia alba*):
Zones 4–8

D. **3 Pink Chinese peonies**
(*Paeonia lactiflora*) such as
'Sarah Bernhardt': Zones 3–8

E. **3 Purple Siberian irises**
(*Iris sibirica*) such as 'Caesar's
Brother': Zones 4–9

F. **3 White Siberian irises**
(*Iris sibirica*) such as 'White Swirl':
Zones 4–9

Brilliant Yellow and Red

This dynamic color duo plays off each other, creating a sizzling combination that can't be ignored.

PUNCTUATED WITH A TOUCH OF WHITE AND LAVENDER, A YELLOW AND RED LANDSCAPE BED GRABS ATTENTION.

Some of the brightest colors that you can find in nature are yellows and reds. This garden has plenty of both, and the two are irresistible together.

Ideal along a sidewalk or as a foundation planting in front of a house where it would be a showstopper, this garden is filled with plants that demand full sun—at least 6 hours a day.

It overflows with Dutch irises, snapdragons, verbena, lavender, marguerite daisies, and other sun-worshippers. In the front, low, spreading plants drape gracefully over the edge of the bed, making this plan a good candidate for a raised bed or terraced wall. Persian buttercups in red and yellow fill in the middle of the border while tall irises, snapdragons, and lavender rise up in the back.

WORKING WITH HOT COLORS

Hot colors are those you find in a sunset—vivid pinks, oranges, reds, and yellows. They make things sizzle. Their in-your-face vibrancy instantly draws attention. Plant them where you want a bold accent.

To prevent hot colors from becoming overwhelming, consider planting some white or cream-color flowers among the vibrant hues to dilute the effect. You can also cool down a hot color scheme with greenery. Tuck in foliage plants such as hosta, ajuga, or coral bells to create a little breathing space among the explosion of color. Or tuck in an unexpected blue or purple bloomer to cool things down.

Each square = 1 foot

COLD-CLIMATE OPTIONS

This flowerbed has a number of perennials that perform best in milder climates, such as the southern half of the U.S. and the Pacific Northwest.

In colder climates, swap out the Dutch iris for yellow bearded irises. Instead of the tender Persian buttercups, consider tall African marigolds (Tagetes erecta). And instead of the trailing perennial verbena, use a red annual verbena or red petunias.

PLANT LIST

A. **5 Yellow Dutch irises** *(Iris × hollandica)* such as 'Golden Harvest' : Zones 5–9

B. **3 Marguerite daisies** *(Argyranthemum frutescens)*: Annual

C. **5 Creamy white snapdragons** *(Antirrhinum majus)*: Annual

D. **9 Red and yellow Persian buttercups** *(Ranunculus asiaticus)*: Zones 7–9

E. **3 Lavenders** *(Lavandula angustifolia)*: Zones 5–9

F. **6 Red verbenas** *(Verbena × hybrida)* such as 'Taylortown Red': Zones 7–9; annual elsewhere

G. **6 Feverfews** *(Tanacetum parthenium)*: Zones 4–9

H. **3 Yellow or cream French marigolds** *(Tagetes patula)*: Annual

Red Hot!

Just try to ignore a red garden—it clamors for attention and energizes the entire landscape.

RED CAN BE TRICKY TO WORK WITH—SOME REDS CLASH WITH OTHERS. BUT THIS BEAUTIFULLY COORDINATED RED GARDEN PACKS A WALLOP OF COLOR TO IGNITE YOUR DAY.

This red border makes a stunning front garden, where it can catch the eye of passersby. Or put it in your backyard where even from a distance, you can appreciate its blazing color.

Red flowers abound in nature. Consider the numerous botanical names that include Latin origins of red: *cardinalis, coccineus, rosea, rubra, ruber,* and *sanguineus* (a reference to blood).

Most red-flowered plants are sun-lovers, needing at least 6 full hours of sun a day. Fewer red-blooming plants thrive in shade. However, impatiens, wax and tuberous begonias, Lenten roses, scarlet sage *(Salvia splendens),* and nicotiana are available in shades of red and grow with 6 or fewer hours of sun a day. If your garden is shady, substitute some of these low-light tolerant plants to adapt the design to shade. Also consider the plants that have splashes of red in their foliage, such as coleus and caladiums.

USING RED

Understand the many tones of red. **Some reds are scarlet (orangish red), others are crimson (purplish red), and still others border on magenta (pinkish red). Furthermore, reds range from rosy pinks to rusty browns. All this is why it takes care to combine red flowers. Some shades and hues don't always go together. Experiment and see what's pleasing to your eye.**

Red flowers attract hummingbirds and butterflies. **Tubular red flowers, such as penstemon and scarlet sage, are especially attractive to hummingbirds.**

Green is the perfect foil to red. **Deep emerald and forest greens work best. Yellow-greens detract from red flowers. However, purplish maroon foliage can set off red dramatically. One example: purple-leaved cannas with red flowers.**

Clear, bright reds enliven cool, rainy spring days. **Red tulips are an excellent choice for this reason. In fall, deeper reds with elements of orange or burgundy blend beautifully with other rich autumn colors in the garden.**

Each square = 1 foot

PLANT LIST

A. **6 Red impatiens** (*Impatiens walleriana*)
such as 'Dazzler Red': Annual

B. **1 White flowering tobacco** (*Nicotiana alata*): Annual

C. **2 Red dahlias** (*Dahlia* hybrids)
such as 'Bishop of Llandaff' or 'Red Pygmy':
Zones 8–10, annual elsewhere

D. **3 Red bee balms** (*Monarda didyma*)
such as 'Jacob Kline': Zones 3–9

E. **3 Lenten roses** (*Helleborus orientalis* 'Red Lady'):
Zones 4–9

F. **2 Littleleaf boxwoods**
(*Buxus microphylla* 'Compacta'): Zones 6–9

G. **5 Lucky clovers** (*Oxalis tetraphylla*)
such as 'Iron Cross': Zones 8–9, annual elsewhere

H. **2 Purple hybrid lobelias**
(*Lobelia × speciosa*) such as 'Grape Knee-Hi':
Zones 6–9

I. **1 Red Asiatic lily** (*Lilium* hybrids)
such as 'Monte Negro': Zones 3–8

Singing the Blues

Tranquil blue evokes the sea and sky. Mix up blues in every shade and hue to create this soothing border.

IS IT ANY WONDER THAT BLUE IS A FAVORITE COLOR OF MANY GARDENERS? IT'S COOLING AND CALMING, THE PERFECT PLANTING SCHEME FOR A GARDEN THAT HELPS YOU RELAX AND RESTORE AFTER A LONG DAY.

It's difficult to find true blue in most flowers. But that's okay—the purples, blue-violets, and lavenders that are so abundant in the gardening world come close to true blue and are gorgeous to boot.

This garden, which needs full sun, is filled with beautiful blue flowers—delphinium, salvia, wishbone flower, aster, pansy, and browallia. You could substitute additional sun-loving blue flowers, such as petunia, speedwell, forget-me-not, heliotrope, hydrangea, iris, morning glory, statice, or grape hyacinth.

Add a personal touch to this blue garden, if you like, by punching it up with touches of white, pink, or yellow. The added color will make it more vibrant and less dreamy.

USING BLUE

Make blue stand out. Accent blue plantings with white flowers or plants with gray foliage.

Use blue to visually expand a space. Try blue flowers along the sides of a narrow garden or along a bed at the back of your yard. Blue recedes, making small spaces seem larger.

Include blue foliage in the mix. Some hostas, many succulents, and evergreens such as junipers and spruces have a beautiful blue cast to their leaves.

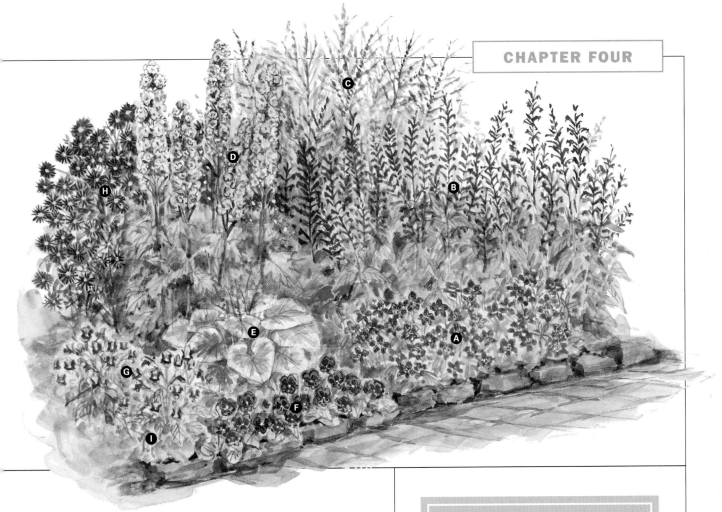

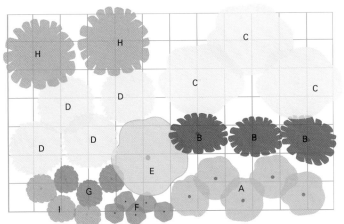

Each square = 1 foot

BHG DESIGN TIP

Have a larger space to fill? Extend the blue border with amsonia and sea holly.

Amsonia

Sea holly

PLANT LIST

A. **5 Browallias**
(*Browallia speciosa*):
Zones 10–11, annual elsewhere

B. **3 Anise-scented sages**
(*Salvia guaranitica*):
Zones 8–10, annual elsewhere

C. **3 Russian sages**
(*Perovskia atriplicifolia*):
Zones 5–9

D. **4 Hybrid delphiniums**
(*Delphinium* hybrids)
such as 'Magic Fountain Sky Blue':
Zones 3–7

E. **1 Variegated heart-leaf brunnera**
(*Brunnera macrophylla*)
such as 'Variegata':
Zones 3–7

F. **5 Blue or purple pansies**
(*Viola × wittrockiana*)
such as 'Blue Denim':
Zones 4–8

G. **3 Blue wishbone flowers**
(*Torenia fournieri*)
such as 'Summer Wave Blue':
Annual

H. **2 Blue or lavender New York asters**
(*Aster novi-belgii*) such as 'Royal Velvet':
Zones 4–8

I. **3 Ageratums** (*Ageratum houstonianum*):
Annual

Plant a Garden In Cheerful Yellow

Is there a happier hue than yellow? Grow a garden in sunny hues and enjoy a color combination that's at once joyful and sophisticated.

YELLOW IS THE COLOR OF JOY. IT STIMULATES CREATIVE AND INTELLECTUAL ENERGY AND EVOKES A SENSE OF WELL-BEING. IN SHORT, YELLOW SPARKS A SMILE.

And yet, a yellow garden also looks elegant, perhaps due to the discipline of designing with a single color. Subdued creams and deep, rich golds add to the elegance.

This simple garden features just a few yellow blooming plants, but they're bright enough to have a big impact. The bed is filled with creamy yellow daylilies, golden plume celosia, sunny yellow zinnias, pastel yellow angel's trumpet (which is also wonderfully fragrant), and a tower of climbing black-eyed susan vine, which you can plant from seed indoors or purchase as a small plant.

Add more punch to this garden by playing around with foliage colors. Incorporate a chartreuse sweet potato vine or cushion spurge with yellow-green foliage and yellow springtime flowers.

True to its sunny color scheme, this garden loves the sun, requiring at least 6 hours daily. Daylilies will do well with a little less sun, but if you want to adapt this design to shade, substitute cream-color astilbe, white or yellow impatiens, yellow tuberous begonias, and gold variegated hostas for the other sun-lovers.

USING YELLOW

Explore the full range of yellow. Pale creamy white, clear sunny yellow, deep gold, and yellow-orange all work together beautifully.

Expand a space with yellow. Plant a yellow garden in a tight spot and it's as though you brought in additional light. The nook feels more expansive.

Plant yellow flowers for a fresh, radiant look even in hot weather. Late summer yellow and gold blooms add spark to a heat-stressed landscape.

Catch a moonbeam with pale yellow. Creamy whites and pale yellows catch moonlight especially well, creating the effect of being illuminated from within. Use pale yellow flowers in night gardens or areas where you'll be sitting in the evening.

BHG
MONEY
SAVER

**SUBSTITUTE
LESS EXPENSIVE
MATERIALS**
*The wrought-iron tuteur
and brick path lend an air
of elegance to this bed, but
they can be expensive. To
save money you can use a
wood obelisk or lath trellis
for the tuteur and wood
chips or pea gravel for the
path. The less expensive
materials not only look
nice, but they also are
easy to install.*

PLANT LIST

A. **7 Yellow zinnias** *(Zinnia elegans)* such as
'Barry's Giant Golden Yellow': Annual

B. **1 Yellow angel's trumpet** *(Brugmansia*
spp.): Zones 10–11, annual elsewhere

C. **1 Black-eyed susan vine** *(Thunbergia alata)*:
Zones 9–11, annual elsewhere

D. **9 Yellow or gold plume celosias**
(Celosia argentea plumosa)
such as 'Sparkler Yellow': Annual

E. **2 Yellow or gold miniature daylilies**
(Hemerocallis hybrids) such as 'Stella de Oro':
Zones 3–9

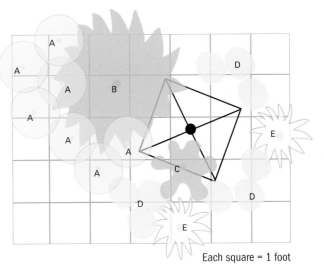

Each square = 1 foot

Wow 'em With White

An all-white garden sparkles with clean, clear color that looks fresh all season long.

PLANT A HANGING BASKET

For instant fullness when planting a large container, such as the urn shown here planted with million bells, purchase an established hanging basket instead of a few smaller individual plants.

To transplant the hanging basket, cut away the plastic hanger with a garden shears. Gently remove the plants' roots from the basket and transfer to the new container partly filled with potting soil. Fill in around the roots with more potting soil as needed, tamp down with your fingers, pushing the soil in around the sides, and water well.

FOR CENTURIES, GARDENERS HAVE PRIZED ALL-WHITE GARDENS AS THE PINNACLE OF UNDERSTATED ELEGANCE.

The restraint practiced in planting only white flowers in a garden is indeed sophisticated. But white gardens also have a charming, clean, childlike quality. They look pure and wholesome.

And white flowers stand out visually, whether it's early in the morning when they're covered in dew or late at night when the moon illuminates them.

It's simple to mix and match cream and white blooms.

The monochromatic palette ensures color coordination. Just be sure to include a variety of leaf shapes and textures, as well as varied flower sizes and shapes, to prevent the design from becoming monotonous.

This full-sun garden has large-flowered Shasta daisies, marigolds, and bearded irises. A container planted with daintier million bells serves as a focal point and adds structure to the garden.

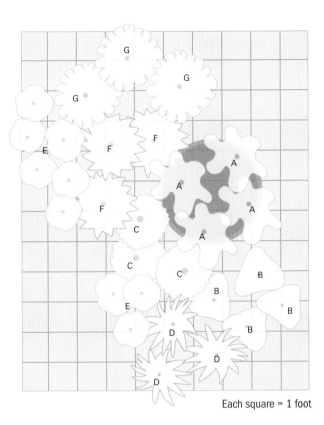

Each square = 1 foot

PLANT LIST

A. **4 White million bells** (*Calibrachoa* hybrids)
such as 'Superbells White':
Annual

B. **4 White sweet violets** (*Viola odorata*):
Zones 8–9

C. **3 White zinnias** (*Zinnia elegans*)
such as 'Peter Pan White':
Annual

D. **3 White sun-tolerant impatiens**
(*Impatiens walleriana*)
such as Sunpatiens 'Compact White':
Annual

E. **9 Cream-colored African marigolds** (*Tagetes erecta*)
such as 'French Vanilla':
Annual

F. **3 White bearded irises** (*Iris hybrids*)
such as 'Immortality':
Zones 4–10

G. **3 Shasta daisies** (*Leucanthemum × superbum*)
such as 'Becky':
Zones 4–9

USING WHITE

Use white's calming effect. White gardens are ideal in a space that you want to tone down visually.

Note the details in white flowers. Many have hints of other colors in them. White snapdragons, for example, often have soft yellow at the base of their petals. White vinca typically has a bright pink center. White salvia may have a bluish cast on portions of its petals. Keep these variations in mind when designing an all-white bed.

Use leaf textures and colors to set off white flowers. Gray foliage is especially striking in a white garden. So is variegated foliage with a touch of white, such as hostas, goutweed, and white-striped ornamental grasses.

Plant white flowers in the shade. White is highly reflective and considerably brightens a dark corner. White impatiens, tuberous begonias, wax begonias, hydrangeas, bleeding hearts, salvias, lilies-of-the-valley, azaleas, daylilies, and nicotianas are examples of white flowers that like shade.

Meticulously deadhead spent white flowers. More so than blooms of other colors, white flowers quickly morph to unattractive brown. Pinch or trim off dead flowers to keep the planting looking good.

Roses, Roses, Roses

There's a reason the rose is called the queen of flowers. Consider its rich history and romance, the exquisite form of this regal flower, its evocative fragrance, and the pleasure of cutting just a single bloom. *Since ancient times gardeners have been drawn to roses. Today gardeners have an astounding selection of roses to choose from that are as easy and disease-resistant as they are lovely. Turn the pages to find entire gardens inspired by the beauty of roses.*

Rose Growing Basics

Roses are easy plants to grow if you make the right choices. Plant the lowest-maintenance types and then sit back and enjoy the show!

There's a host of low-maintenance roses available that are beautiful, fragrant, and fend off diseases and pests like never before.

Regular deadheading discourages pests, encourages further bloom, and keeps your garden looking well-groomed.

It's a myth that beautiful roses are hard to grow. Choose the right rose for your climate and it will be nearly maintenance-free.

Roses are beautiful grown alone or mixed with other flowers. They come in a wide variety of sizes—from miniatures that grow no more than a foot tall to giant ramblers that sprawl 40 feet or more.

Red, pink, and yellow may be the most popular, but roses are available in almost every color except true blue and black. (There are even greenish roses!) And rose plants have various forms.

Choose right. Many newer landscape roses need minimal maintenance. They're different from hybrid tea and other roses gardeners grew 50 to 75 years ago. Previously the emphasis was on large, beautiful flowers on long stems perfect for cutting. Hybrid tea roses need lots of winter protection in cold climates, ample fertilizer, and usually pest and disease controls.

Landscape roses are also different from antique roses favored 100 years ago. Antiques usually bloom just once per year, although the flowers are beautiful with outstanding fragrance.

Consult the lists of the best roses for specific locations on the next page to decide which roses are best for your site.

Fertilize well. Most roses need ample nutrients. Plant them in soil heavily amended with compost. Then fertilize every 2 to 6 weeks during the growing season. In Zones 6 and colder, stop fertilizing 2 months before your region's first frost date to avoid forcing tender new late-season growth that will fail to harden off properly before winter's cold arrives.

Prune smart. Pruning needs vary from one type of rose to another. For all types, trim out any dead or damaged plant parts any time they are observed. Most rugosas, ramblers, and low-maintenance landscape roses need little additional pruning other than to thin out weak stems and canes. Others, such as climbers and hybrid teas may need hard pruning in late winter or early spring, just as the leaves are beginning to expand to force strong new basal cane growth. As the rose blooms fade, trim off spent flowers to encourage further bloom.

Prevent pests and diseases. Climate plays a big role in susceptibility of roses to various pests and diseases. Roses grown in humid regions tend to have more problems with pest and diseases.

Even in pest-prone regions you can thwart disease and insect problems by choosing pest-resistant roses. Although some rose gardeners spray disease and insect controls as a preventative measure, this usually is unnecessary. A more environmentally sound alternative is to wait until a problem occurs, identify the problem; and then use an appropriate low-impact control.

PLANT SUPERSTARS

'Morden Centennial'

Carefree Beauty

Knock Out

'Fragrant Cloud'

EASIEST ROSES FOR COLD CLIMATES

THE CANADIAN EXPLORER ROSES such as 'Henry Hudson' and 'John Cabot'

DAVID AUSTIN ROSES including 'Mary Rose', 'Heritage', and 'Abraham Darby'

THE FLOWER CARPET SERIES such as Flower Carpet Scarlet and Flower Carpet Pink Supreme

GRIFFITH BUCK ROSES such as Carefree Beauty, 'Earth Song', and 'Country Dancer'

THE KNOCK OUT SERIES such as Knock Out, Double Knock Out, and Pink Double Knock Out

RUGOSA ROSES such as 'Therese Bugnet', 'Linda Campbell', 'Fru Dagmar Hastrup', and 'Simplicity'

PARKLAND ROSES such as 'Morden Centennial', 'Morden Blush', and 'Adelaide Hoodless'

NOTE: *Avoid hybrid teas. They're marginally hardy even in Zone 5.*

EASIEST ROSES FOR WARM CLIMATES

EARTHKIND ROSES such as Carefree Beauty, 'The Fairy', and Perle d'Or

ANTIQUE ROSES such as 'Harison's Yellow', 'Duchesse de Brabant', and 'Lady Banks'

THE KNOCK OUT SERIES such as Knock Out, Double Knock Out, and Pink Double Knock Out

CERTAIN HYBRID TEAS such as 'Mister Lincoln' and 'St. Patrick'

NOTE: *Roses grafted onto the rootstock of* Rosa fortuniana *are extremely resistant to the root knot nematode, which is prevalent in the South.*

MOST FRAGRANT ROSES

CANADIAN EXPLORER ROSES such as 'Henry Hudson' and 'John Cabot'

DAVID AUSTIN ROSES including 'Mary Rose,' 'Heritage', and 'Abraham Darby'

THE FLOWER CARPET SERIES such as Flower Carpet Scarlet and Flower Carpet Pink Supreme

GRIFFITH BUCK ROSES such as Carefree Beauty, 'Earth Song', and 'Country Dancer'

THE KNOCK-OUT SERIES such as Knock Out, Double Knock Out, and Home Run

RUGOSA ROSES such as 'Therese Bugnet', 'Linda Campbell', and 'Fru Dagmar Hastrup'

PARKLAND ROSES such as 'Morden Centennial', 'Morden Blush', and 'Adelaide Hoodless'

NOTE: *Some hybrid teas have no scent, but those that mention strong scent in their descriptions, such as 'Fragrant Cloud', are usually outstanding.*

BEST ROSES FOR CUTTING

HYBRID TEA ROSES are excellent for cutting. They produce single large flowers on top of long stems. 'Mister Lincoln' has beautiful red velvety petals and is fragrant. 'Double Delight' has gorgeous coloring and fragrance. 'Gold Medal' has glowing yellow flowers.

FLORIBUNDA ROSES, which have clusters of roses, also are nice for casual arrangements. White 'Iceberg', and pink 'Sexy Rexy' are two good examples.

NOTE: *Avoid rugosa, David Austin, and most landscape roses for cutting because the flowers shatter easily after a day or so.*

Love 'em and Leave 'em

This rose bed may look high-maintenance, but it takes less care than a bed of annual flowers. The bonus: It comes back year after year!

TUCK THIS SEMICIRCULAR BED INTO A SUNNY SPOT IN YOUR LANDSCAPE, BY THE DRIVEWAY, OR IN A CORNER OF THE YARD. IT'S QUICK TO PLANT AND IS FILLED WITH NO-FUSS ROSES AND PERENNIALS.

Are you a beginning rose gardener? This combination bed is great for a novice.

It consists of a few easy-care roses, rimmed with lady's mantle, a low edging plant that's a classic with roses. Its pretty green foliage and chartreuse flowers blend easily with nearly any kind of rose.

A climbing rose in the back, 'New Dawn', is fairly cold-hardy and tough. It adds a helpful vertical element to the planting, integrating it with whatever background. Train this climber up a gazebo, as shown, or grow it along a fence or hedge (with the help of a trellis to give it some support).

The other roses are among the lowest-maintenance roses available today, and most will bloom heavily in late spring with light flowering until frost. Follow this plan exactly, or substitute other easy roses that you can find in your local garden center. It's pretty to do a mix of colors—red, pink, and white—though you could also do a planting of nothing but one particular rose.

Be sure to plant any rose bed in full sun—at least 8 hours of direct, unfiltered light. This bed will also appreciate a sprinkling of a granular, balanced slow-release fertilizer once in the spring and a good inch or two of mulch. But other than that, it needs little care.

Polar Joy

PLANT SUPERSTAR
TREE ROSES

In this or other rose plantings, consider working in tree roses. Tree roses are lovely accents for the landscape, but in Zones 6 and colder, they need extensive winter protection. Many gardeners resort to partially digging them up, tipping them over into a trench, and burying them each winter to protect them from the cold.

That's because most tree roses are grafted onto a trunk which is very tender and can be killed by winter cold.

Polar Joy is a particularly cold hardy variety that is shaped into a tree form without the extra step of grafting. That means it can grow in Zones 4 and warmer with no winter protection. It has soft pink 2-inch-diameter flowers. The plant will grow 5 to 6 feet tall although it can be pruned shorter if desired.

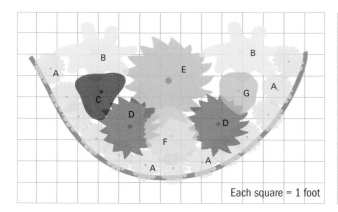

Each square = 1 foot

PLANT LIST

A.	**13 Lady's mantle** (*Alchemilla mollis*): Zones 4–8
B.	**2 Light pink climbing roses** such as 'New Dawn': Zones 5–9
C.	**1 Red shrub rose** such as 'La Sevillana': Zones 4–10
D.	**2 Red shrub roses** such as 'Knock Out': Zones 4–10
E.	**1 Deep pink shrub rose** such as 'William Baffin'*: Zones 3–8
F.	**1 Light pink shrub rose** such as 'The Fairy': Zones 4–9
G.	**1 Apricot–pink shrub rose** such as 'Perdita': Zones 4–9

* Climbing form also available.

An Easy Arbor Planting

This pleasant mix of perennials and roses is sure to set off any arbor.

EXPAND YOUR PLANTING FROM JUST A COUPLE OF CLIMBING ROSES ON AN ARBOR TO A SIMPLE BUT ELEGANT ROSE GARDEN BY ADDING A FEW EASY-CARE PERENNIALS AND SHRUBS.

This landscaping project can be completed in a few hours, yet will look terrific for years to come.

The arbor sports a 'New Dawn' rose, a classic climber. It grows to 20 feet tall (keep it in check with spring pruning) and bears lovely 3-inch-diameter blooms with soft pink petals and a light fragrance. 'Ballerina', planted at the base of the arbor, is another classic rose choice. It's one of the best blooming shrub roses around, producing numerous clusters of pink-tinged single blooms. It can grow up to 5 feet tall and

wide, but is easy to keep smaller by pruning severely in early spring.

'Annabelle' hydrangea reaches nearly the same size as 'Ballerina' rose. Large panicles of flowers produced by the hydrangea echo the shape of the rose bloom clusters. It produces beautiful puffs of creamy white blooms in midsummer.

Other lower-growing perennials surround the larger elements of this arbor-focused garden, adding color all season long.

PLANT LIST

A.   **2 'New Dawn' climbing roses:** Zones 5–9

B.   **1 'Ballerina' rose:** Zones 5–9

C.   **8 Rose verbenas** (*Verbena canadensis*): Zones 4–8

D.   **3 Pinks** (*Dianthus* spp.): Zones 3–10

E.   **1 Annabelle smooth hydrangea**
(*Hydrangea arborescens* 'Annabelle'): Zones 4–9

F.   **3 Foxgloves** (*Digitalis purpurea*): Zones 4–8

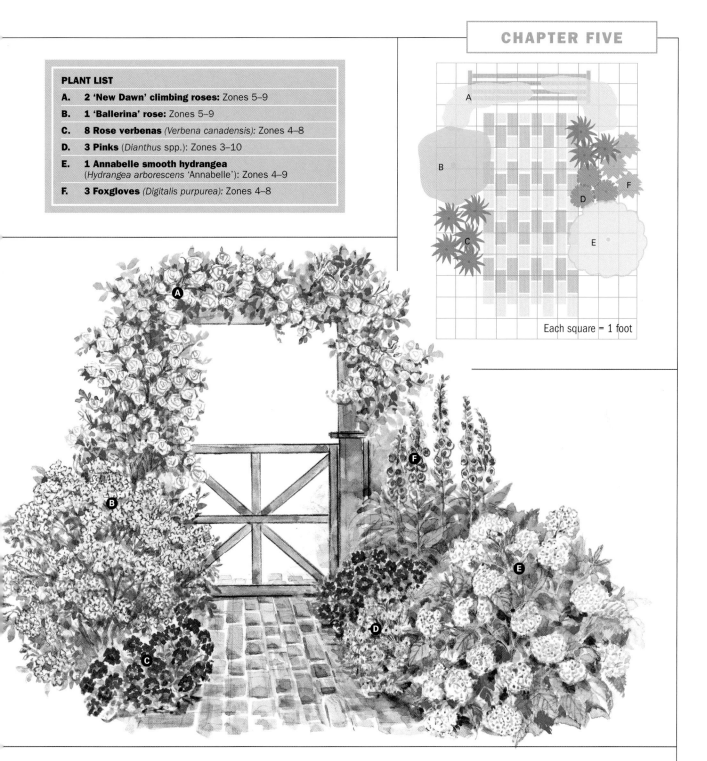

Each square = 1 foot

GARDEN SMARTER

WHEN TO PLANT ROSES

What time of year should roses be planted? It depends on the region and the type of rose.

As a rule of thumb, plant container-grown roses any time of year except during temperature extremes. Avoid periods when hard freezes (below 25°F) or extended heat (above 90°F) are likely. In most regions this means planting container-grown roses from early spring through autumn. In warmer climates plant them from fall through late winter.

Bare-root roses have a narrower window for planting. They need temperate, moist conditions to get established. Plant bare-root roses in spring about the same time that other plants are leafing out, but before daytime temperatures regularly climb into the 80s. In the southern quarter of the U.S., you can also plant them in fall and winter.

In Zone 6 and colder, it's best to avoid planting container-grown roses in the fall. They don't have enough time to get established before winter cold hits and their chances of dying are much higher.

Combine Climbers and Clematis

The perfect pair: climbing roses and vining clematis. Together they intertwine, bloom, and prove that when it comes to flowers, more is definitely better!

LIKE CHAMPAGNE AND STRAWBERRIES, CLIMBING ROSES AND CLEMATIS ARE AN ELEGANT, CLASSIC COMBO THAT HAS STOOD THE TEST OF TIME. FOR CENTURIES GARDENERS HAVE ENJOYED PLANTING THE TWO TOGETHER TO WATCH THE SPECTACULAR RELATIONSHIP GROW AND FLOWER.

Climbing roses are rambling woody plants that need support to sprawl on. Clematises, on the other hand, have nimble, flexible stems that need a support to climb. Roses, with their many branches, give the clematis excellent purchase to scramble skyward. But unlike some vines, which can be rampant, clematises are moderate growers that will not smother a rose. Instead, most clematises have sparse enough foliage to allow in enough sunlight for the roses to thrive.

Some climbing roses and clematises bloom at the same time. If the two are of contrasting colors, such as a pink rose with a purple clematis or a red rose with a white clematis, the sight can be breathtaking. Other pairings of climbing roses and clematises can extend the blooming season. For example, pair an early-summer blooming climbing rose with a late-summer blooming clematis, and you'll be treated to a few weeks of bloom from the rose and then a few weeks of bloom from the clematis.

In the garden shown, repeat-blooming 'New Dawn' climbing roses intertwine with deep purple Jackman clematises to embellish a classic white arbor and picket fence, the destination of a gently rising walk. The walk is flanked with low-maintenance red barberries, junipers, and delicate pink 'The Fairy' roses that are easy to grow.

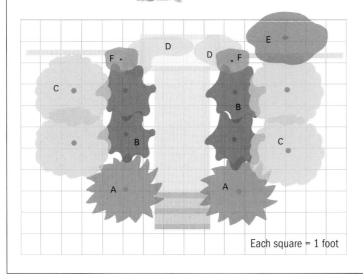

Each square = 1 foot

PLANT LIST

A. **2 Creeping junipers**
(*Juniperus horizontalis* 'Bar Harbor'):
Zones 5–9

B. **4 Red Japanese barberries**
(*Berberis thunbergii* 'Atropurpurea'):
Zones 5–8

C. **4 'The Fairy' roses:**
Zones 5–9

D. **2 'New Dawn' climbing roses:**
Zones 5–9

E. **1 'Constance Spry' shrub rose:**
Zones 5–9

F. **2 Jackman clematises**
(*Clematis* 'Jackmanii'): Zones 4–8

'New Dawn' rose and
'Jackmanii' clematis

BHG
DESIGN
NOTE

MATCH THE CLEMATIS WITH THE ROSE

It's important to choose the right size of clematis so that it doesn't overwhelm or get lost in the rose.

Rambling roses, which can sprawl 40 feet, combine well with sweet autumn clematis (Clematis terniflora), which grows to 20 feet.

For most climbing roses, which range in size from 10 to 20 feet, choose large-flowered clematises, most of which get no taller than 10 to 15 feet.

Pair shrub roses with one of the small clematises, such as Durand's clematis (Clematis × durandii), alpine clematis (C. alpina), or Italian clematis (C. viticella), that climb no more than 4 or 5 feet high.

A Rosy Outlook

Line a walk with a variety of roses edged in boxwood for a time-honored display of flowers and an undulating ribbon of foliage.

IT'S AN ELEGANT LOOK: A GENTLY CURVED SIDEWALK FLANKED WITH BOXWOOD AND ROSES. THE PLAN CAN BE ADAPTED TO NEARLY ANY STRETCH OF SUNNY PATH.

This is lined primarily with hybrid tea roses. It's a showy way to display a collection of hybrid teas and display the breadth of their color range.

Hybrid teas are a smart selection for a rose planting that also serves as an excellent source of cut flowers to bring indoors. The more flowers you cut, the more roses are produced. That's because the goal of any flowering plant is to set seed and reproduce. By constantly trimming off flowers, either for cut flower arrangements or by deadheading spent blooms, the plant's attempt to set seed is circumvented. This makes it go into flowering double-time in an attempt to produce more flowers that have a higher chance to set seed.

Landscape roses are a lower-maintenance choice for this rose-lined front path. Make the planting more cold-hardy and less work by planting a row of Knock Out, Flower Carpet, or Easy Elegance Series roses, which are among the most cold-hardy and disease-resistant roses around. They also need minimal pruning.

Antique rose fanciers could also use this general design to show off a collection of old roses. Or adapt the plan to a particular color theme, such as a garden entirely of red roses or entirely of white roses.

PLANT LIST

A. **25 Boxwoods** (*Buxus* 'Green Gem'):
Zones 5–9

B. **2 Carefree Wonder roses:**
Zones 5–9

C. **1 'Gold Medal' rose:**
Zones 5–9

D. **1 'Perfume Delight' rose:**
Zones 5–9

E. **1 'Queen Elizabeth' rose:**
Zones 5–9

F. **1 'Royal Highness' rose:**
Zones 5–9

G. **1 'Rio Samba' rose:**
Zones 5–9

H. **2 'Blaze' climbing roses:**
Zones 5–9

I. **1 'Mister Lincoln' rose:**
Zones 5–9

J. **1 'Sunbright' rose:**
Zones 5–9

K. **1 'Sexy Rexy' rose:**
Zones 5–9

L. **1 'Playboy' rose:**
Zones 5–9

M. **1 'John F. Kennedy' rose:**
Zones 5–9

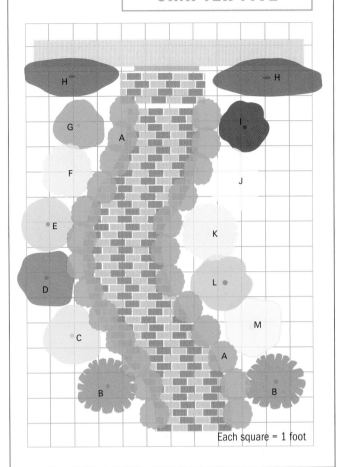

Each square = 1 foot

BHG DESIGN TIP

UNDERSTANDING HYBRID TEA ROSES

Hybrid tea roses have long been a favorite of rose connoisseurs, florists, and those who want to grow roses for shows.

They love the classic vase-shaped buds that unfurl into many-petaled rose blossoms. They are borne on long stems that make them perfect for cut flower arrangements.

Hybrid tea roses bloom from early summer through hard freezes in fall and many have wonderful fragrance. Hybrid tea roses come in a wide array of colors, including bicolors.

Ring Around The Roses

Plant roses in a circle and weave in perennials. It's an elegant centerpiece for a sunny yard.

PLANT LIST

A. **1 Climbing rose** such as 'Colette': Zones 5–9

B. **8 Chrysanthemums** (*Chrysanthemum × morifolium*): Zones 5–10

C. **10 Romantica shrub roses** such as 'Auguste Renoir', 'Comtesse de Provence', 'Francois Rabelais', 'Guy de Maupassant', 'Johann Strauss', 'Tchaikovsky', 'Yves Piaget', and 'Peter Mayle': Zones 5–9

D. **6 Miniature roses** such as 'Alfie', 'Baby Paradise', and 'Rainbow's End': Zones 5–9

E. **6 Tall sedums** (*Sedum spectabile*) such as 'Brilliant': Zones 4–9

F. **6 Perennial salvias** (*Salvia × sylvestris* 'May Night'): Zones 5–9

G. **3 Lady's mantles** (*Alchemilla mollis*): Zones 4–7

H. **3 Lamb's ears** (*Stachys byzantina* 'Silver Carpet'): Zones 4–8

THIS CIRCULAR GARDEN GROWS ARMSFUL OF ROSES SET OFF WITH THE MOODY BLUES OF LAVENDER AND SALVIA WITH BRIGHTENING TOUCHES OF SILVERY LAMBS' EARS.

A French tuteur is an elegant, freestanding plant support that usually rises 5 to 7 feet high. It makes an excellent support for a rose that rambles, providing a means to grow a climbing rose in the middle of a flower bed.

The French inspiration in the garden carries through to the choice of roses. Bred in Provence, Romantica roses have beautiful flowers with long stems perfect for cutting—or just enjoying in the garden from early summer through fall.

Many Romantica roses are wonderfully fragrant and all are highly disease-resistant, making this a low-maintenance garden. Romantica roses are teamed with miniature roses and low-care perennials, such as sedum, perennial salvia, and lambs' ears, to create a garden that's long-blooming and easy-care.

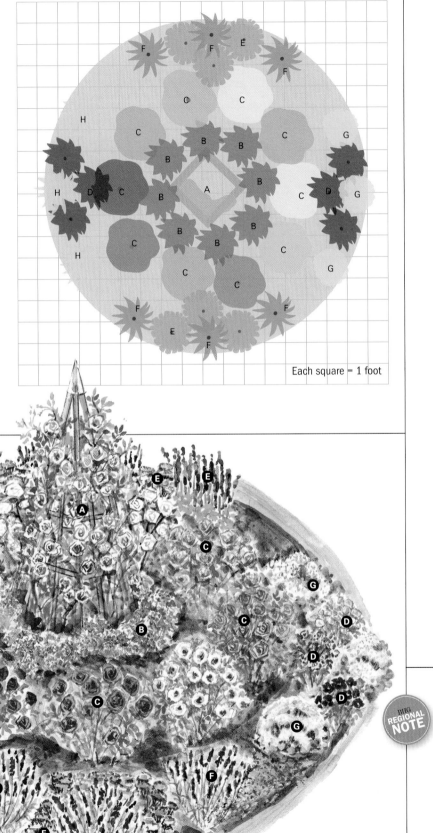

Each square = 1 foot

'Jean Giaono'
Romantica rose

PLANT SUPERSTAR
ROMANTICA ROSES

Call them English roses with a French accent. Similar to David Austin roses (which are also known as English roses), Romantica roses are modern roses that have been crossed with antique roses in an effort to capture the best characteristics of both. They were bred in Provence by the famed House of Meilland, which is known for producing tough, beautiful roses.

David Austin roses also are valued for their cold-hardiness (to Zone 5), but they often do not bloom well in warmer climates. Romantica roses, on the other hand, do better in the heat, bearing larger flowers in hotter regions of the country.

David Austin rose bushes have a shrubby, full shape. Romantica roses tend to be smaller but upright, as are floribunda and hybrid tea roses. The Romantica flower form is similar to that of a hybrid tea rose while David Austin roses have a fuller, rounded, old-fashioned flower form.

David Austin roses are renowned for their fragrance while most but not all Romantica roses have a notable fragrance.

BIG REGIONAL NOTE

Make this garden more drought-tolerant by leaving out the lady's mantle, which likes cool, moist conditions. Instead, plant more lamb's-ears in place of the lady's mantle.

Cottage Gardens

Cottage gardens are as old as cottages themselves, but their appeal is timeless. *While the definition of what constitutes a cottage garden might vary, in all cases it embraces an unpretentious, exuberant, casual mix of flowers and other plants— sometimes even edibles.*

An appealing element of cottage gardens is that you can easily add on to them. Plant a small bed or border one season, then expand it or install additional beds as time and budget allow. The eclectic, relaxed mix works beautifully with minimum forethought.

Plant Along A Walk

Line a path with a tumble of perennials that are sure to please the eye.

THIS CHEERFUL MIX OF WATER–THRIFTY FLOWERS WILL COME BACK YEAR AFTER YEAR. THEY LINE THIS PATHWAY TO TURN A MERE WALK INTO A PLEASANT JOURNEY.

In classic cottage design, nothing is too regimented. A path seldom runs straight. Plants hardly ever are planted in rows or geometric blocks. Instead, it's a happy mishmash of many different plants with no straight lines to be found.

This garden, designed for a sunny locale, is an excellent example. On one side, there is a long, curving drift of low-growing sedum groundcover (or you could simply grow grass on that side). But on the other, there are a number of perennials and shrubs planted with no particular rhyme or reason other than to make sure the taller ones are in the back and that there's contrast in colors and shapes.

True to cottage style, some of the plants, such as the lady's mantle, might reseed in the cracks of the flagstone. And the sedum may spread into the cracks.

The planting plan doesn't specifically include plantings in the cracks, but experiment with tucking in sweet alyssum (an annual) or perennial herbs such as creeping thyme or mint here and there where space permits. It's delightful to see how some plants such as these prefer a tight space with little soil and water.

If you want more reseeders, let the flowers ripen and go to seed on the plant. If you want fewer, trim spent blooms immediately. In early spring, you can also edit reseeders by weeding out the ones you don't want and transplanting the ones you do want to just the right spot.

Overall, this garden is reasonably drought-tolerant. Substitute thyme or another type of sedum for the lady's mantle, one of the thirstier plants in this group, for a very drought-tolerant garden.

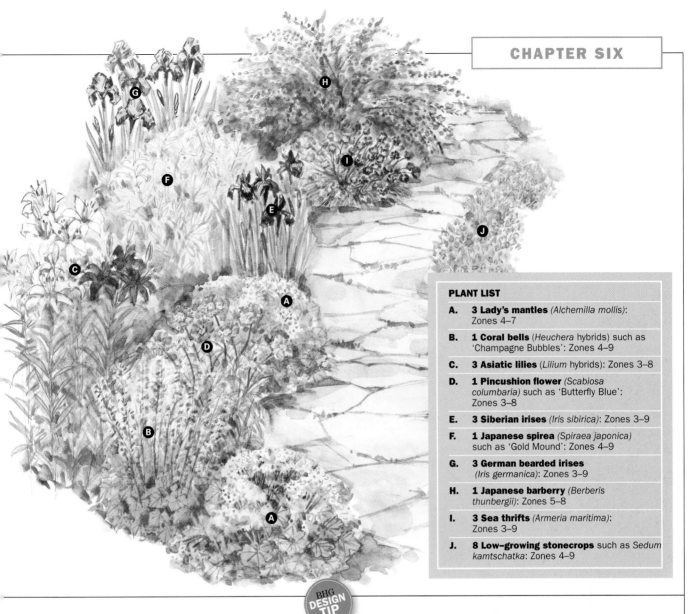

PLANT LIST

A. **3 Lady's mantles** (*Alchemilla mollis*):
Zones 4–7

B. **1 Coral bells** (*Heuchera* hybrids) such as
'Champagne Bubbles': Zones 4–9

C. **3 Asiatic lilies** (*Lilium* hybrids): Zones 3–8

D. **1 Pincushion flower** (*Scabiosa
columbaria*) such as 'Butterfly Blue':
Zones 3–8

E. **3 Siberian irises** (*Iris sibirica*): Zones 3–9

F. **1 Japanese spirea** (*Spiraea japonica*)
such as 'Gold Mound': Zones 4–9

G. **3 German bearded irises**
(*Iris germanica*): Zones 3–9

H. **1 Japanese barberry** (*Berberis
thunbergii*): Zones 5–8

I. **3 Sea thrifts** (*Armeria maritima*):
Zones 3–9

J. **8 Low-growing stonecrops** such as *Sedum
kamtschatka*: Zones 4–9

Each square = 1 foot

WHAT IS COTTAGE STYLE?

Cottage gardens share a handful of characteristics:

They're informal. Most cottage gardens are a higgledy–piggledy mix of plants, the more eclectic the better. Put cabbages with the roses, tuck in annuals next to a shrub—there are few rules for mixing and matching.

They're easy-care. Cottage gardens started out as peasant gardens, so very expensive, rare, or high-maintenance plants can look out of place. Use plants that grow easily in your area. And if they're divisions from friends and neighbors, so much the better. It's fitting to the spirit of the humble cottage garden.

They're full. Cottage gardens tend to be lush and tumble all over each other with abandon. Place plants as close as common sense allows and don't worry about positioning them too evenly. (Tip: Intensively planted gardens like this do best with good soil. Work in as much compost as possible at planting time and add more compost to the soil each year.)

They're usually asymmetrical. In formal gardens, straight lines, geometry, and strict balance rule. In cottage gardens, the less planned out a garden looks, the more successfully it adheres to the cottage philosophy.

Pedestal With a Pot

Give a bed or border a casual focal point by topping a stack of bricks with a pot brimming with roses.

BEDS AND BORDERS LOOK BEST IF THEY HAVE A FOCAL POINT. IT CAN BE A BIRDBATH, A SUNDIAL, A SCULPTURE, OR IN THIS CASE, A SIMPLE POT SET ON A BRICK COLUMN.

Plant the pot with something vivid. In this case, it's a red rose. While nearly any rose will grow in a pot, a good choice would be a tough, long-blooming type, such as one of the Flower Carpet or Knock Out roses.

In warm climates, Zones 8 and warmer (see page 216), the rose will grow fine in the pot year-round. However, in colder regions the soil would freeze and kill the rose. In these colder areas, it's best to plant the pot with bright red annuals, such as a red Martha Washington or other cascading geranium. After the first hard frost, empty and store the pot indoors until spring. This sun-loving border gets a secondary focal point from the pine standard. Standards are simply plants

trained into a lollipop shape. In this garden, it's, a pine. Or experiment with substituting any other type of standard, such as one from rosemary, hibiscus, or a rose. Evergreen standards are usually cold-hardy through Zone 4 while other standards have variable cold-hardiness, so factor that into the selection.

If standards aren't to your taste or in your budget—they're usually pricey—just leave them out. Corn poppies are seeded throughout this planting, weaving in and out of other plantings, creating bright spots of scarlet. They're easy on the budget too, since they do best from seed.

Corn Poppy

PLANT SUPERSTAR
CORN POPPIES

Also called Shirley poppies or sometimes Flanders poppies, these are the real-life version of the crimson paper flowers handed out as a fundraiser for war veterans. Corn poppies are seldom available as established seedlings since they have a long taproot that makes transplanting difficult.

Instead, start them from seed directly in the ground. In cold winter areas (Zones 7 and colder), plant them from seed as soon as the soil can be worked in late winter or early spring. In warmer regions, sow in September for winter color and very early spring for a second show.

Do not cover the seeds; they need light to germinate. Keep lightly moist by watering daily with the fine mister of a hose spray attachment.

Once the seeds germinate, thin them—that is, pull up all but selected seedings—so that there's just one poppy seedling every 8 or so inches.

PLANT LIST

A. **1 Spiderwort** (*Tradescantia* spp.): Zones 5–9

B. **2 Rose campions** (*Lychnis coronaria*) such as 'Alba': Zones 4–8

C. **3 Yarrows** (*Achillea milliefolium*) such as 'Cerise Queen': Zones 3–9

D. **1 Variegated boxwood** (*Buxus sempervirens* 'Variegata'): Zones 6–9

E. **1 Rose** such as Flower Carpet Red: will survive winters in a pot in Zones 7–9 in colder climates. If desired, plant red trailing geraniums, which are annuals, in colder climates.

F. **3 Lamb's ears** (*Stachys byzantina*): Zones 4–8

G. **1 Dwarf pine standard** (*Pinus* spp.): Zones 3–10, depending on the type

H. **6 Asiatic lilies** (*Lilium* spp.): Zones 2–8

I. **1 or 2 Seed packets of corn poppy** (*Papaver rhoeas*): Annual

The pedestal shown here is made of mortared brick, which takes time and skill to construct. Create a smaller, easier, faster version with two square concrete pavers and 8 bricks.

Place one of the concrete pavers on the soil, making sure it's level. Then lay two bricks, touching side by side, on the paver. Then stack two more bricks, running the other direction, on top of that. Repeat with one or two more layers.

Top with the second concrete paver to act as a cap. Place the pot on top.

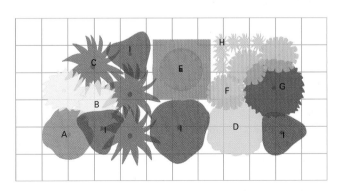

Each square = 1 foot

Turn a Patio Into A Lush Retreat

Embellish a sitting area with pots of flowers set against rich background plantings.

THERE'S SOMETHING SLIGHTLY EXTRAVAGANT ABOUT PUTTING GENEROUSLY SIZED POTS, OVERFLOWING WITH FLOWERS, IN FRONT OF A FLOWER BED. THE EFFECT IS WONDERFULLY LAYERED, BLOOM UPON BLOOM UPON BLOOM.

This patio would be perfectly attractive with just the plantings shown alongside it. But the addition of the pots, which are planted with some of the same flowers in the beds, makes the flower bed seem to leap out of the ground and embrace whoever is lucky enough to enjoy a relaxing morning or restful afternoon reclining nearby. Pots add color, interest, and detail.

This patio is an asymmetrical shape, but the idea would also work with nearly any shape patio or low deck, as long as the area receives at least part sun. Simply plant the edge with billowy flowers and tuck in a few pots alongside.

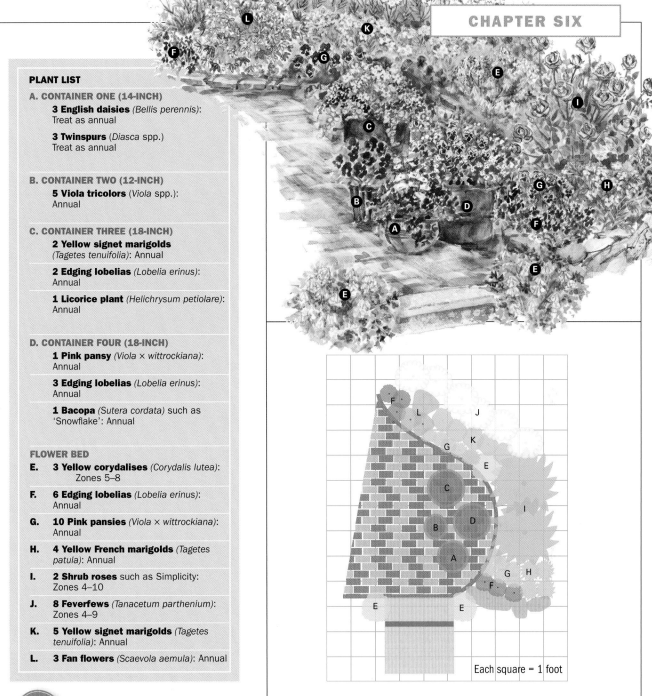

PLANT LIST

A. CONTAINER ONE (14-INCH)

3 English daisies (*Bellis perennis*): Treat as annual

3 Twinspurs (*Diasca* spp.) Treat as annual

B. CONTAINER TWO (12-INCH)

5 Viola tricolors (*Viola* spp.): Annual

C. CONTAINER THREE (18-INCH)

2 Yellow signet marigolds (*Tagetes tenuifolia*): Annual

2 Edging lobelias (*Lobelia erinus*): Annual

1 Licorice plant (*Helichrysum petiolare*): Annual

D. CONTAINER FOUR (18-INCH)

1 Pink pansy (*Viola × wittrockiana*): Annual

3 Edging lobelias (*Lobelia erinus*): Annual

1 Bacopa (*Sutera cordata*) such as 'Snowflake': Annual

FLOWER BED

E. **3 Yellow corydalises** (*Corydalis lutea*): Zones 5–8

F. **6 Edging lobelias** (*Lobelia erinus*): Annual

G. **10 Pink pansies** (*Viola × wittrockiana*): Annual

H. **4 Yellow French marigolds** (*Tagetes patula*): Annual

I. **2 Shrub roses** such as Simplicity: Zones 4–10

J. **8 Feverfews** (*Tanacetum parthenium*): Zones 4–9

K. **5 Yellow signet marigolds** (*Tagetes tenuifolia*): Annual

L. **3 Fan flowers** (*Scaevola aemula*): Annual

Each square = 1 foot

THE BEST PATIOSIDE PLANTINGS

Choose plants that look good for long periods of time. Rely on plants that have a tidy growth habit since you'll be looking at these plants up close and personal—a lot. Position plants with more rangy, wild, open growth habits farther out in the garden where they can be appreciated from a distance.

Whenever possible, choose plants that are fragrant. Since people are often sitting with their noses right at plant height, it's a wonderful opportunity to really enjoy the scent. Compact fragrant plants for patioside settings include Oriental lilies, hyacinths, stock, heliotropes, azaleas, dwarf lilacs, gardenias, some types of roses, and some types of flowering tobacco. Conveniently, most plants release their fragrance best in the late afternoon or early evening, just when you're getting home from work and need a fragrant, relaxing setting the most.

Fertilize judiciously. Be sure to work in plenty of compost at planting time. And feed plants regularly throughout the growing season so they're at peak performance longer. But don't overfertilize, which will stimulate too much lush, green growth and make plants floppy.

Keep plants well groomed. This is likely the flower bed you're going to view the most. Keep it tidy so it can be truly enjoyed. Fortunately, this is easy since it's a cinch to pull a few weeds and do a little deadheading every time you go outside.

Make a Curbside Bloom

Plant a broad sweep of tough perennials to soften and brighten a corner lot curb.

A WASH OF BLOOMING PLANTS FILLS THE EDGE OF THIS WIDE, CURVING CORNER LOT. ADAPT THE IDEA TO A NARROW MEDIAN STRIP BETWEEN A SIDEWALK AND A STREET, WHETHER IT TURNS AND TWISTS OR NOT.

Tired of having a front yard that looks like everyone else's on the block? This gardener was, so she planted vast sweeps of easy-care perennials that thrive in full sun and fill her front yard with blooms.

The catmint, cushion spurge, sedum, and wallflower all need very little care yet bloom for several weeks at a time. Among these low masses of flowers, other perennials, such as giant allium and foxglove, add a vertical element, like exclamation points.

This curbside planting is in a neighborhood without sidewalks, so it could stretch as wide as the homeowners wanted. In neighborhoods with sidewalks, you could end the flower bed at the walk or—even better—extend past the sidewalk to the curb for maximum impact.

A major benefit of a planting like this is that it minimizes lawn. Lawn is thirstier than this collection of plants and needs more fertilizer and weed control. The amount of time needed to maintain either one is a toss-up, but certainly, most homeowners feel that tending flowers is more fun than simply mowing week after week. The neighbors like it too!

PLANT LIST

A. **7 Cushion spurges** (*Euphorbia polychroma*): Zones 4–8

B. **2 Tall sedums** (*Sedum spectabile*) such as 'Autumn Joy': Zones 3–10

C. **6 Oriental poppies** (*Papaver orientale*): Zones 4–9

D. **6 Columbines** (*Aquilegia* spp.): Zones 3–9

E. **5 Giant ornamental onions** (*Allium giganteum*) such as 'Globemaster': Zones 4–9

F. **2 Large catmints** (*Nepeta* spp.) such as 'Six Hills Giant' or 'Walker's Low': Zones 4–8

G. **3 Foxgloves** (*Digitalis purpurea*): Zones 4–8

H. **9 Wallflower** (*Erysimum* spp.) such as 'Bowles Mauve': Zones 6–10

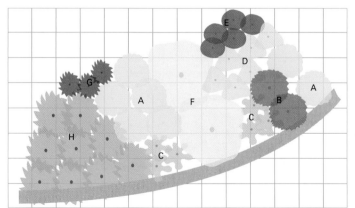

Each square = 1 foot

BHG MONEY SAVER This bed has large swaths of perennials. If it's not in the budget to plant such a large bed, plant just the front half of this planting, the part right along the street. Then, two or three years later, after the perennials have established themselves, divide them and plant the other half.

GARDEN SMARTER

TIPS FOR SUCCESSFUL CURBSIDE PLANTINGS

Check with local zoning offices. There may be height and planting restrictions. Many won't let homeowners grow plants over a certain height.

Consider salt-tolerance. In cold-weather areas, plants are likely to get doused with salt spread on the road to melt ice. Choose those that can handle it.

Choose lower-water plants. As much as possible, choose plants that will need little watering. If there's an irrigation system, that's a huge help; Otherwise watering a curb means hauling the hose a long way from the house.

Consider foliage. Choose those plants that have good-looking leaves as well as flowers. Curbside plantings are on display all the time and are under close observation by anyone walking by. They should look good much of the growing season.

Don't be afraid of broad sweeps of color. Much of the viewing of a curbside planting is from a moving car. Bold blasts of color are eye-catching even at 20 miles per hour.

Avoid mounding soil. Keep the soil level no higher than the sidewalk and curb. Otherwise, soil and mulch will wash onto the walk and water will be diverted onto the walk. This can be tricky since tilling or adding soil amendments increases the soil volume. Be prepared to haul some of the soil away to another location in the yard as needed. Or install a raised edging that will hold the soil in place.

A Protected Pocket

English gardeners have become masters at finding sheltered spots to nurture favorite plants like these.

PROTECT TALL, DELICATE FLOWERS FROM HARSH WINDS AND LOW TEMPERATURES BY TUCKING THEM INTO A CORNER CREATED BY A WALL, FENCE, OR A SECTION OF THE HOUSE.

Working with the existing structure of your landscape is key to any good design. Many gardeners look at a corner and see a problem, but in this case, a corner of a wall and stairs is the perfect place to grow tender plants protected from cold and damaging winds. That's especially important when growing statuesque plants, such as delphiniums, or plants just borderline hardy in your area.

In just about any garden, in fact, there are protected spots where plants will do better than they would in open areas. These are usually on the east and south side of houses, garages, fences, and hedges—away from the beating western sun and cold north wind. In some cases, you can gain an entire zone (see page 216) by planting in a protected spot.

Case in point: The Peruvian lily is hardy only to Zone 8. But in a protected spot, you might be able to get it to survive the winter as far north as Zone 7.

If the protecting structure is made of brick, stone, concrete, or stucco, there's an additional benefit. These materials are good at gathering heat during the day and then releasing the heat at night. Amazingly, in some cases, that tiny benefit can be the difference between a plant thriving or not.

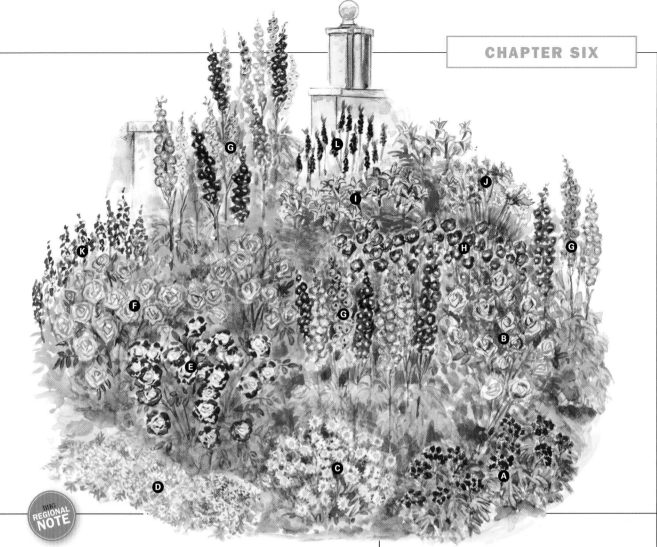

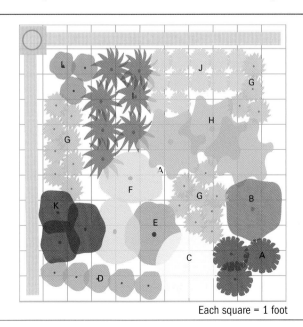

Each square = 1 foot

REGIONAL NOTE

Several of the plants in this garden are cold-hardy only to Zones 7 or 8 (see page 216). Gardeners in colder-weather gardens may want to substitute Shasta daisies for the marguerite daisies, pink yarrow for the cistus, Asiatic lilies for the Peruvian lilies, a smaller allium for the society garlic, and perennial salvia for the Mexican bush sage and lavender.

PLANT LIST

A. 3 Rose-type geraniums (*Pelargonium hortorum*) such as a 'Graveolens': Annual

B. 1 Medium-size rose such as 'Fragrant Memory': Zones 5–9

C. 1 Marguerite daisy (*Argyranthemum frutescens*): Zones 10–11, annual elsewhere

D. 5 Moss phloxes (*Phlox subulata*): Zones 3–8

E. 1 Medium-size rose such as 'Double Delight': Zones 5–9

F. 2 Other medium-size roses such as 'Chicago Peace': Zones 5–9

G. 20 Tall delphiniums (*Delphinium* hybrids): Zones 3–7

H. 3 Rock roses (*Cistus creticus*): Zones 7–10

I. 7 Peruvian lilies (*Alstroemeria* cultivars): Zones 8–10

J. 12 Society garlics (*Tulbaghia violacea*): Zones 7–10

K. 3 Mexican bush sages (*Salvia leucantha*): Zones 10–11

L. 3 Spanish lavenders (*Lavandula stoechas*): Zones 8–9

Ring Around A Lawn

Edge grass or other open areas with a classic border of mixed perennials to add fun and interest.

A RELIABLE MIX OF YELLOWS, PINKS, AND BLUES MAKES THIS A VERSATILE COTTAGE BED THAT EMBELLISHES A LAWN OR ALMOST ANY OTHER SUNNY SITE.

Who doesn't love a bed of pink, blue, and yellow flowers? They're as happy as a sunny day and fit in well with a variety of house styles and personal tastes.

This bed also has a few small boxwoods tucked in so that it always has something green and beautiful, even in winter when the surrounding perennials die back to the ground.

The slightly crescent-shape bed would work well in other settings too. Put it in a front lawn. Or use it at the far end of a sunny backyard. Straighten it out and plant it along a driveway. And if you have a larger space to cover, just repeat the planting pattern to run around the perimeter of a backyard.

For an even longer period of bloom, tuck in daffodils and tulips among the perennials for spring color. For fall color, add a few tall asters in the back and low-growing cushion mums in front.

Nearly all the flowers in this garden are good for cutting. And since cutting flowers is really just a highly pleasurable way to deadhead, you'll be grooming your garden and encouraging longer bloom times while you decorate your home. The reward will be wave after wave of bloom from early spring through frost.

PLANT LIST

A. **3 Dwarf boxwoods** (*Buxus* spp.): Zones 5–9

B. **4 Dame's rockets** (*Hesperis matronalis*): Zones 4–9

C. **1 Lamb's ears** (*Stachys byzantina*): Zones 4–8

D. **4 Hardy geraniums** (*Geranium* spp.): Zones 4–8

E. **1 Blue or purple beardtongue** (*Penstemon* spp.) such as 'Sour Grapes': Zones 7–10

F. **2 Peach-leaf bellflowers** (*Campanula persicifolia*) such as 'Alba': Zones 3–8

G. **4 Leopard's bane** (*Doronicum orientale*): Zones 4–8

H. **2 Yellow yarrows** (*Achillea filipendulina*) such as 'Coronation Gold': Zones 3–9

I. **9 Tall delphiniums** (*Delphinium* spp.) such as the Pacific Giants series: Zones 4–7

J. **1 Tall sedum** (*Sedum spectabile*) such as 'Autumn Joy': Zones 3–10

Each square = 1 foot

Delphinium

False indigo

GARDEN SMARTER
TOUGHER SPIRES OF BLUE

Delphiniums are gorgeous, but in very hot or cold climates, or those areas with severe weather, they can be difficult to grow as tall and gorgeous as they are pictured here.

An easier, more reliable alternative would be blue false indigo (*Baptisia australis*). It also produces beautiful spires of deep blue flowers but has a more shrubby growth habit. It grows 3 to 4 feet tall and grows 2 to 3 feet wide. Plant one blue false indigo for every three delphiniums in this or other plans in this book.

A Beautiful Mix

Contrasting heights, shapes, textures, and colors are key to any planting. This plan has it all!

A GOOD-LOOKING FLOWER BED ISN'T AN ACCIDENT. FOLLOW BASIC DESIGN RULES TO FOLLOW THAT ALLOW FLOWERS TO MIX AND MATCH GRACEFULLY.

In this garden, tall plants soar upward in the back while low plants sprawl forward. Grasses arc outward, spikey plants rise upward, and globelike flowers provide interesting accents.

Good flower garden design isn't difficult to do. Here's how simplify the process:

MAKE 'EM BIG. Design beds and borders deep enough to allow for a variety of shapes and heights. That means at least 3 feet deep for most beds and borders, but don't be afraid to extend the bed even 6 or 9 feet deep. (Put a narrow, mulched access path along the back to make it easy to care for the garden.)

PLACE TALL PLANTS IN BACK. Those that climb trellises or fences or that rise 3 feet or more are like the tall kids in the photo. They go in the back row. In island beds, they go in the center.

SITE LOW PLANTS IN FRONT. Look for climbing or sprawling plants that don't grow much more than a foot tall to gracefully fill out the front. They can be annuals, perennials, or small ornamental grasses.

FIND GOOD MIDDLE-GROUND PLANTS. Those plants that grow 1 to 3 feet tall can go in the middle.

CONSIDER THE LEAVES. Go for a mix of foliage types that are different colors, shapes, sizes, and textures. If you get the leaves right, the planting will look good even when things aren't in bloom.

BHG REGIONAL NOTE

If cardoon isn't cold hardy in your zone (see page 216), plant four purple spider flowers (*Cleome*) instead. They're anuals and so last only until frost, but they're far less expensive with interesting flowers and an interesting shape.

PLANT LIST

A. **1 Maiden grass** (*Miscanthus sinensis* 'Gracillimus'): Zones 4–9

B. **8 Giant alliums** (*Allium giganteum*): Zones 5–10

C. **1 Coral bells** (*Heuchera* spp.): Zones 3–10, depending on species

D. **1 Boxwood** (*Buxus sempervirens*) such as 'Wintergreen': Zones 5–8

E. **6 Fleabanes** (*Erigeron karvinskianus*): Zones 5–7

F. **3 Pincushion flowers** (*Scabiosa columbaria*): Zones 4–9

G. **1 Lamb's ears** (*Stachys byzantina*): Zones 4–8

H. **1 Purple-leaf plantain** (*Plantago major* 'Rubrifolia'): Annual

I. **2 Blue fescues** (*Festuca glauca*) such as 'Elijah Blue': Zones 4–8

J. **3 Sea hollies** (*Eryngium* spp.): Zones 4–9

K. **5 Rose verbenas** (*Verbena × hybrida*): Annual

L. **3 Cosmoses** (*Cosmos bipinnatus*): Annual

M. **1 Shasta daisy** (*Leucanthemum × superbum*): Zones 5–8

N. **1 Hardy geranium** (*Geranium* spp.): Zones 5–9

O. **3 Pinks** (*Dianthus* spp.) such as 'Bath's Pink': Zone 4–9

P. **1 Large-flowered clematis** (*Clematis* hybrids): Zones 4–9

Q. **1 Low-growing sedum**, such as *Sedum sieboldii*: Zones 6–9

R. **3 Firecracker plants** (*Bouvardia ternifolia*): Annual

S. **1 Blue false indigo** (*Baptisia australis*): Zones 3–9

T. **1 Meadow rue** (*Thalictrum delavayi*): Zones 5–9

U. **12 Irises** (*Iris* hybrids): Zones 5–9

V. **4 African daisies** (*Osteospermum jucundum*) such as 'Nairobi Purple': Annual

W. **1 Joseph's coat** (*Alternanthera ficoidea* var. *amoena* 'Versicolor'): Annual

X. **1 Cardoon** (*Cynara cardunculus*): Zones 7–9

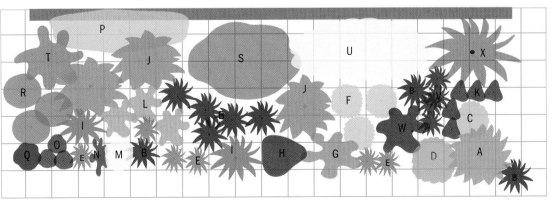

Each square = 1 foot

Marathon Bloomers

Make your garden go the distance with colorful flowers artfully arranged in a casual cottage planting.

THERE'S A SAYING THAT IT'S EASY TO HAVE A PRETTY GARDEN IN MAY; THE TOUGH PART IS KEEPING IT GREAT-LOOKING IN AUGUST. THIS PLAN SOLVES THAT PROBLEM WITH PLANTS THAT GIVE AND GIVE FOR MONTHS.

If you've ever had a planting that flowered beautifully for a little while and then stopped, you'll appreciate this combo's ability to keep going even in the worst of summer's heat.

Ornamental grasses—a maiden grass would be elegant—are attractive from the moment they pop out of the ground in spring. They look fresh in summer and then produce beautiful seed heads in late summer and early autumn. Leave the grasses standing over winter to allow you to appreciate snow and ice on their by-then buff-colored foliage.

Some of the plants in this garden are tropicals, plants that originate where it's super hot and humid. When your garden is a steambath in August, they'll be lovin' it. The canna, annual red salvia, vinca flowers (sometimes known as periwinkle), and butter daisies thrive in hot and steamy weather. (Mulch to help conserve moisture; these plants need it.)

Tall bearded iris add color to this garden in spring. And the zinnias are a nice, low-maintenance touch. You can start them directly in the soil from seed, if you like—they're that easy!

PLANT LIST

A. **9 Scarlet sages** (*Salvia splendens*): Annual

B. **2 Tall irises** (*Iris* hybrids): Zones 3–9, depending on species

C. **2 Cannas** such as 'Tropicana': Zones 8–11; annual elsewhere

D. **7 Vincas** (*Catharanthus roseus*): Zone 9–11; annual elsewhere

E. **9 Tall zinnias** (*Zinnia elegans*): Annual

F. **3 Ornamental grasses** such as *Miscanthus sinensis* 'Morning Light': Zones 4–9

G. **4 Gloriosa daisies** (*Rudbeckia hirta*): Zones 4–9

H. **6 Million golds** (*Melampodium paludosum*): Annual

GARDEN SMARTER
MORE COLOR LONGER

Get even more bloom time from this and other plantings by following these pointers:

Deadhead daily. **Trim off spent flowers to encourage plants to keep blooming longer.**

Add bulbs. **For even more color, tuck in a dozen or more daffodil bulbs in fall among the plants for more flowers earlier next year.**

Prune early. **In spring, trim back by about one-third any tall plants that bloom in the fall, such as asters and false sunflower. They will quickly recover and grow into more sturdy plants that don't flop once they reach their mature height.**

Pinch mums. **Snip back new growth until the Fourth of July to encourage stockier, fuller-blooming plants in autumn.**

Mind the basics. **Water regularly, never letting plants wilt. Also fertilize regularly with a bloom-booster formula.**

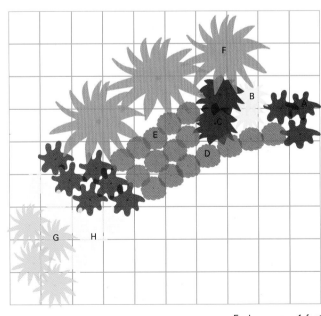

Each square = 1 foot

A Fancy Fence

Double your pleasure and that of passersby by planting both sides of a fence.

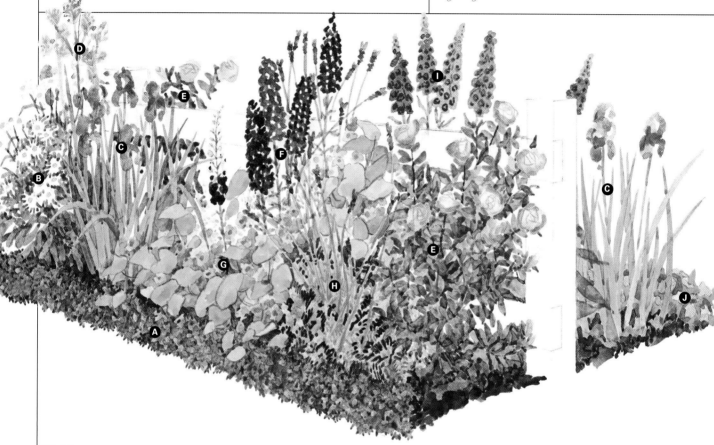

THIS PLANTING WOULD BE BEAUTIFUL WITH JUST ONE SIDE OF THE FENCE PLANTED WITH COLORFUL FLOWERS. BUT WHEN YOU PLANT THE OTHER SIDE TOO, YOU CAN ENJOY THE DISPLAY FROM TWO DIRECTIONS.

Fences are a natural magnet for landscape plantings. They make a reliable backdrop for small trees, shrubs, and flowers. Plus they are a built-in plant support, preventing taller plants from flopping and providing a handy leg up for climbing vines and roses. Tall delphiniums and foxgloves, for example, otherwise would be more time-consuming to grow.

When building or choosing a fence for your landscape, keep in mind how easy or difficult it will be to landscape around it. Open fences like this are the easiest to landscape—they're just one big plant support. Lattice fences are especially good as plant supports because it's so easy for plants to weave in and out of them. You don't need to tie plants to get them started.

Tall, solid fences can be more of a challenge since they often need trellises to help support vines and climbing roses. Also, since they're solid, they cast more shade, which limits plant choices, especially if the fence faces north.

When deciding on a material and finish for your fence, go for those that need minimal maintenance, such as natural wood or metal. (Vinyl fencing is easy-care, but choose carefully to find one with less shine that looks more natural.) You can let the wood weather naturally, though consider a sealant to better protect it from the elements. If you choose to add color, consider a stain, which won't peel the way paint might.

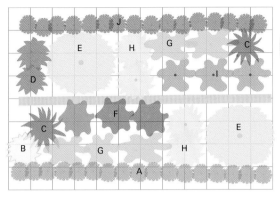

Each square = 1 foot

PLANT LIST

A. **17 Edging lobelias** *(Lobelia erinus)*: Annual

B. **1 Shasta daisy** *(Leucanthemum × superbum)*: Zones 4–9

C. **2 German bearded irises** *(Iris germanica)*: Zones 3–10

D. **2 Brazilian vervains** *(Verbena bonariensis)*: Zones 7–11; annual elsewhere

E. **2 Roses** *(Rosa 'Peace')*: Zones 5–9

F. **3 Tall delphiniums** *(Delphinium hybrids)* such as the Pacific Giant series: Zones 3–7

G. **5 Nasturtiums** *(Tropaeolum hybrids)* such as the Gleam series: Annual

H. **4 Spanish lavenders** *(Lavandula stoechas)*: Zones 8–11*

I. **3 Foxgloves** *(Digitalis purpurea)*: Biennial, Zones 4–9

J. **16 Impatiens** *(Impatiens walleriana)*: Annual

**In colder regions substitute English lavender.*

THE TIE THAT BINDS

Some of the plants in this garden, such as the foxglove and delphiniums, do best with staking or supports.

In most gardens, you can stake by pounding a tall (about 4 feet) stake or pole into the ground right at planting time. As the plant grows, tie it to the stake every several inches.

You can also buy special single plant supports. They're made of green powder–coated metal with a small open hoop a few inches across atop a stake of 3 or so feet. Put these in after the plant is about a foot tall.

However, this garden plan has a fence running through it, which not only is charming but also practical. It serves as an informal support for the delphiniums and foxgloves. It's also a handy support for a rose, should you choose to plant a taller, climbing type.

Tie plants directly to the fence. No need for stakes or other supports. Use dark green twine, which is hard to detect. One caveat: Be sure to position tall plants right up against the fence so they grow close to their support.

A Flowering Foundation

Forget ordinary and go for extraordinary! This front-yard planting will be the talk of the neighborhood.

MOST FOUNDATION PLANTINGS ARE NOTHING MORE THAN SOME EVERGREENS AND A TREE. GET ADVENTUROUS AND MIX UP ROSES, CLEMATIS, DAYLILIES, AND MORE FOR A DECIDEDLY DIFFERENT DESIGN.

The job of a foundation planting is to integrate the house with the landscape so that the two blend seamlessly, creating a welcoming, harmonious look. Without a foundation planting, a house looks stark, as though rises directly from the ground.

Instead of the usual row of evergreens, this foundation planting features low-maintenance shrub roses, fronted by neat rows of perennials and backed by sprawling clematis—a romantic touch that is the hallmark of cottage style.

If you don't have three windows along the front,

simply plant clematis on either side of a larger window or smaller multiple windows. Choose large-flowered clematis, which grow about 6 to 12 feet tall, just the right size for this scheme. Provide the clematis with a trellis for support. Inexpensive prefabricated types from the garden center will do fine. Just make sure the trellis is at least 6 to 8 feet tall. If possible, anchor the top to the house to prevent tipping outward.

It's a simple matter to shorten it or extend this plan as far as needed to fit the planting space by adding or subtracting daylilies, salvias, and shrub roses.

PLANT LIST

A. **2 Miniature roses:** Zones 5–9

B. **3 Dwarf Asiatic lilies** (*Lilium* hybrids) such as 'Lollipop': Zones 3–8

C. **2 Indian hawthorns** (*Raphiolepis indica*): Zones 8–10*

D. **10 Miniature daylilies** (*Hemerocallis* hybrids) such as 'Stella de Oro': Zones 3–10

E. **10 Perennial sages** (*Salvia* × *sylvestris*) 'May Night': Zones 4–8

F. **5 Shrub roses** such as 'Betty Prior': Zones 5–9

G. **3 Large-flowered clematises** (*Clematis* hybrids) such as 'Jackmanii' and 'Henryi': Zones 4–9

* In colder regions, substitute dwarf Korean lilacs (Syringa meyeri).

Each square = 1 foot

Vintage Charm

Relive the past with a planting that your great-grandmother might have strolled through.

IN A SIMPLER ERA, PLANTS NOW TAKEN FOR GRANTED WERE TREASURED. THIS DESIGN, SPREAD OUT ON A LARGE LAWN, USES VINTAGE FLOWERS IN ABUNDANCE TO HELP REDISCOVER THEIR BEAUTY ONCE AGAIN.

This plan is filled with broad sweeps of plants that serious plant designers seldom feature: iris, peonies, dame's rocket, and heavenly fragrant mock orange. It even includes some asparagus for a utilitarian touch so characteristic of gardens a century ago, when water was more precious and time spent on flowers secondary to making sure your family had enough to eat.

This garden would be perfect in the middle of a large lawn, a stylish way to reduce mowing chores.

Adapt it to your own tastes by adding large sweeps of other plants common to Victorian-era gardens, such as daylilies, rose-of–sharon, common lilacs, snowball viburnum, true lilies, lily-of-the-valley, and ferns.

If the design is too large for your space, reduce it by cutting the number of roses in half to make either side of the path smaller. Or simply plant one side of the plan and not the other.

Keep maintenance chores to a minimum by installing edging. Salvaged weathered brick would be an appropriately vintage material.

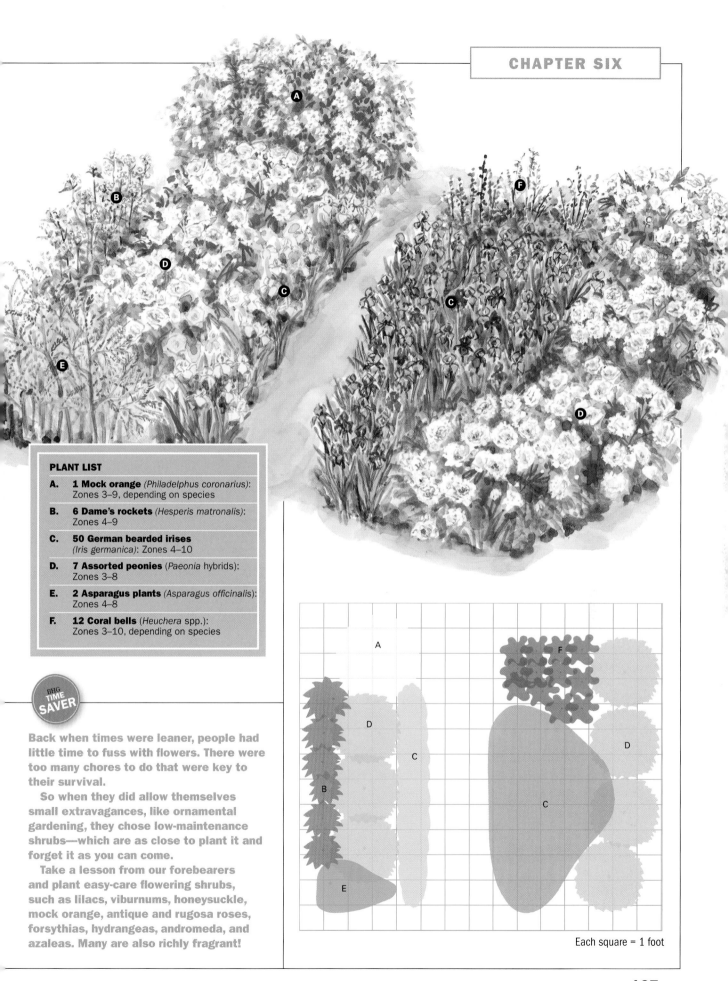

PLANT LIST

A. **1 Mock orange** (*Philadelphus coronarius*):
    Zones 3–9, depending on species

B. **6 Dame's rockets** (*Hesperis matronalis*):
    Zones 4–9

C. **50 German bearded irises**
    (*Iris germanica*): Zones 4–10

D. **7 Assorted peonies** (*Paeonia* hybrids):
    Zones 3–8

E. **2 Asparagus plants** (*Asparagus officinalis*):
    Zones 4–8

F. **12 Coral bells** (*Heuchera* spp.):
    Zones 3–10, depending on species

BHG
TIME
SAVER

Back when times were leaner, people had little time to fuss with flowers. There were too many chores to do that were key to their survival.

So when they did allow themselves small extravagances, like ornamental gardening, they chose low-maintenance shrubs—which are as close to plant it and forget it as you can come.

Take a lesson from our forebearers and plant easy-care flowering shrubs, such as lilacs, viburnums, honeysuckle, mock orange, antique and rugosa roses, forsythias, hydrangeas, andromeda, and azaleas. Many are also richly fragrant!

Each square = 1 foot

Collect Passalong Plants

Create a garden of perennials and herbs shared from family and friends.

PASSALONG PLANTS NOT ONLY SAVE YOU MONEY; THEY PRESERVE MEMORIES OF NEIGHBORS, GARDENING FRIENDS, CHERISHED FAMILY MEMBERS, AND OTHER LOVED ONES. EACH PLANT IS A MEMORY.

Sharing plants is a gardening fundamental. So why not take advantage of this charming tradition and create a garden entirely from plants shared by others?

This garden's focal point is a bench and arbor, which align with a sundial. (All are great gifts to receive for birthdays and special events like Mother's or Father's Day. Drop hints!)

Fill spaces around these focal points with plants gleaned from others' gardens—peonies, daylilies, hardy geraniums, catmints, or daisies that proliferate in others' gardens. Gardeners are by nature generous

people and are usually happy to share.

These are the plants that grow in such abundance that you'll sometimes see them put out on a curb with a sign: "Free to good home."

So if you spy a plant you like, ask politely and offer something in return—preferably another plant, but even a plate of freshly baked cookies would be welcome.

The plan is forgiving. Mix and match freely. However, when designing with these plants, group them according to color. This avoids a look that is too jumbled and patchwork.

PLANT LIST

A. **1 Grape vine** such as 'Concord': Zones 4–9

B. **1 Climbing rose** such as 'Constance Spry': Zones 5–9

C. **3 Monkshoods** (*Aconitum* spp.): Zones 3–7

D. **12 Various daylilies** (*Hemerocallis* hybrids): Zones 3–10

E. **4 Various peonies:** Zones 3–9

F. **2 Dwarf boxwoods** (*Buxus* spp.): Zones 5–10, depending on the type

G. **10 Various irises** such as German bearded or Siberian: Zones 3–9

H. **1 Hardy geranium** (*Geranium* spp.) such as 'Johnson's Blue': Zones 4–8

I. **3 Pink hardy geraniums** such as 'Ballerina': Zones 4–8

J. **9 Wild strawberries** (*Fragaria chiloensis*): Zones 4–7

K. **1 Sage** (*Salvia officinalis*): Zones 5–8

L. **6 Oxeye daisies** (*Leucanthemum vulgare*): Zones 4–7

M. **6 Coral bells** (*Heuchera* spp.): Zones 4–9

N. **10 Lady's mantles** (*Alchemilla mollis*): Zones 4–7

O. **2 Yarrows** (*Achillea* spp.): Zones 4–8

P. **2 China pinks** (*Dianthus* 'Bath's Pink'): Zones 4–9

Q. **1 Geum** (*Geum coccineum*): Zones 5–9

R. **1 Santolina** (*Santolina chamaecyparissus*): Zones 5–9

S. **1 Thyme** (*Thymus* spp.): Zones 4–9

T. **1 Common woadwaxen** (*Genista tinctoria*): Zones 2–8

U. **6 Asiatic lilies** (*Lilium*): Zones 3–8

V. **3 Catmints** (*Nepeta* spp.): Zones 4–9

W. **4 Tickseeds** (*Coreopsis* spp.): Zones 3–8

GARDEN SMARTER
GREAT PASSALONG PLANTS

The best plants for sharing spread well, but not invasively, and are easy to divide. They include:

Bee balm	Larkspur*
Catmint	Lily-of-the-valley
Columbine*	Obedient plant
Crocus	Oxeye daisy*
Daylily	Peony
Hollyhock*	Purple coneflower
Hostas	Tickseed
Iris	Thyme
Joe pye weed	Virginia bluebell
Lady's mantle	Yarrow

Prolific reseeders. Dig up and share seedlings in spring.

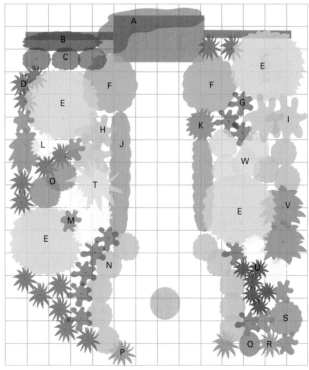

Each square = 1 foot

Elegantly Formal

In this bustling, chaotic world, the serene elegance of a formal garden is wonderfully soothing. *This type of garden somehow bespeaks a kinder, gentler era of order and beauty. But well-ordered doesn't have to translate into stiff or stuffy. A formal garden is simply any garden that is symmetrical, that has a certain element of repetition. That repetition, when done well, is comforting, not confining.*

Mirror Image

Flank either side of a front entry with two undulating beds filled with cheerful flowers.

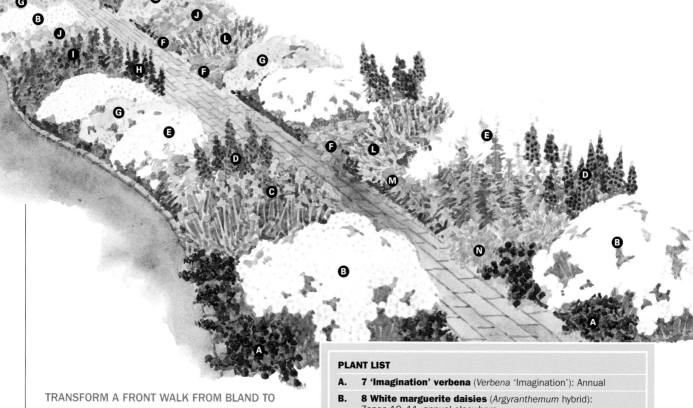

TRANSFORM A FRONT WALK FROM BLAND TO BEAUTIFUL! IT'S EASY TO DO. JUST DIG UP THE TURF ON EITHER SIDE AND FILL WITH A MIX OF ANNUALS AND PERENNIALS.

Two straight strips of plantings lining the sidewalk are a little predictable. So make some waves and liven things up.

By simply curving the edges of the two beds in the snaking pattern shown here, the design becomes more interesting.

The beds are filled with classic cottage flowers: snapdragons, foxgloves, daisies, yarrows, and delphiniums. You can also substitute freely. Add shrub roses or other perennials and annuals.

Install edging to keep grass from creeping into the beds. Brick is a natural choice in front of this brick home, but you could also use other types of barriers.

PLANT LIST

A.	**7 'Imagination' verbena** (*Verbena* 'Imagination'): Annual
B.	**8 White marguerite daisies** (*Argyranthemum* hybrid): Zones 10–11, annual elsewhere
C.	**4 Annual verbenas** (*Verbena × hybrida*): Annual
D.	**6 Foxgloves** (*Digitalis purpurea*): Biennial, Zones 4–9
E.	**1 Spider flower** (*Cleome hassleriana*) such as 'White Queen': Annual
F.	**5 Wax begonia** (*Begonia semperflorens-cultorum*): Annual
G.	**8 Pink marguerite daisies** (*Argyranthemum*) such as 'Mary Wootton' or 'Vancouver': Zones 10–11, annual elsewhere
H.	**3 Snapdragons** (*Antirrhinum majus*): Annual
I.	**4 Delphiniums** (*Delphinium* Belladonna Group): Zones 3–7
J.	**2 Yarrows** (*Achillea filipendulina*) such as 'Coronation Gold': Zones 3–9
K.	**6 Violet sages** (*Salvia nemorosa*) such as 'Pink Friesland': Zones 5–11
L.	**2 Spanish lavenders** (*Lavandula stoechas pedunculata*): Zones 8–11
M.	**1 Common yarrow** (*Achillea millefolium*) such as 'Paprika': Zones 3–8
N.	**1 Mugwort** (*Artemisia vulgaris*) such as 'Oriental Limelight': Zones 4–8

BHG REGIONAL NOTE

COLD-WEATHER SUBSTITUTES

The garden pictured is located in an area with mild winters where temperatures seldom dip below freezing. In colder regions, substitute more hardy English lavender for the Spanish lavender. And instead of the marguerite daisy, substitute Shasta daisies.

BHG DESIGN TIP

ELEMENTS OF FORMAL GARDEN STYLE

What makes a garden formal? Here are key aspects:

Symmetry. One half is shaped like or closely resembles the other half. Circles, rectangles, squares, and other geometric shapes set the tone of most formal gardens. Mix up plantings within the formal framework to keep them from looking stuffy or staid.

Repetition. Most formal gardens repeat elements, such as a certain plant, a series of trellises, or accents that mirror each other.

Edging. Most formal gardens incorporate edging. Boxwood is classic. Choose dwarf varieties, and trim regularly to keep in check. But nearly any neatly growing plant can be used. Or use hardscape, such as brick, raised bed edging, or stone to give it definition all year.

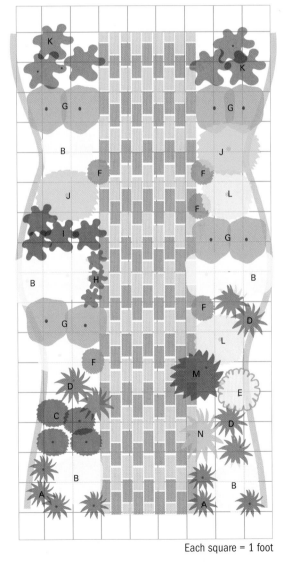

Each square = 1 foot

Plant a Bouquet

Enjoy flowers indoors and out with this formal cutting garden.

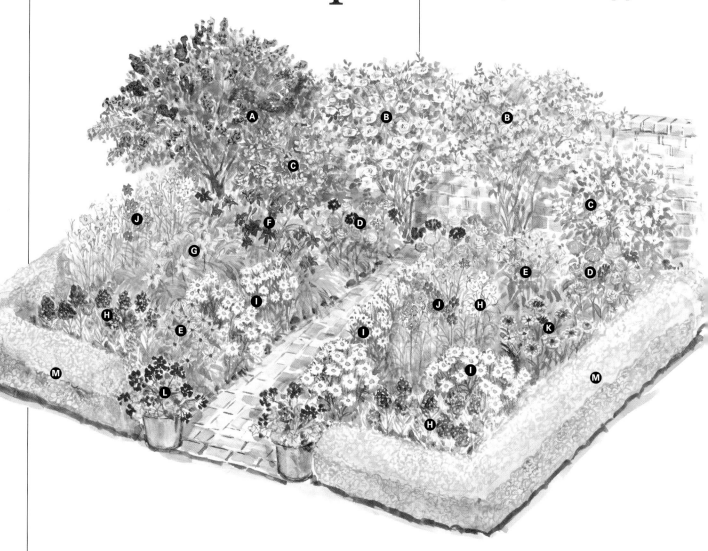

CREATE AN OUTLINE WITH LOW-GROWING BOXWOOD AND THEN FILL THIS GARDEN WITH A RAINBOW OF FLOWERS THAT YOU CAN CUT ALL GROWING SEASON LONG.

Even if you never pluck a single posy from this garden, it's so attractive you could plant it just to gaze at from afar. And that's an accomplishment, since too often, cutting gardens look like utilitarian farms rather than attractive landscaping.

This design is an exception. It's no plant-it-all-in-rows cutting garden. Instead, flowers are planted in relaxed drifts here and there so this garden is as pretty to look at as the arrangements you'll create from it.

Two pots, filled with annuals for cutting, make cheerful sentries to the entrance. A spectacular crape

myrtle adds a vertical element, as do the two climbing roses scaling the back wall.

Since there are no paths for easy access into the beds, you may want to strategically place stepping stones, pavers, or flagstones to give you a handy landing pad as you snip plants.

And while the garden shown is backed by a wall, you could easily adapt the design by extending the low hedge around the back and adding two more pots. Plant shrub roses instead of climbers, and you'll be set for armloads of flowers spring through fall.

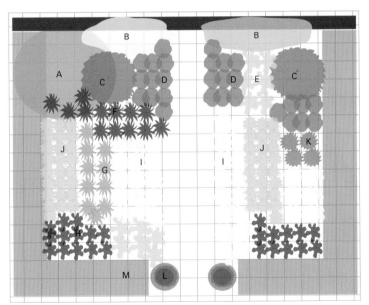

Each square = 1 foot

In colder regions, substitute dwarf Korean lilac for the camellia and saucer magnolia for the crape myrtle. Both are hardy through Zone 4.

PLANT LIST

A. **1 Crape myrtle** (*Lagerstroemia indica*): Zones 7–9

B. **2 Climbing roses** (*Rosa* hybrids): Zones 5–10

C. **2 Camellias** (*Camellia japonica*): Zones 6–8

D. **28 Tall zinnias** (*Zinnia elegans*): Annual

E. **12 Black-eyed susans** (*Rudbeckia fulgida*): Zones 4–9

F. **13 Red Asiatic lilies** (*Lilium* hybrids): Zones 4–9

G. **10 Yellow Asiatic lilies** (*Lilium* hybrids): Zones 4–9

H. **24 Stocks** (*Matthiola incana*) or **snapdragons** (*Antirrhinum majus*) or a mix: Annuals

I. **39 Shasta daisies** (*Leucanthemum × superbum*) or **Ox-eye daisies** (*Leucanthemum vulgare*): Zones 4–8

J. **50 Cosmoses** (*Cosmos bipinnatus*): Annual

K. **4 Gloriosa daisies** (*Rudbeckia hirta*): Zones 3–7

L. **8 Martha Washington geraniums** (*Pelargonium × domesticum*): Annual

M. **22 Dwarf boxwoods** (*Buxus* spp.): Zones 5–8*

* In Zone 5, choose a cold-hardy cultivar, such as 'Green Gem' and wrap in burlap for winter protection.

Lovely With Lavender

Outline a bed with circles and squares. Then fill with easy-care boxwood and fragrant lavender.

WITH A STRIKING PIECE OF FOUND ART AND CHARMING LAYOUT, THIS GARDEN WOULD BE A BEAUTIFUL FOCAL POINT FOR NEARLY ANY LANDSCAPE.

The sphere in the center is one-of-a-kind, but you could substitute any salvaged garden art, such as a lightning rod, weathervane, or other upright, interesting piece.

Surround the sphere or other accent with lavender and boxwood, though you could skip the boxwood and fill the entire bed with lavender. In Zones 5 and colder where lavender is marginally hardy, substitute catmint, fragrant shrub roses, or perennial blue salvia, which are more cold-hardy.

Wattling—rustic woven fence—is easy to craft yourself out of flexible, long slender branches from around the yard (willow is the classic wood for this).

If you're feeling not-so-crafty, use attractive low edging fencing available at garden centers. You can even leave the edging out altogether, but it adds a nice architectural element to the garden.

A shredded bark path makes for easy viewing and low maintenance. Tepees made of branches, long lengths of bamboo, or wooden lath add additional vertical elements.

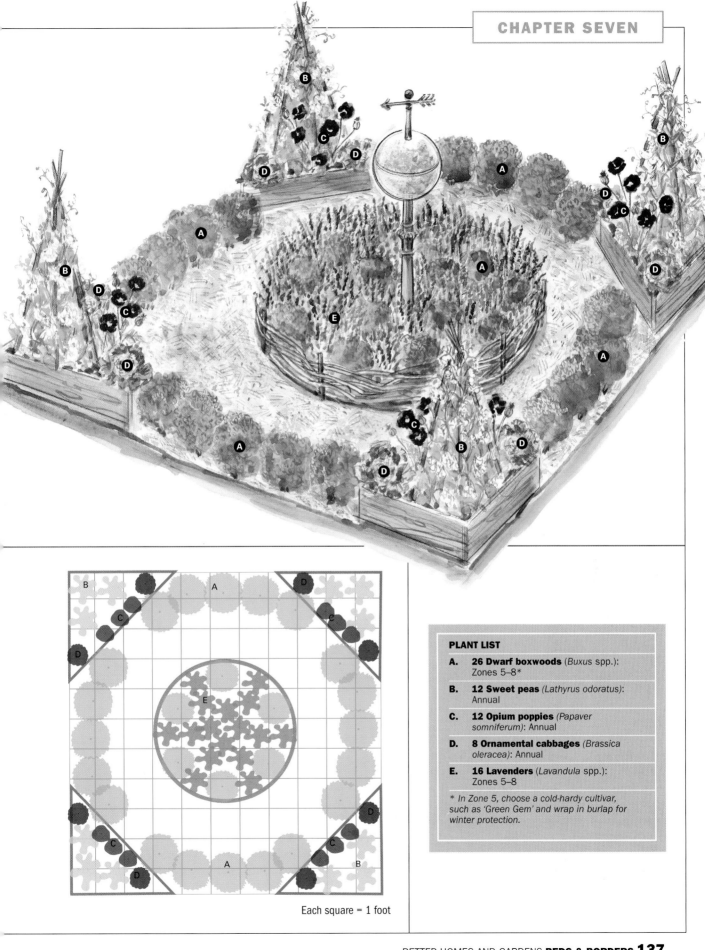

Each square = 1 foot

PLANT LIST

A. **26 Dwarf boxwoods** (*Buxus* spp.):
Zones 5–8*

B. **12 Sweet peas** (*Lathyrus odoratus*):
Annual

C. **12 Opium poppies** (*Papaver
somniferum*): Annual

D. **8 Ornamental cabbages** (*Brassica
oleracea*): Annual

E. **16 Lavenders** (*Lavandula* spp.):
Zones 5–8

** In Zone 5, choose a cold-hardy cultivar,
such as 'Green Gem' and wrap in burlap for
winter protection.*

Weave a Classic Knot Garden

This pretty planting is edged in low boxwood and filled with an assortment of flowers and herbs.

SINCE MEDIEVAL TIMES, KNOT GARDENS HAVE BEEN PRIZED IN LANDSCAPES FOR THEIR ELEGANT LINES AND TRIM APPEARANCE. AND IN MODERN TIMES THEY CAN BE AN OASIS OF ORDER IN THE LANDSCAPE.

Knot gardens can be quite elaborate, with low edges of different-color foliage creating an interwoven pattern. Or they can be simple, like the knot garden here. Its straightforward design makes it easier to achieve, lay out, and maintain.

Follow this pattern exactly or alter it to better fit your own yard and personal style. The planting plan includes excellent suggestions for filling the shapes but you may substitute freely. Include more colorful annuals, herbs,

or more perennials to avoid replanting each year. Just be sure to use small plants that have a tidy growing habit to keep the neat, sharp appearance crucial to a well-tended knot garden.

Also select plants that contrast with the emerald green foliage of the boxwood hedges so the design stands out. Choose brightly colored flowers or plants with contrasting foliage in silvery grays, yellow-greens, or deep purples.

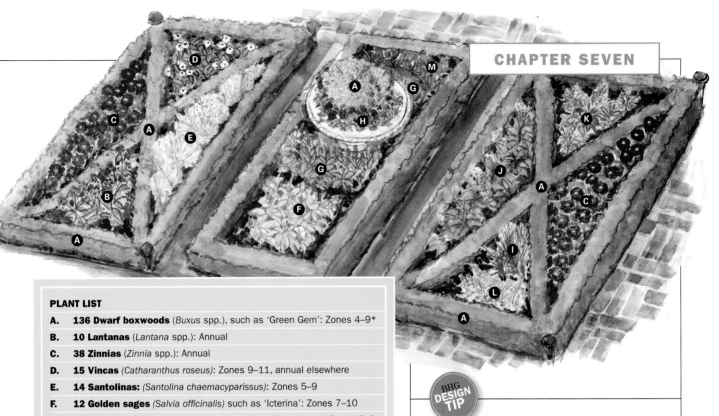

PLANT LIST

A. **136 Dwarf boxwoods** (*Buxus* spp.), such as 'Green Gem': Zones 4–9*

B. **10 Lantanas** (*Lantana* spp.): Annual

C. **38 Zinnias** (*Zinnia* spp.): Annual

D. **15 Vincas** (*Catharanthus roseus)*: Zones 9–11, annual elsewhere

E. **14 Santolinas:** (*Santolina chaemacyparissus)*: Zones 5–9

F. **12 Golden sages** (*Salvia officinalis)* such as 'Icterina': Zones 7–10

G. **16 Common sages** (*Saliva officinalis)* such as 'Berggarten': Zones 5–9

H. **6 Petunias** (*Petunia hybrida)*: Annual

I. **3 Chives** (*Allium schoenoprasum)*: Zones 3–9

J. **8 Sorrels** (*Rumex acetosa)*: Zones 5–9

K. **10 Mixed sweet and purple basils** (*Ocimum basilicum)*: Annual

L. **3 Thymes** (*Thymus* spp.): Zones 5–9

M. **12 Purple variegated sages** (*Salvia officinalis)* such as 'Tricolor': Zones 6–9

In Zones 4 to 5, wrap in burlap for winter protection.

BHG DESIGN TIP

Formal boxwood edging needs frequent shearing to stay its best. Trim it four or so times a year in warm-winter climates; two or three times in colder climates.

Mark your cutting lines with string and stakes, and then use a power hedge trimmer (corded electric models are very light and inexpensive) to make quick work of the task.

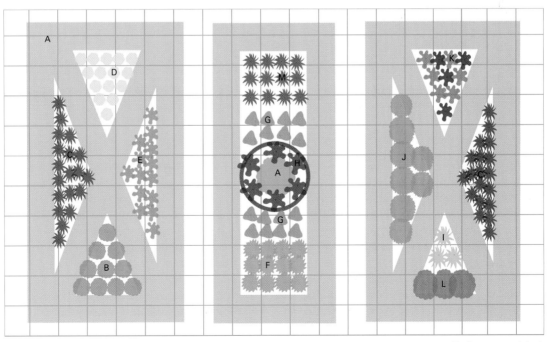

Each square = 1 foot

A Subtle Circle

Small and simple, this garden in blues and shimmering whites is ideal for the middle of a small lawn or other sunny spot.

LIKE SO MANY FORMAL GARDENS, THIS ONE STARTS WITH A FOCAL POINT—IN THIS CASE, A NICELY SHAPED POT. IT'S THEN RINGED IN UNDERSTATED WHITE ROSES AND SILVER-LEAVED MEALYCUP SAGE WITH BLUE FLOWERS.

This formal design is easy to create. It's one of those gardens you can dig and plant in an afternoon.

Simply use a stake with a string on it to mark out the perimeter. (Put the stake in the middle and rotate the string around to mark the edge). Remove the sod from the circle. Then add plenty of soil amendments, such as compost. Fill the container with top-quality potting soil. Then plant it with a boxwood.

Choose small shrub roses for the garden. 'Iceberg' is a classic, but any rose that remains under 3 or 4 feet tall and wide will do. (Hard pruning in spring helps control the size.)

For early spring color, consider tucking in white daffodils among the mealycup sage. About the time the daffodil foliage is fading, the annuals will cover the browning bulb leaves with their new foliage.

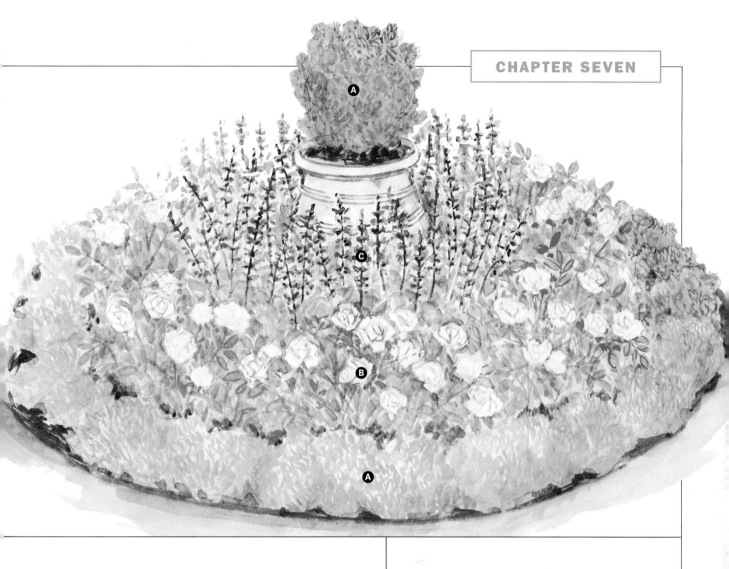

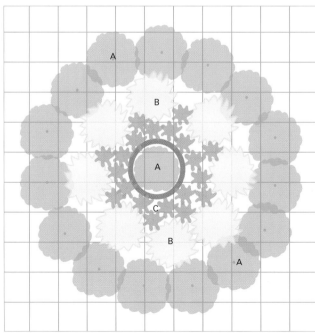

Each square = 1 foot

PLANT LIST

A. **16 Dwarf boxwoods** (*Buxus* spp.) such as 'Green Gem': Zones 4–7

B. **8 Small white shrub roses** such as 'Iceberg': Zones 5–9

C. **20 Mealycup sages** (*Salvia farinacea*) such as 'Victoria Blue': Annual

* In Zones 4 to 5, wrap boxwood in burlap for winter protection.

The mealycup sage in this plan provides a bolt of deep blue thoughout the growing season. But also consider substituting catmint or perennial sage (such as 'May Night'). These perennials cost a little more up front but save money and time in replanting.

Go Grand With a Grid

Calming blues, silvers, and greens make for a serene and sophisticated checkerboard.

LAY OUT A MEMORABLE GARDEN BY THINKING *INSIDE* THE BOX. GRAB SOME STRING AND STAKES AND START TURNING OVER SOIL FOR A REFINED DESIGN WITH CLEAN LINES AND RESTFUL COLORS.

A limited palette of plants with a formal layout makes for a simple but luxurious garden that would be the star of any landscape.

The cool green of boxwood outlines the design. More boxwood is used to create graceful curves around upright evergreens. The pyramid-shape yews in each corner serve as punctuation marks to add vertical interest and drama.

Plant mealycup sage and dusty miller in neat rows to form tidy boxes that repeat throughout the garden. The number of plants suggested here will quickly fill in to form a solid mass. You can save some money by purchasing fewer plants and spacing them 9 inches apart rather than 6 inches.

For a more permanent planting, substitute perennial blue salvia for the mealycup sage and perennial sage *(Salvia officinalis)* for the dusty miller.

PLANT LIST

A.	**72 Dwarf boxwoods** (*Buxus* spp.) such as 'Green Gem': Zones 4–9*
B.	**72 Dusty millers** (*Senecio cineraria*): Zones 8–10, annual elsewhere
C.	**36 Blue mealycup sages** (*Salvia farinacea*) such as 'Victoria Blue': Zones 8–10, annual elsewhere
D.	**25 Heliotropes** (*Heliotropium arborescens*): Annual
E.	**4 Pyramidal Japanese yews** (*Taxus cuspidata*) such as 'Capitata': Zones 4–7
F.	**3 Cape leadworts** (*Plumbago auriculata*): Zones 9–10, annual elsewhere.

* In Zones 4 and 5, wrap in burlap for winter protection.

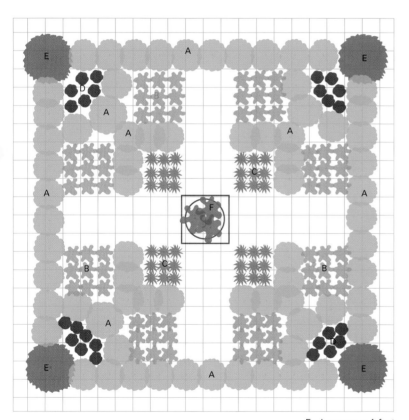

Each square = 1 foot

Feeling a little intimidated about planting such a large garden? Plant just the center portion with the mealycup sage. In the second stage, add the portion around it with the dusty miller and heliotrope. Finally, add the outer rim of boxwood and yews.

PLANT SUPERSTAR
BEAUTIFUL BOXWOOD

Boxwood is an excellent edging material for formal gardens. However, some boxwoods can soar to well over 12 feet, so be sure to choose a dwarf variety for your knot garden.

For the low hedges shown here, avoid common boxwood (*Buxus sempervirens*), which can grow 5 to 12 feet. Also avoid Japanese boxwood (*Buxus microphylla japonica*) since it grows too high—3 to 6 feet—for the edging shown here.

Also avoid boxwoods that have pyramidal shapes, such as 'Green Mountain', since they don't work well for trimming into a low hedge. Excellent choices for this edging would be:

DWARF ENGLISH BOXWOOD (*Buxus sempervirens* 'Suffruticosa'), which grows just 2 to 4 feet tall.

LITTLELEAF BOXWOOD (*Buxus microphylla*), which gets 3 to 4 feet tall.

KOREAN BOXWOOD (*Buxus sinica insularis*), which grows 2 to 3 feet high. It is the most cold-hardy type of boxwood.

HYBRID BOXWOODS (*Buxus* cultivars) 'Green Gem' is a perfect size for edging (18 inches tall and wide) and is one of the most cold-hardy, growing well in Zones 5 to 9. It is marginally hardy in Zone 4. In Zones 4 and 5, wrap boxwoods in winter to prevent winter burn, which can disfigure the shrubs. 'Green Mound' is hardy in Zones 5 to 7 and grows 3 feet high and wide.

Team Daylilies And Hostas

Create a large formal garden easily and economically with hostas and daylilies.

YOU DON'T HAVE TO EMPTY THE BANK TO DESIGN A LARGE, LOW-MAINTENANCE LANDSCAPE. THIS FORMAL GARDEN IS SO ELEGANT YOU'D NEVER KNOW THAT MOST OF THE PLANTS WERE FREEBIES.

This garden does well in light shade, costs little to create, and takes little time to tend once planted.

Daylilies and hostas form the backbone of this garden. And if you have any friends or family who garden, you know that these are plants that green thumbs love to give away when it's time to divide them.

Plant lush tropical caladiums at the center of each quadrant as a focal point. (In all but the warmest regions of the country, caladiums need to be dug and stored each fall.)

Then plant the daylilies and hostas, filling in around them with thread-leaf tickseed for variety. This type of tickseed is easy to divide and share, so you may be able to get plants for free. All three are perennials that will return year after year.

As you plant the caladiums and flowering perennials, leave pockets for bright red impatiens. They'll add punches of color from spring through frost each year.

A fountain is the focal point of this garden, but if you're on a tight budget, you could substitute a birdbath or garden art. Make paths out of salvaged brick or go with inexpensive shredded bark mulch.

This garden likes moderate moisture, so be sure to mulch around plants. It will conserve moisture and minimize weeding chores.

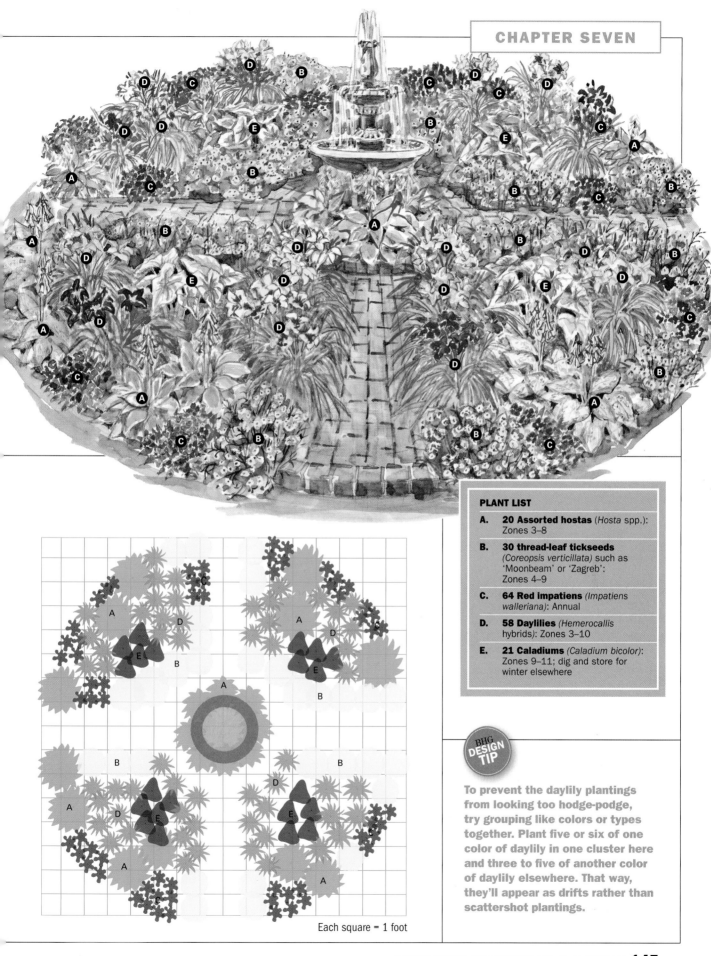

PLANT LIST

A. **20 Assorted hostas** (*Hosta* spp.): Zones 3–8

B. **30 thread-leaf tickseeds** (*Coreopsis verticillata*) such as 'Moonbeam' or 'Zagreb': Zones 4–9

C. **64 Red impatiens** (*Impatiens walleriana*): Annual

D. **58 Daylilies** (*Hemerocallis* hybrids): Zones 3–10

E. **21 Caladiums** (*Caladium bicolor*): Zones 9–11; dig and store for winter elsewhere

Each square = 1 foot

BHG DESIGN TIP

To prevent the daylily plantings from looking too hodge-podge, try grouping like colors or types together. Plant five or six of one color of daylily in one cluster here and three to five of another color of daylily elsewhere. That way, they'll appear as drifts rather than scattershot plantings.

Making a Grand Entrance

If you've ever gone house hunting, you know how much the front entrance matters in creating a welcoming atmosphere. *Even in simply visiting someone's house, the appearance of the front entry sets the tone for the entire stay.*

That old saw about first impressions is true. Even if wonderful things lie beyond the front door, it's what you see first that creates a lasting mood.

Gardening Front and Center

Take a little time and effort to make your front entry special. Visitors won't be the only ones who appreciate it; you will too, every time you come home!

Add an arbor and a fence to a front yard to increase architectural interest and to serve as a directive to an entry door.

Even modest landscaping can get the drama queen treatment with outdoor lighting. Lighting also makes a landscape more secure and safe.

It's surprising how much impact front landscaping makes. Little more than a few nice plantings and a well-designed path are needed to create a welcoming entrance for guests and to set off the home.

A well-designed front garden pays off in other ways. Curb appeal is all-important when it comes to selling a home, so a nicely landscaped front yard can enhance a home's value.

Go for a variety of plant shapes and sizes. Put a plant with feathery leaves, such as a fern, next to one with a large, solid leaf, such as a hosta. Or contrast bold foliage with a spikey-leafed plant, such as liriope.

Have fun with color. Lots of colorful flowers add punch and personality to your home's front yard. It doesn't take much. Just a few well-placed flowers show that the home is well cared for.

Set out containers. They're an easy way to add bright color all season long. One or two large containers look better than a hodgepodge of small containers. (Larger pots are also easier to keep watered.) For a unified, streamlined look, select coordinating containers, such as all-white wood or all terra-cotta pots.

Consider structures. An arbor, a pergola over the front door, or decorative railings add instant appeal and style to your home.

Fence yourself in. A front yard fence adds old-fashioned charm. Keep it low and open so that it's welcoming rather than defensive. Match the style of the fence to the architecture, scale, and period of your home. Consider placing just a section or two of fence in the front yard (see page 164 for an example). The sections provide a suggestion of enclosure and become a handy focal point or backdrop for plantings. Erect a corner of a fence (as on page 122) or flank the front walk with two sections of fence and plant around both.

Light up your life. Low-voltage outdoor lighting systems are perfect for illuminating front paths for safety and for showing off plantings 24 hours a day. Consider uplighting under shrubs or to wash the front door or facade of the house in light.

A traditional entry light or yard light provides more illumination, but both require weatherproof wiring. Do it yourself if you're experienced, but otherwise hire an electrician.

Skillful landscaping bumps up the curb appeal of this modest home and adds significant value.

GARDEN SMARTER

THE FOUNDATION PLANTING FORMULA

Stumped for ideas on how to landscape the front of your house? Follow these guidelines.

Start with foundation shrubs. Choose yew, boxwood, holly, or other low-growing evergreens that are easy to keep trimmed to run along expanses of your home. These quiet, classic shrubs aren't flashy, but they provide greenery all year long.

Add height at the corners. At either end of the house, add upright plants for vertical interest. Ideally the mature height of these corner anchors should reach two-thirds the height of the roofline. That means you'll need taller plants for a two-story home than a ranch-style.

Allow enough distance. Plant far enough from the home for the tree or shrub to spread to its full width. If the plant is only a few feet away from the house, choose an upright or columnar small tree or shrub. Upright junipers, yews, and arborvitae are easy choices. Plant crabapples, redbuds, Japanese maples, or other small flowering trees at least 10 to 15 feet away from the foundation.

Add color. Leave some room in front of or between evergreen shrubs for a cluster or two of annuals or perennials. Plant them in drifts of a dozen or more small plants or three to five larger ones for maximum impact.

This front entrance is mainly driveway, but with the addition of plants and a low wall, it becomes a welcoming nook.

Create a Vibrant Entrance

Flank your front walk with long in-ground or raised beds to say "Welcome!"

FILLED WITH VIBRANT COLORS AND LUSH TROPICAL PLANTS, THIS IS A GARDEN THAT HITS ITS STRIDE IN HEAT AND HUMIDITY.

Gardeners today have an astounding selection of plants from around the globe at their disposal. This garden takes advantage of that, with several tropical stars blazing in neon colors.

Citrus-green sweet potato vine is a prime example. A native of South and Central America, it grows profusely in hot, humid weather and like most of the plantings here, needs ample water that simulates its rain forest origins.

Other plants in the plan with tropical heritages include elephant's ear from Southeast Asia, as well as vinca, also called Madagascar periwinkle.

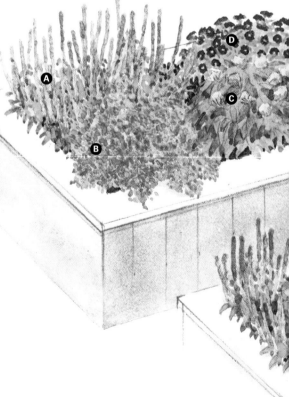

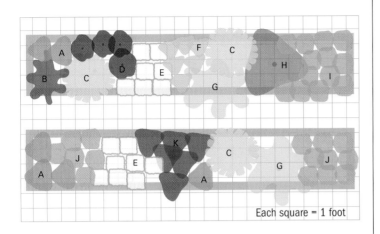

Each square = 1 foot

PLANT LIST

A. **6 Perennial sages** (*Salvia* × *superba*) such as 'May Night': Zones 4–7

B. **1 Fan flower** (*Scaevola aemula*): Annual

C. **3 Peonies** (*Paeonia lactiflora*): Zones 2–8

D. **4 Zinnias 'Profusion Cherry'** (*Zinnia* spp.): Annual

E. **15 White vincas** (*Catharanthus roseus*) such as 'Victory Pure White': Annual

F. **6 Petunias** (*Petunia* × *hybrida*): Annual

G. **2 Sweet potato vines** (*Ipomoea batatas*) such as 'Margarita': Zone 11, annual elsewhere

H. **1 Elephant's ear** (*Colocasia esculenta*): Zones 9–11

I. **13 Red vincas** (*Catharanthus roseus*) such as 'Pacifica Red': Annual

J. **15 Pink vincas** (*Catharanthus roseus*) such as 'Raspberry Cooler': Annual

K. **6 Zinnias 'Profusion Fire'** (*Zinnia* spp.): Annual

Plant For the Neighborhood

Be the most popular homeowner on the street by planting this pedestrian-friendly garden that rewards the nose as well as the eye.

A FENCE CAN BE A BARRIER TO KEEP OUT INTRUDERS OR AN INVITATION TO EXPLORE. THIS FENCE SENDS THE RIGHT KIND OF MESSAGE—FRIENDLY AND WELCOMING—BECAUSE IT'S LOW, OPEN, AND POSITIONED JUST FAR ENOUGH FROM THE SIDEWALK TO ALLOW FOR COLORFUL PLANTINGS.

A Victorian house is a good candidate for an old-time picket fence. Fences were once a must in small communities because many people had chickens and other livestock that roamed the streets, nibbling on prized plantings. Picket fences kept out the animals.

Today, a front fence is more likely erected for visual appeal or to keep little ones near the house, safe from busy streets. In this yard, the low fence also serves as a casual plant support, preventing the Oriental lilies and daylilies from toppling.

The strip in front of the fence has a softening effect, allowing plantings to weave through both sides, establishing the illusion that the fence has been there

for years. The Oriental lilies have an intense fragrance that carries for several feet, so passersby will certainly get a whiff of their perfume.

Repeat this sun-loving plan as many times as needed to span the length of a fence. Or work in other plants, such as shrub roses, to substitute for some of the lilies. For an even lower-maintenance perennial planting, consider swapping catmint for the lobelia and coreopsis for the nasturtiums.

If your yard is shaded, substitute impatiens or hostas for the nasturtiums and fragrant, hardy azaleas, such as the Bright Lights Series, for the lilies.

'Star Gazer'
Oriental Lily

STAR GAZER LILY

Many Oriental lilies are fragrant, but 'Star Gazer' is outstanding in that department. It has gained much attention in recent years in part because of its deep, rich scent. Add the fact that it has deep pink petals with red freckles and white edging, and its popularity is understandable.

'Star Gazer' makes an excellent cut flower. Include just one or two in an arrangement because indoors, the scent can be overpowering. (Tip: The stamens are coated with deep golden pollen that can stain tablecloths, clothing, and hands. Trim them off when cutting lilies for indoors.)

However, outside it's impossible to have too many of these spicy, sweet-scented flowers. Cluster them in groups for best visual effect and to help them support each other. In rich soils you may need to stake them.

Most Oriental lilies have excellent fragrance. They need full sun and deep, well-drained, fertile soil—work in plenty of compost. Grow them with moderate moisture and excellent drainage or they'll rot. Plant bulbs in fall (the most economical way to plant these gems) or purchase them as nursery-grown blooming pots in the spring.

After bloom time, cut the stalks back to remove spent flowers, but allow the foliage to die back completely before removing it.

PLANT LIST

A. **3 Eging lobelias** (*Lobelia erinus*): Annual

B. **5 Nasturtiums** (*Tropaeolum majus*): Annual

C. **5 Star Gazer' Oriental lilies** (*Lilium* 'Star Gazer'): Zones 4–8

D. **3 Daylilies** (*Hemerocallis* hybrids): Zones 3–10

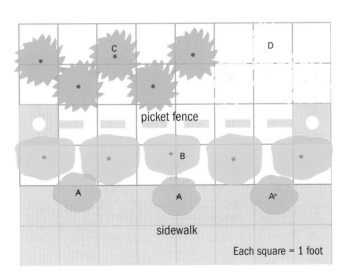

picket fence

C

D

B

A   A   A

sidewalk

Each square = 1 foot

Set Off an Arbor

An arbor is a welcoming addition to nearly any front walkway. Accent it with old-fashioned flowers.

AN ARBOR ADDS DRAMA AND ARCHITECTURAL INTEREST TO THIS FRONT GARDEN, WHILE ROSES AND OTHER PERENNIALS SOFTEN ITS EFFECT AND MARRY IT TO THE LANDSCAPE.

Arbors add vertical interest and create an outdoor doorway leading to the front entrance of the home. This latticework arbor also has a gate to create continuity with the fence.

This unique arbor is outfitted with outdoor lanterns that are mounted on the posts. The wires run down the arbor, through conduit buried into the yard, and to a power source by the house. It's an especially elegant alternative to a freestanding yard light. And like a yard light, it promotes safety and is welcoming.

The plantings in the plan run 10 feet along the sidewalk. You could repeat the planting to extend the entire length of a longer front fence. Or add your own mix of favorite shrub roses and perennials. You could also repeat the planting in mirror image on the other side of the arbor.

PLANT LIST

A. **1 David Austin rose** such as 'Mary Rose': Zones 5–9

B. **1 Hybrid tea rose** such as 'First Prize': Zones 5–9

C. **5 Foxgloves** (*Digitalis purpurea*): Zones 4–8

D. **3 Twinspurs** (*Diascia* hybrids): Zones 6–9, annual elsewhere

E. **1 Spanish lavender** (*Lavandula stoechas*): Zones 6–8

F. **1 Red verbena** (*Verbena* × *hybrida*): Annual

G. **3 Bacopas** (*Sutera cordata*) such as 'Snowstorm': Annual

H. **1 Purple verbena** (*Verbena* × *hybrida*): Annual

I. **5 Snapdragons** (*Antirrhinum majus*): Annual

J. **2 Calla lilies** (*Zantedeschia elliottiana*): Zones 9–10, annual elsewhere

K. **1 Hybrid tea rose** such as 'Mister Lincoln': Zones 5–9

L. **1 Ground morning glory** (*Convolvulus sabatius*): Zones 8–11, annual elsewhere

M. **1 Cheddar pink** (*Dianthus gratianopolitanus*): Zones 3–9

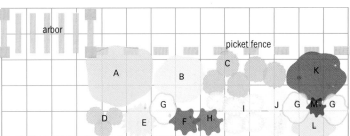

Each square = 1 foot

BHG DESIGN TIP

FRONT-YARD ARBOR HOW-TO

Make it wide. You can get away with a narrow backyard arbor, but a front-entry arbor must accommodate people who may be carrying a suitcase or large shopping bags. Keep the passageway a minimum of 3 feet wide; 4 feet is ideal.

Plant it with care. Vines and roses look gorgeous growing up an arbor, but check the mature size of your choice first. Some vines, such as trumpetvine and bittersweet, can reach 40 feet in length, engulfing your arbor and making it difficult for people to pass through. Prune roses regularly to make sure the thorny canes inflict no damage to pedestrians.

Create a destination. Remember that an arbor is a doorway. It should lead to something. Position the arbor at the beginning or end of a sidewalk or path rather than in the middle of the lawn.

Add a fence. An arbor looks even more at home when attached to a fence. The fence anchors the arbor physically and visually. High winds can upend a solitary arbor.

Cope with A Slope

Convert a problematic front slope into an inviting front yard flower garden.

FORGET ABOUT MOWING GRASS ON A STEEP INCLINE. INSTEAD, PLANT A GRACEFUL MIX OF EVERGREENS, GROUNDCOVERS, AND FLOWERS.

In nearly all creative endeavors, it's a problem that sparks the most interesting solution. In this landscape, a low sunny slope in the front yard was the challenge. It was dificult to mow and erosion was an issue. The interesting solution turned out to be planting a fetching combination of evergreens, low-growing sedum, and a variety of flowering perennials.

A front gate without an adjoining fence provides a whimsical touch. To anchor it visually, boxwoods flank the gateposts. Another boxwood in the flower bed ties the areas together.

The gardeners also partly buried a series of small boulders in the slope. Rocks help hold soil in place and provide convenient stepping stones while weeding and maintaining the bed.

Boxwood flanks the fence. It's a wise choice for many climates, but can suffer cold damage in harsher areas. Consider substituting yews for cold, moist climates or junipers in cold, dry regions.

The pots on the steps are optional. But their colorful annuals add nonstop color all season long and draw attention to the steps and gate.

PLANT LIST

A. **3 Boxwoods** (*Buxus* spp.): Zones 5–9

B. **6 Delphiniums** (*Delphinium* Pacific Giant series): Zones 4–7

C. **3 Peach-leaf bellflowers** (*Campanula persicifolia*): Zones 3–8

D. **6 Shasta daisies** (*Leucanthemum × superbum*) such as 'Becky': Zones 4–9

E. **9 Sedums** (*Sedum acre*): Zones 3–8

F. **6 Rose campions** (*Lychnis coronaria*): Zones 4–8

Delphinium

DELPHINIUM

Delphinium is one of the most dramatic perennials. In the right setting, a stand of delphiniums is stunning, with tall purple, white, or blue spires rising as high as 7 feet.

However, the right setting can be hard to come by. Delphiniums dislike extreme heat and cold. Even the occassional drought, wind, or pelting rain wreaks havoc with their large leaves and stately stalks.

They thrive beautifully in the evenly cool conditions of the Pacific Northwest and coastal California, true to the name of one of the most popular types of tall delphiniums, Pacific Giant hybrids.

Shorter forms of delphinium, which are less fussy, can be grown successfully in much of the rest of the country. Try Magic Fountains series, which tops out at 3 feet tall.

Delphiniums are short-lived perennials. They live for a few years and then die out, even in favorable climates. In the Pacific Northwest, they may live for up to five years. In other parts of the country, it's usually just two or three years.

Give them rich, well-drained soil in a sunny (but not baked) spot. Water and fertilize amply and you'll be rewarded with gorgeous spires.

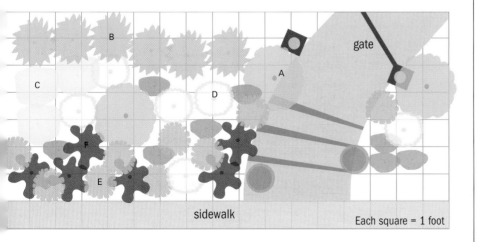

gate

A

B

C

D

F

E

sidewalk

Each square = 1 foot

Step It Up

A few stairs provide the perfect opportunity to nurture plants that love full sun and excellent drainage.

WHILE SOME PLANTS LIKE PLENTY OF WATER, THERE ARE OTHERS THAT HATE WET FEET AND DEMAND EXCELLENT DRAINAGE. A SMALL FRONT SLOPE IS JUST THE TICKET, PROVIDING THE PERFECT MICROCLIMATE.

Whether you have rustic stone steps like those shown here or steps made of concrete or brick, this planting will take advantage of the excellent drainage and tough, dry conditions found around stone and pavement that receive full sun.

This garden showcases a variety of low-growing plants that originate on hilly, stony mountainsides in their native countries. Some of these plants will reseed into cracks; others, such as the sedums, will slowly spread outward and fill in wherever they can in among stones and cracks.

The plan shows groundcovers growing out of narrow gaps between stones. If your walk has no gaps, leave out the space-filling spreaders.

The boulders shown here are a nice touch, especially on a slope where they help hold soil in place. However, you can substitute a few low-growing shrubs or more perennials in place of the stones.

BHG DESIGN TIP

TIPS FOR SLOPES

Solve slope problems by adopting these few simple strategies.

Love your roots. Select perennials and shrubs that thrive in dry soil and have dense, far-reaching root systems, such as daylilies (*Hemerocallis* spp.) and California fuchsia (*Zauschneria* spp.). Their roots form tight-knit mats to hold soil in place.

Puddle up. Because water collects at the base of slopes, choose plants for the bottom of the hill that tolerate (or even need) occasional wet feet.

Be a drip. Use soaker hoses or a drip irrigation system to ensure that water moves into the ground rather than runs off.

Prevent erosion during planting. To prevent bare soil from eroding while plants settle in, pin landscape cloth to the slope and cut slits in it to plant through. Top with a layer of mulch.

PLANT LIST

A. **3 White stonecrops**
(*Sedum album*) such as 'Chubby Fingers': Zones 4–8

B. **5 Golden carpet sedums**
(*Sedum acre*):
Zones 3–8

C. **1 Barrenwort**
(*Epimedium rubrum*):
Zones 4–9

D. **6 Sea thrifts**
(*Armeria maritima*):
Zones 3–9

E. **4 Creeping thymes**
(*Thymus coccineus*):
Zones 4–9

F. **1 New Zealand flax**
(*Phormium tenax*):
Zones 8–10

G. **4 Purple-leaved sedums**
(*Sedum* spp.) such as 'Purple Emperor': Zones 3–7

H. **1 Sea lavender**
(*Limonium latifolium*):
Zones 5–9

I. **2 Oregon stonecrops**
(*Sedum oreganum*):
Zones 2–9

J. **1 Two-row stonecrop**
(*Sedum spurium* 'Voodoo'):
Zones 4–9

Each square = 1 foot

Walk Through Spring Blooms

Welcome winter's end with a jubilant planting of daffodils, pansies, and poppies.

AFTER A COLD, GRAY WINTER, CELEBRATE SPRING WITH A FRONT YARD PLANTING EXPLODING WITH COLOR. THIS PATH IS LINED WITH A RIOT OF BULBS AND SPRING ANNUALS TO TURN A SHORT WALK INTO A BEAUTIFUL JOURNEY.

Nothing is more cheering than sunny daffodils, and this design has plenty.

This plan is shown as part of a front courtyard, but it will work for either a streetside walkway or a more open path leading to the front door.

This bed thrives in full sun and measures about 16 feet long by 4 feet wide. It can easily be adapted to wider or longer spaces. If it's to run along a front walk, consider creating a balanced effect by duplicating the strip on both sides of the walk.

To extend the length of the bed, repeat the entire planting lengthwise, or add an extension by inserting a carbon copy of the middle of the bed. (Either a 4- or 8-foot-long extension works well.) If you need to plant a wider bed, ring the entire garden in trimmed boxwoods.

Prepare the bed in fall. If it's next to a lawn, minimize later maintenance by installing brick, stone, or metal edging material.

Plant the daffodils in fall. In mild winter areas (Zones 6 and warmer), plant pansies in the fall too. Otherwise, wait to plant pansies until early spring. In spring, also plant the boxwoods, Iceland poppies, and gerberas.

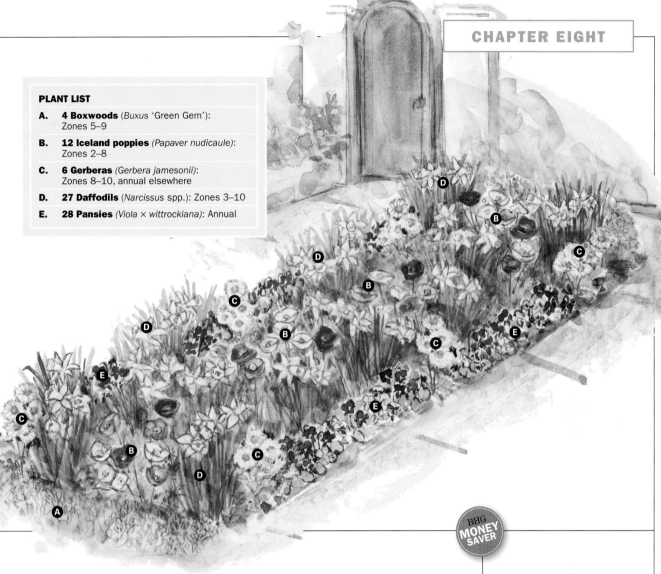

PLANT LIST

A. **4 Boxwoods** (*Buxus* 'Green Gem'):
Zones 5–9

B. **12 Iceland poppies** (*Papaver nudicaule*):
Zones 2–8

C. **6 Gerberas** (*Gerbera jamesonii*):
Zones 8–10, annual elsewhere

D. **27 Daffodils** (*Narcissus* spp.): Zones 3–10

E. **28 Pansies** (*Viola* × *wittrockiana*): Annual

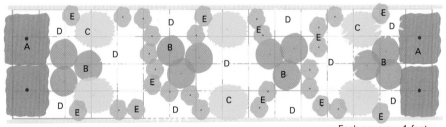

Each square = 1 foot

PERENNIAL SOLUTION
To reduce the number of plants necessary to replant this bed each year, increase the amount of daffodils and Iceland poppies, which are perennials. You can also substitute self-seeding Johnny-jump-ups (Viola tricolor) for the pansies.

Consider outlining the bed in 'Stella de Oro' daylilies or lavender. These easy-care perennials have attractive green or gray-green color in spring with a bonus of summer flowers.

This garden will look fantastic in early spring, when the daffodils and spring annuals are at their peak. As spring temperatures rise, however, most of the plants will brown and fade. At that time, fill in bare or unattractive spots with warm-season annuals, such as marigolds and petunias. Leave daffodil foliage to brown and ripen naturally. The bulbs need it to rejuvenate for next year.

Define an Entry With an Arbor

An arbor makes a wonderful centerpiece for an entry garden. It creates a sense of arrival and guides visitors to the main path.

THIS GARDEN PROVIDES OPTIONAL POINTS OF ENTRY WITH BOTH AN OPEN GATEWAY AND AN ARBOR. THE PICKET FENCE BACKDROP ALLOWS FOR RICH LANDSCAPING OPPORTUNITIES ON BOTH SIDES.

Landscaping around a front-yard arbor is especially rewarding because it's close to the street, where all who drive or stroll by can enjoy your handiwork. And working out front, tending your border, is a delightful way to meet neighbors.

This garden is full of lush bloomers that peak in late spring to early summer—peonies, irises, and roses. The perennial sage and roses will rebloom throughout the summer, adding splashes of deep rose and purple to the evergreen blue holly and boxwoods that provide 12-month-long structure and greenery. The redbud casts filtered shade, bears vibrant early spring blooms, and provides a transition to the tall arbor.

To pack additional color punch, tuck in pink geraniums in gaps between shrubs and perennials, as shown in the photo. The geraniums will bloom all summer, carrying on the color theme established by the roses.

PLANT LIST

A.	**2 Peonies** (*Paeonia lactiflora*): Zones 4–8
B.	**3 Perennial sages** (*Salvia × sylvestris*) such as 'May Night': Zones 5–9
C.	**1 Blue holly** (*Ilex × meserveae*): Zones 4–9
D.	**3 German bearded irises** (*Iris germanica*): Zones 3–9
E.	**7 Boxwoods** (*Buxus* spp.): Zones 5–9
F.	**4 Knock Out roses**: (*Rosa* spp.) Zones 5–9
G.	**1 Redbud** (*Cercis canadensis*): Zones 5–9

GARDEN SMARTER
FRONT-YARD FLOWERS

What makes an ideal front-yard flower? It should possess the following characteristics:

It always looks good. Front-yard flowers should look good all growing season long. This can be tough to accomplish with perennials. Look for perennials with attractive foliage as well as colorful blooms. Sedum is an excellent example of this. A plant such as Oriental poppy, which is gorgeous during its brief bloom but soon develops brown foliage, is better placed in out-of-the-way areas, surrounded by other foliage that covers it once it's through blooming.

It's tidy. Avoid plants with rangy, floppy, or loose growth habits. Wildflowers are wonderful in a casual meadow but can appear unkempt when viewed at close range. Also steer clear of flowers that develop messy seedpods.

It's petite. Front-yard flowers should frame views, not block them. Low growers draw attention to the yard without creating a visual barrier.

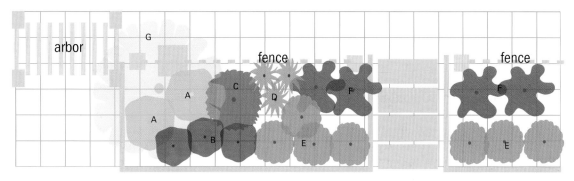

Each square = 1 foot

A Corner on Colonial Charm

With visitors approaching from both sides, this corner lot needed a showy route to the main door.

WHEN YOU HAVE A BIG, SUNNY, OPEN CORNER LOT TO PLAY WITH, WHY WASTE THAT SPACE WITH NOTHING BUT LAWN? PUMP UP THE CURB APPEAL WITH A DELIGHTFUL ARBOR GARDEN FILLED WITH FLOWERS.

A corner lot can be tricky to landscape. It's a little like theatre-in-the-round, with eyes peering from at least two directions. And so entrances need to be designed from two perspectives also.

This plan makes for a delightful journey filled with flowers—and even a birdbath—for those who approach from the side. It provides some privacy in the form of a fence and tall plantings that provide a partial screen.

At the same time, it also is inviting, with an arbor beckoning visitors to stroll through to the front door. Colorful perennials, annuals, and shrubs greet visitors as they approach.

If your yard is shaded, substitute impatiens or hostas for the nasturtiums, and replace the lilies with fragrant hardy azaleas, such as the Bright Lights series.

PLANT LIST

A. **1 White rose** such as 'Summer Snow': Zones 5–10

B. **1 Pink rose** such as 'Sharifa Asma': Zones 5–10

C. **1 Red rose** such as 'Chuckles': Zones 4–7

D. **8 Miniature daylilies** (*Hemerocallis* spp.) such as 'Stella de Oro': Zones 3–10

E. **5 Bee balms** (*Monarda* spp.): Zones 4–8

F. **1 Rhododendron** (*Rhododendron* spp.) such as 'Blue Peter': Zones 6–9

G. **2 Italian clematises** (*Clematis viticella* 'Purpurea Plena Elegans'): Zones 5–9

H. **8 Creeping phloxes** (*Phlox subulata*) such as 'Sea Pink': Zones 4–8

I. **1 Yarrow** (*Achillea* spp.): Zones 3–9

J. **3 New York asters** (*Aster novi-belgii*) such as 'Professor Anton Kippenberg': Zones 4–8

K. **1 Variegated hosta** (*Hosta* spp.) such as 'Patriot': Zones 4-9

L. **7 Wax begonias** (*Begonia* × *semperflorens-cultorum*): Annual

M. **4 Red daylilies** (*Hemerocallis* spp.): Zones 3–10

N. **1 False sunflower** (*Heliopsis helianthoides*): Zones 4–9

O. **1 Japanese yew** (*Taxus cuspidata nana*): Zones 5–10

P. **6 Asiatic lilies** (*Lilium asiaticum*): Zones 3–8

Q. **1 Apricot daylily** (*Hemerocallis* spp.): Zones 3–10

R. **1 Winter honeysuckle** (*Lonicera fragrantissima*): Zones 5–8

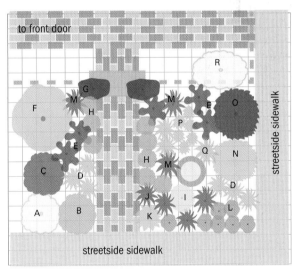

Each square = 1 foot

GARDEN SMARTER
LANDSCAPING CORNER LOTS

Divide and conquer. If the distinction between front and back yards is unclear, define the areas by separating them with a hedge or fence.

Create a private space. Enclose the backyard with more fencing or hedges for complete privacy.

Direct traffic. Plant a low hedge or flowerbeds in the front to direct foot traffic to the main entrance.

Go with the flow. Provide entry from both streets because people will want to take the most direct route to the door regardless of their direction of arrival.

Artful & Edible

Who made the rule that vegetable and herb gardens must be laid out in straight lines? *The designs in this chapter show that an edible planting can look as good as it tastes. You'll find attractive and innovative ideas for growing vegetables, salad greens, fruits, edible flowers, and herbs.*

These gardens also make smart use of space. Most are intensively planted, so they take up little ground, perfect for tucking into a side yard or next to the garage. But with gardens this pretty, why hide them? They're attractive enough to go out front!

A Square Of Greens

This tiny garden is big on good looks. And it's easy. You can assemble and plant it in just a few hours.

GARDEN SMARTER
BUILDING BLOCKS

Looking to start a vegetable garden for the first time? Begin with just one 4×4-foot raised bed. Each year, add another square raised bed or two, leaving a 2-foot-wide mulched path between.

Your garden will grow as your skill and interest does, and you'll never break the bank.

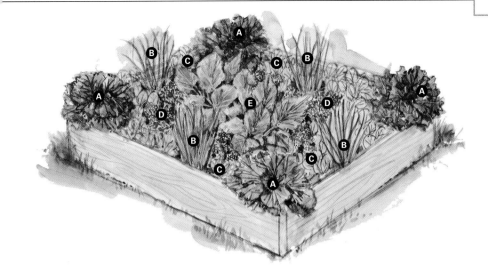

WHEN SPRING HITS AND YOU'RE EAGER TO GET GOING ON A VEGETABLE GARDEN, COOL-SEASON GREENS AND HERBS HIT THE MARK.

To make this simple garden, hammer together 4-foot-long sections of rot-resistant 2×8 lumber. Then give the wood a coat of colorful paint, and fill with a blend of good-quality topsoil and compost. Then plant.

Go for instant impact by setting out transplants. Or save a little money and plant the lettuces from seed. Use a single type of lettuce for a uniform look, or purchase a mix of lettuces for a variety of colors, textures, and flavors.

Anchor the corners of the garden with flowering kale and the center with red cabbage. (Can't tell the difference? Flowering kale has fringed or deeply notched leaf edges. Cabbage has nearly smooth edges.) Flowering kale is edible, but is most often used as a garnish. If your family prefers the taste of broccoli or cauliflower to that of cabbage, substitute either in the center of the bed.

Purple sweet alyssum carpets the planting to add color and fragrance. However, it isn't edible. You could substitute violas instead. Like the other plants in this garden, these pansy relatives thrive in cool weather. Their petals make charming edible additions to salads or garnishes on desserts.

When daytime temperatures reach the mid-80s, this cool-season garden will fade. Replant the bed with your favorite warm-season vegetables and herbs such as tomatoes, peppers, basil, and beans.

PLANT LIST

A. **4 Flowering kales**
(*Brassica oleracea*):
Annual

B. **4 Chives**
(*Allium schoenoprasum*):
Zones 3–9

C. **20 Lettuces**
(*Lactuca sativa*):
Annual

D. **14 Sweet alyssums**
(*Lobularia maritima*):
Annual

E. **4 Cabbages**
(*Brassica oleracea*):
Annual

MATCH PLANTINGS TO THE SEASON

Cool-season vegetables thrive in the cool, moist weather of spring and fall (or through winter in frost-free regions). When the longer days of summer hit, they may quickly bolt and go to seed or simply shut down in the heat. The list of cool-season vegetables includes lettuce, spinach, most other salad greens, cabbage, broccoli, cauliflower, and peas.

In the North, plant cool-season vegetables in early spring, about 6 to 8 weeks before your region's average last frost. In most areas you can also grow cool-season vegetables as fall crops by planting 6 to 8 weeks before the average first fall freeze.

Warm-season vegetables are just the opposite. They thrive in warm temperatures and are easily damaged by frost or prolonged cool weather. Wait until soil adequately warms and all danger of frost is past before planting them. Warm-season vegetables include tomatoes, peppers, eggplants, beans, cucumbers, summer squashes, winter squashes, and pumpkins.

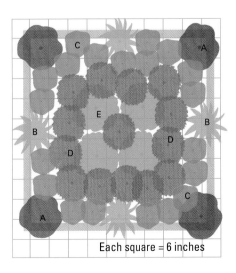

Each square = 6 inches

Vegetables On the Side

This sunny side yard is converted into a convenient kitchen garden with tasty treats and pretty flowers.

THIS FRENCH NORMANDY-INSPIRED PROPERTY INCLUDES A DELIGHTFUL SIDE YARD OF VEGETABLES AND HERBS THAT PROVIDE MONTHS OF GARDEN-FRESH MEALS.

The French long ago learned to make productive use of every inch of garden space. That's because unlike Americans, Europeans for centuries have had to cope with limited land.

This potager, or kitchen garden, is a charming example of how Europeans overcame gardening in a small space. Measuring only 6 feet deep by 16 feet long, the raised bed is defined in whitewashed brick to match the house.

The raised bed is filled with a blend of compost and good-quality topsoil. Trellises are painted the same lavender-blue as the shutters and planted with small climbing roses that remain under 10 feet tall.

The trumpet vine in the corner will sprawl up the side of the house 40 feet or more. In tighter quarters, clematis or another rose would be a better choice. (Note: Trumpet vine is not edible. The roses and marigolds, however, are edible. Use petals of either in salads or as a garnish for drinks and desserts.)

Set out transplants of lettuces or save money and sow seed directly in the row, thinning seedlings to the correct spacing. Use the thinned seedlings as tender baby lettuce greens.

PLANT LIST

A. **5 Climbing roses** such as 'Joseph's Coat': Zones 5–9

B. **6 Looseleaf lettuces** (*Lactuca sativa*) such as 'Salad Bowl': Annual

C. **3 Lavenders** (*Lavandula angustifolia*): Zones 5–10

D. **45 Onions** (*Allium cepa*): Annual

E. **7 Butterhead lettuces** (*Lactuca sativa* 'Bibb'): Annual

F. **35 French marigolds** (*Tagetes patula*): Annual

G. **16 Spinaches** (*Spinacea oleracea*) such as 'Melody': Annual

H. **19 Romaine lettuces** (*Lactuca sativa*) such as 'Parris Island Cos': Annual

I. **7 Looseleaf lettuces** (*Lactuca sativa*) such as 'Black Seeded Simpson': Annual

J. **8 Spinaches** (*Spinacia oleracea*) such as 'Tyee': Annual

K. **3 Korean boxwoods** (*Buxus sinica* 'Wintergreen'): Zones 5–9

L. **1 Yellow trumpet vine** (*Campsis radicans* 'Flava'): Zones 5–9

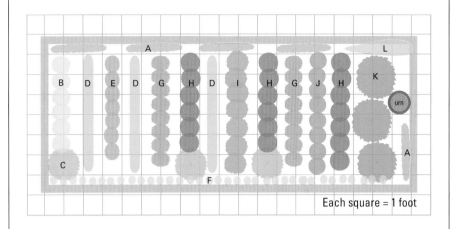

Each square = 1 foot

GARDEN SMARTER
SUNNY DISPOSITIONS

Vegetable gardens need full sun, so they're a good choice for locating along the south and west sides of houses and other buildings.

Vegetables can also do well along the east side of a house as long as trees or shrubs aren't filtering any of the light, which is less intense on this side of a building. In fact, vegetables that don't like extreme heat, such as peas, lettuces, greens, cabbage, and broccoli, often do better on the east sides of houses, where they're protected from the hot afternoon light. This is especially true in the southern half of the U.S., where the sun is more intense.

North sides are usually too shady. Because of the way the sun is positioned with the house, it creates a long shadow that keeps anything planted within several feet of the building in shadow for much of the day.

Flowers And Food

Mix in flowers freely with greens for a garden that is a feast not only for the palate but also for the eyes.

THIS GARDEN IS A FOOD MACHINE, PRODUCING HARVESTS FOR MANY MEALS. BUT IT ALSO INCLUDES MANY ANNUAL AND PERENNIAL FLOWERS THAT CAN BE ENJOYED IN THE GARDEN OR CUT AND BROUGHT INDOORS FOR FLOWER ARRANGEMENTS.

For some inexplicable reason, most gardeners relegate vegetables to one section of the garden and flowers to another. But when it comes to garden design, there are no hard and fast rules. Often the most striking and successful designs are those that break with convention.

This garden happily ignores any division between pretty and tasty. Instead, it mixes flowers with food crops, creating a spirited design that blurs the line between edible and ornamental.

It's a practical solution if you lack space for vegetables. A mixed garden this attractive and tidy could fill an entire backyard and bring rave reviews, both when viewing and tasting.

Forget about saving the sunny spot for a stretch of lawn. Instead, fill it with raised beds. The two rectangular beds shown here are part of a larger garden that includes whiskey barrels, trellises, arbors, and several other raised beds of various shapes. Throughout, lettuces, small shrubs, johnny-jump-ups, cabbages, and herbs intermingle.

A clay pot has been partially buried in one bed to serve as not only a decorative element but also as a practical watering device. When filled with water, the pot allows water to gradually seep into surrounding soil, moistening the growing medium without wasting water.

The bonus to this type of garden is that it's ideal for growing flowers for cutting. In traditional ornamental beds and borders, cut flowers leave gaps after they've been harvested. In a garden such as this, with constant harvesting and planting, any hole quickly fills with new plants.

PLANT LIST

A. **8 Boxwoods** (*Buxus sempervirens*):
Zones 5–9

B. **21 Johnny-jump-ups** (*Viola tricolor*):
Annual

C. **2 Chards** (*Beta vulgaris cicla*) such as
'Fordhook Giant': Annual

D. **2 Red cabbages** (*Brassica oleracea*)
such as 'Ruby Ball': Annual

E. **2 Golden lemon balms** (*Melissa officinalis*
'Aurea'): Zones 4–11

F. **5 Onions** (*Allium cepa*) such as 'Copra':
Annual

G. **1 Golden oregano** (*Origanum vulgare*
'Aureum'): Zones 5–11

H. **19 Looseleaf lettuces** (*Lactuca sativa*)
such as 'Royal Oak Leaf': Annual

I. **1 Purple bearded iris** (*Iris germanica*) such as
'Hello Darkness': Zones 3–10

J. **2 Broccolis** (*Brassica oleracea*) such as
'Packman': Annual

K. **3 Parsleys** (*Petroselinum crispum*): Biennial
grown as annual

L. **1 Tall delphinium** (*Delphinium elatum*
'Pacific Giant'): Perennial 4–8

M. **15 carrots** (*Daucus carota sativus*) such as
'Scarlet Nantes': Annual

N. **1 Borage** (*Borago officinalis*): Annual

O. **10 Pole beans** (*Phaseolus vulgaris*) such as
'Blue Lake Pole': Annual

P. **22 White and yellow johnny-jump-ups**
(*Viola tricolor*): Annual

Q. **6 Heliotropes** (*Heliotropium arborescens*):
Zone 11, annual elsewhere

R. **1 Rhubarb** (*Rheum rhabarbarum*):
Zones 2–9

S. **4 Hot peppers** (*Capsicum annuum*): Annual

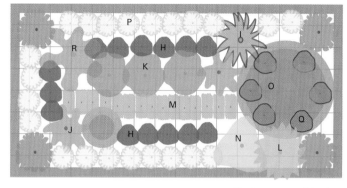

Each square = 6 inches

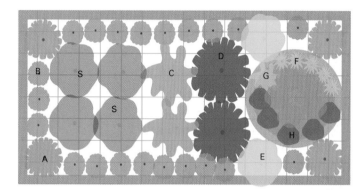

GARDEN SMARTER
SMART
SOWING

You can grow cutting
flowers inexpensively in
the vegetable garden. Zinnias,
marigolds, cosmos, sunflowers,
sweet peas, and bachelor's buttons are
all excellent cutting flowers that are a snap
to start from seed directly in the ground.

Sow these cutting flower seeds in rows, just as
you do vegetables. And then harvest them, just as you
would produce. After a few weeks, the plant is likely to
send out more flowers.

Perennial flowers for cutting also are excellent in the vegetable
garden. This garden has delphinium and iris. Other perennial favorites
for cutting that work well planted in rows in a vegetable garden are
Asiatic lilies and perennial poppies. Many homeowners like to plant
tender flowering bulbs such as dahlia and gladiolus in the vegetable
garden too, because fall digging for winter storage is easier.

A Circle Of Herbs

Enliven a vegetable garden with a ring of herbs in the middle of your yard.

A BED OF HERBS IS LIKE A LIVING SPICE CABINET. JUST STROLL OUT TO THE GARDEN BEFORE DINNER AND SNIP A FEW HERBS TO PERK UP THE MEAL.

This herb bed is especially practical. The herbs tumble into one another, making efficient use of space. The reach from garden's edge to the herbs planted in the center is convenient at no more than 4 feet. A circle of stones rings the bed, containing the garden's sprawl and elevating the soil for a raised bed.

Nearly all herbs like the good drainage that raised beds provide. The stone edging absorbs the sun's heat and passes it along to the herbs. Since so many herbs are natives of hot, arid climates, they thrive on the reflected heat of the stone edging. A trailing plant, such as woolly thyme, scrambles across the stones' surface keeping the herb leaves high and dry the way they like it.

Further, most herbs grow best in sandy or gravelly soil. They develop more intense flavor with minimal nutrients, reflective of the poor, rocky soils of arid regions in which they originated. So avoid filling the raised bed with moist, rich compost. Instead, fill it with a sandy soil mix.

The center of the bed has a vertical support called a tuteur (pronounced too-TOOR). It can be purchased premade or you can build one yourself. Or opt for a more informal tepee (see the facing page).

On the tuteur shown here, red cypress vine winds its way through the supports. If you prefer to stick with edibles, cherry tomatoes or scarlet runner beans would make attractive substitutes.

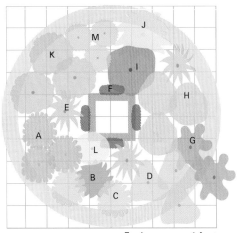

Each square = 1 foot

PLANT LIST

A. **3 Basils** (*Ocimum basilicum*): Annual

B. **1 Flat-leaf parsley** (*Petroselinum crispum*):
    Biennial grown as annual

C. **2 Curly-leaf parsleys** (*Petroselinum crispum*
    'Moss Curled'): Biennial grown as annual

D. **3 Woolly thymes** (*Thymus pseudolanuginosus*):
    Zones 5–8

E. **3 Chives** (*Allium schoenoprasum*): Zones 3–9

F. **4 Red cypress vine** (*Ipomoea quamoclit*):
    Annual

G. **2 Common thymes** (*Thymus vulgaris*):
    Zones 5–9

H. **3 Tricolor sages** (*Salvia officinalis* 'Tricolor'):
    Zones 5–8

I. **1 Lemon balm** (*Melissa officinalis*): Zones 4–11

J. **1 Rosemary** (*Rosmarinus officinalis*):
    Zones 8–10, annual elsewhere

K. **3 Oreganos** (*Origanum vulgare*): Zones 5–9

L. **1 Tarragon** (*Artemisia dracunculus sativa*):
    Zones 5–9

M. **3 Dills** (*Anethum graveolens*): Annual

REGIONAL NOTE

ROSEMARY FOR ANY CLIMATE

Rosemary is a wonderful herb that adds distinctive flavor to chicken, lamb, soups, pastas, and many Mediterranean dishes.

True to its Mediterranean roots, rosemary likes hot, dry climates. In places like Italy, Greece, France, and many parts of the West Coast, it grows as a medium to large shrub.

However, most varieties are cold hardy only in Zones 8 to 11. In the rest of the country, overwinter rosemary in a large pot indoors. Grow it in a cool (60°F or cooler) sunroom or next to a window in a room that is not excessively dry. (When the air is too warm and dry indoors, this plant browns and drops needles.) Another option is to place it next to a window in an unheated garage, as long as the temperature remains above 25°F. You may harvest sprigs sparingly through winter.

In the spring, replant the potted rosemary by partially burying the container in the ground, or simply continue to grow the plant aboveground directly in the pot.

GARDEN SMARTER
TERRIFIC TEPEES

Grow vining plants on a teepee of poles to save space and ensure healthier plants. Training plants on poles provides excellent air circulation, preventing many fungal disease problems.

Indeterminate tomatoes (types that grow several feet tall), pole beans, and cucumbers are good candidates for pole teepees. Branches, bamboo, wood lath, copper, or PVC pipe may be fashioned into a teepee. A rough surface on the pole prevents support ties from slipping.

Fashion a circle out of the poles with their bases spaced at least 1 foot apart. Erect as few as three or as many as six or seven. Insert the base into the soil and then pull their tops together and tie with twine.

Place a transplant or sow several seeds at the base of each pole. In the case of tomatoes, plant one directly under the center of the teepee, and then as it grows, tie the vine to the poles with strips of soft fabric.

Greens On The Patio

With a vegetable garden this eye-catching, it would be a shame to tuck these gorgeous greens out of sight!

BHG MONEY SAVER

MORE CHIVES FAST
Chives multiply freely. To cut the initial investment, purchase one chive plant instead of the 3 shown. Within a couple of years, you'll be able to divide the clump to fill in the area in the plan.

THIS SUN-SOAKED SIDE PATIO IS A FAVORITE SPOT FOR LOUNGING. INSTEAD OF USING THE SPACE FOR TRADITIONAL LANDSCAPING, THE HOMEOWNERS DECIDED TO CREATE A GARDEN THAT'S AS FUNCTIONAL AS IT IS ATTRACTIVE.

This small but productive garden is inexpensive and easy to manage. The brick patio surface eliminates any worries of tracking in mud from the garden. Rot-resistant lumber forms an edging for the bricks and keeps the compost and topsoil contained in the garden.

Most of the plants in this garden can be sown from seed directly in the soil. A few, such as the chives, cardoon, and broccoli, are easiest to purchase as seedlings from the greenhouse.

The apple tree is permanent. A dwarf tree is small enough to grow in this kitchen garden without shading the other plants. In this garden, it's trained as an espalier with branches extending in pairs parallel to the wall in order to save space.

The lettuces edging the beds fade once the heat of summer arrives. In the larger bed, heat-loving New Zealand spinach in summer fills the space vacated by the lettuce. Plant bush beans, peppers, or other warm-season crops to replace the lettuce in the smaller bed.

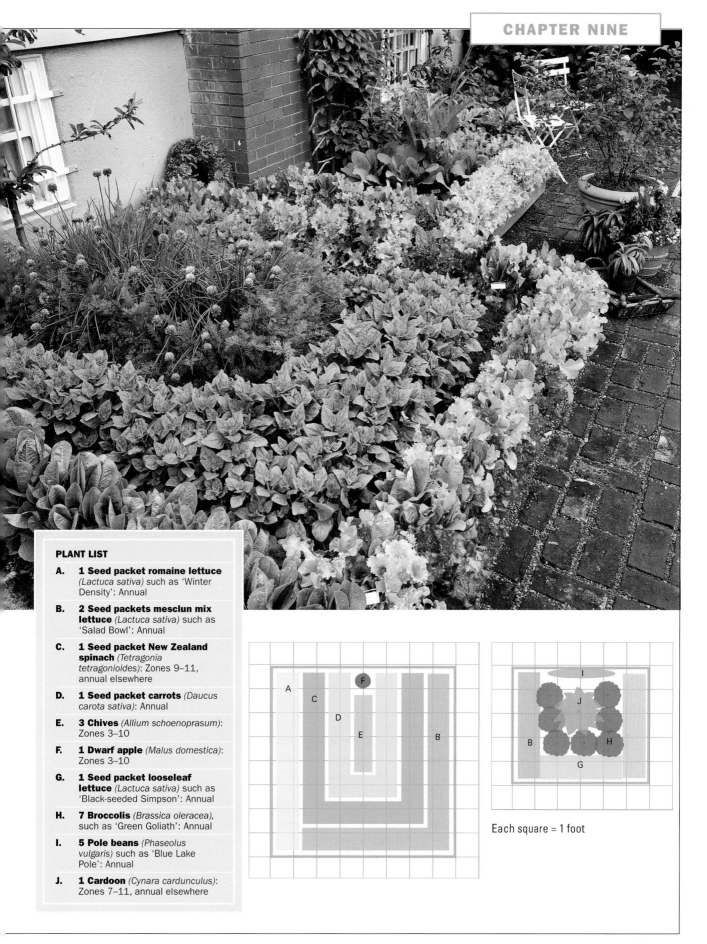

PLANT LIST

A. **1 Seed packet romaine lettuce** *(Lactuca sativa)* such as 'Winter Density': Annual

B. **2 Seed packets mesclun mix lettuce** *(Lactuca sativa)* such as 'Salad Bowl': Annual

C. **1 Seed packet New Zealand spinach** *(Tetragonia tetragonioides)*: Zones 9–11, annual elsewhere

D. **1 Seed packet carrots** *(Daucus carota sativa)*: Annual

E. **3 Chives** *(Allium schoenoprasum)*: Zones 3–10

F. **1 Dwarf apple** *(Malus domestica)*: Zones 3–10

G. **1 Seed packet looseleaf lettuce** *(Lactuca sativa)* such as 'Black-seeded Simpson': Annual

H. **7 Broccolis** *(Brassica oleracea)*, such as 'Green Goliath': Annual

I. **5 Pole beans** *(Phaseolus vulgaris)* such as 'Blue Lake Pole': Annual

J. **1 Cardoon** *(Cynara cardunculus)*: Zones 7–11, annual elsewhere

Each square = 1 foot

Cool To Be Square

Square cedar raised beds are among the easiest of vegetable gardens to maintain. Their convenient height makes vegetable growing a breeze.

THAT OLD SAW ABOUT WORKING SMARTER, NOT HARDER, IS TRUE. INVEST SOME TIME AND EFFORT UP FRONT TO CONSTRUCT THESE STURDY RAISED BEDS. THEY SMOOTH THE WAY FOR EFFORTLESS VEGETABLE GARDENING FOR DECADES TO COME.

These 12-inch-deep raised beds provide plenty of rooting depth to grow any vegetable imaginable, including root vegetables such as carrots and potatoes.

They're wisely designed with a narrow ledge around the top, positioned at an ideal height for perching on the side to plant, weed, and harvest. The ledge also makes a convenient place to set tools and small buckets to prevent stooping.

Fill the raised beds with a mix of good-quality topsoil and compost. Use up to one-third compost by volume. The result will be excellent soil that provides ample nutrients for an intensively planted garden.

The trellis along the back of one of the planters makes this garden even more productive by taking advantage of vertical space. Scarlet runner beans, which have pretty red flowers as well as edible beans, climb one corner of the trellis. Cucumbers and peas also reach skyward on latticework and strings. Basil and broccoli round out the edible delights in the bed. Zinnias, lobelias, and wallflowers enliven the bed with color.

In the other bed, beefsteak tomatoes, peppers, and an eggplant are confined by cages, which keep fruits off the ground and prevent the plants from becoming a jungle-like mess. Bright orange and gold nasturtiums and signet marigolds are both attractive and edible.

Build just one of these user-friendly raised beds, or several. Arrange in a row or in blocks or wherever you have enough sun for edibles.

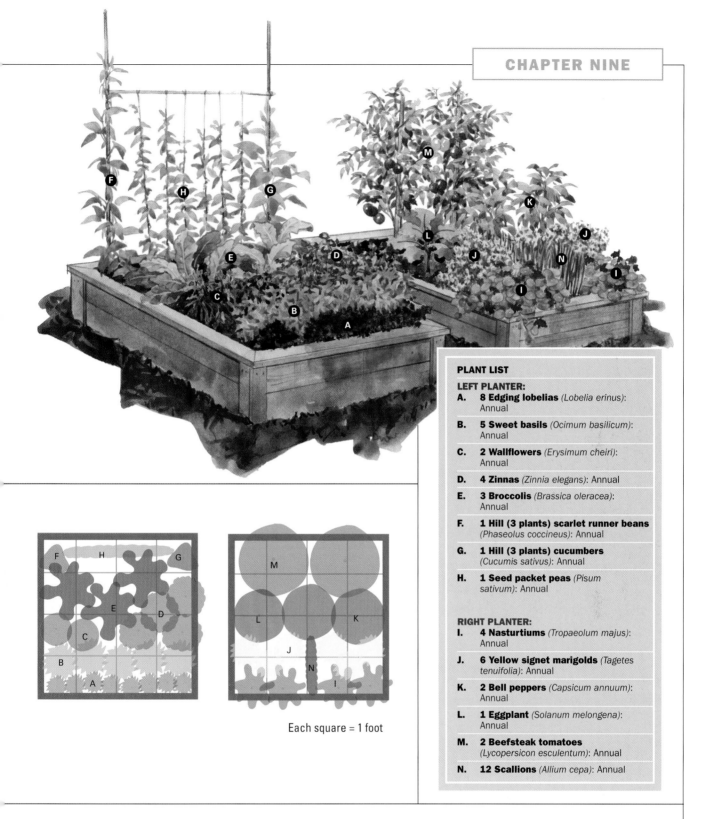

Each square = 1 foot

PLANT LIST

LEFT PLANTER:

A. **8 Edging lobelias** (*Lobelia erinus*): Annual

B. **5 Sweet basils** (*Ocimum basilicum*): Annual

C. **2 Wallflowers** (*Erysimum cheiri*): Annual

D. **4 Zinnas** (*Zinnia elegans*): Annual

E. **3 Broccolis** (*Brassica oleracea*): Annual

F. **1 Hill (3 plants) scarlet runner beans** (*Phaseolus coccineus*): Annual

G. **1 Hill (3 plants) cucumbers** (*Cucumis sativus*): Annual

H. **1 Seed packet peas** (*Pisum sativum*): Annual

RIGHT PLANTER:

I. **4 Nasturtiums** (*Tropaeolum majus*): Annual

J. **6 Yellow signet marigolds** (*Tagetes tenuifolia*): Annual

K. **2 Bell peppers** (*Capsicum annuum*): Annual

L. **1 Eggplant** (*Solanum melongena*): Annual

M. **2 Beefsteak tomatoes** (*Lycopersicon esculentum*): Annual

N. **12 Scallions** (*Allium cepa*): Annual

GARDEN SMARTER
MINIMAL SPACE, MAXIMUM HARVESTS

Most edibles are well suited to growing in the confined spaces of these small raised beds. Train plants that might otherwise sprawl onto a trellis.

A handful of edibles, however, demand more space than these raised beds provide. Corn, for example, must be planted in blocks for proper cross-pollination. Pumpkin vines sprawl many yards wide. While they could be planted in these raised beds, they would eventually spread well beyond the bed and walkway. Most melons and squashes also need room to sprawl.

For small raised beds such as these, look for bush forms of vining vegetables. Bush cucumbers and squashes spread no more than 2 to 3 feet wide, a nicely limited size.

Plant a Potager

Say "poh-tah-zhay." It's French for kitchen garden. This one uses elegant formal design, making it as pretty as it is practical.

DECADES AGO, GARDENERS DIVIDED LANDSCAPES INTO TWO TYPES: ENGLISH AND FRENCH. TODAY, THINGS HAVE LOOSENED A BIT AND NOW THEY'RE DEFINED SIMPLY AS INFORMAL AND FORMAL.

Even those garden distinctions have relaxed, but most gardens can be categorized as formal or informal. And this vegetable garden is decidedly formal.

It's divided into quadrants with paths serving as partitions. This means that it is also a parterre (par-tehr), literally meaning on the ground. In English the term is used for any ornamental garden with paths between the beds.

The combination of potager and parterre creates a vegetable garden that emphasizes beauty and function. It translates into a large, orderly, and highly productive vegetable garden that is gorgeous.

This plan calls for a great number of certain vegetables—perhaps more than most households could eat. However, the vegetables also play an important design role. For example, cabbages outline each quadrant of the garden. (Not so much a fan of cabbage? Substitute herbs such as basil, rosemary, tarragon, lavender, or parsley.) The design calls for repeated planting beds of 12 French marigolds. As with the cabbage, the repetition creates visual unity. For more variety, plant half the designated sections with annual cutting flowers, such as zinnias or cosmos.

The paths are made of flagstone. Add creeping thyme between the stones for a softer finishing touch. To simplify and economize you could substitute wood chip mulch or gravel for the pathways.

PLANT LIST

A. **4 Moonflowers** (*Ipomoea alba*): Annual

B. **1 Seed packet carrots** (*Daucus carota sativus*): Annual

C. **6 Jalapeno peppers** (*Capsicum annuum*): Annual

D. **10 Chards** (*Beta vulgaris cicla*): Annual

E. **36 Cabbages** (*Brassica oleracea*): Annual

F. **4 Boxwoods** (*Buxus sempervirens*): Zones 5–9

G. **1 Packet spinach** (*Spinacia oleracea*): Annual

H. **96 French marigolds** (*Tagetes patula*): Annual

I. **6 Tomatoes** (*Lycopersicon esculentum*): Annual

J. **1 Seed packet pole beans** (*Phaseolus vulgaris*): Annual

K. **8 Cherry tomatoes** (*Lycopersicon esculentum*): Annual

L. **2 Seed packets peas** (*Pisum sativum*): Annual

M. **2 Hills cucumbers** (*Cucumis sativus*): Annual

N. **72 Strawberries** (*Fragaria ananassa*): Zones 3–10

O. **8 Bell peppers** (*Capsicum annuum*): Annual

P. **1 Seed packet bush beans** (*Phaseolus vulgaris*): Annual

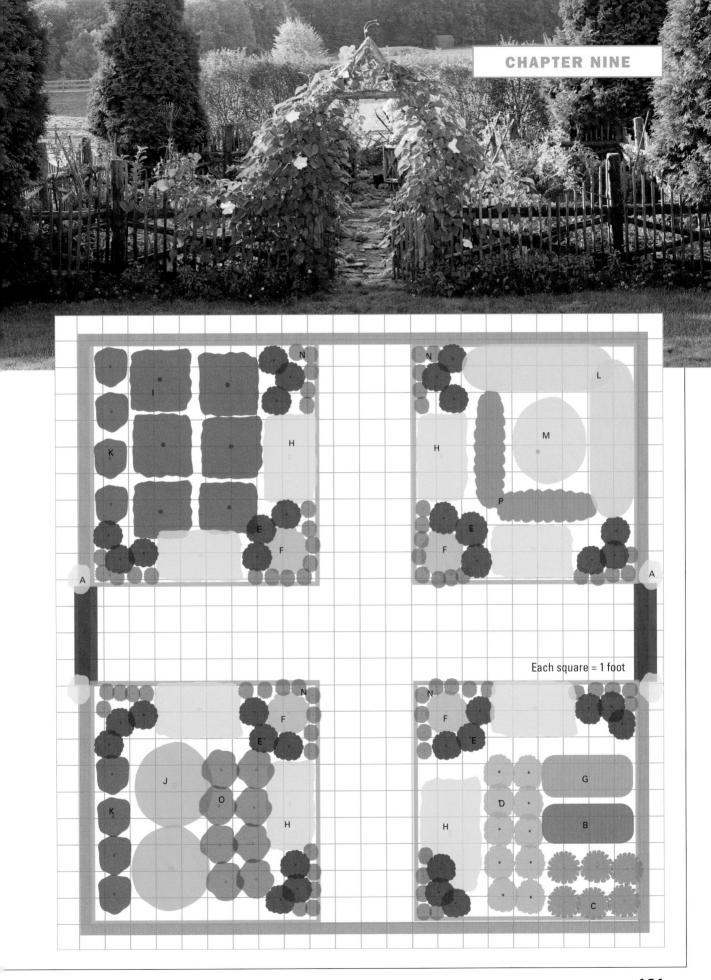

Each square = 1 foot

For Everything There Is a Season

Celebrate the changing seasons with a planting that plays them to the hilt. Try a spring garden that explodes with color and fragrance, a summer garden that goes the distance in heat and drought, or a fall garden filled with the rich colors of autumn. *Plant the gardens in this chapter all by themselves, or incorporate them into a larger bed or border to make that space a showcase for a month or two of the year. It's a great way to make a big bang in a small space and to help you enjoy your garden even more—all growing season long!*

Gardening With the Seasons

Create plantings that are filled with the color and exuberance of the ever-changing year.

Pastels are a hallmark of spring gardens. Here, tulips and forget-me-nots blend beautifully.

By late summer, most gardens are taking on richer, deeper hues, such as those in golden black-eyed susan.

Fall gardens are filled with colors that reflect the changing trees—deep, warm tones found in sunsets.

Imagine what life would be like without any parties or holidays. They're the moments that focus one's attention on the unique, bittersweet pleasure of fleeting time. In much the same way, seasonal gardens also capture that mood. A seasonal garden contains spots where you can jam in the most spectacular plants of that quickly passing time of year. Here's how to create successful gardens that capitalize on seasonality.

Design a spring garden. After a long, cold winter, an early spring garden filled with spring-flowering plants, such as pansies, tulips, daffodils, flowering shrubs, and lobelias, is nothing less than a spring festival—a celebration of the end of winter and the beginning of the gardening season.

Plan for a late-summer garden. When everything else is flagging and burning up from the heat, a garden filled with black-eyed susans, lilies, liatris, and other plants that peak late bursts into fresh, restorative color.

Enjoy a fall garden. An autumn garden allows you to concentrate all the best and beautiful fall colors—deep, jewel tones in saturated reds, purples, golds, and oranges—in one place.

Understand seasonal peaks. Seasonal gardens are at their prime only for a short time. Elsewhere in your landscape, you likely have plantings that will go the distance all growing season—shrubs that bloom for a few weeks and then grace the landscape with their greenery the rest of the year. Or perhaps you have lots of perennials that bloom for a few weeks and then recede quietly into your flowerbeds and borders. Tuck annuals into beds and borders to add bright spots of color here and there for months on end.

Groom for good looks. For the most part, the gardens in this chapter will look fairly fresh (though not showy) all growing season. They are designed to include foliage that is attractive even the plants aren't in bloom.

Cool-season annuals in spring gardens start to fade when daytime temperatures start hitting the 90s. Replant with warm-season annuals.

And in all gardens, deadhead most perennial flowers to keep flowers neat looking and to encourage a second flush of bloom.

Find spots to create these seasonal gardens in your landscape. You'll be glad you did!

SPRING CONTAINER GARDEN

Spring In a Pot

What could be a better way to blow winter away than with tulips and pansies?

PUT THIS CHEERY CONTAINER GARDEN BY YOUR FRONT DOOR TO GREET GUESTS.

This small pot has big impact. It's bright and mood-lifting, a much-needed boost of color after a dreary winter.

Start with a pot at least 18 inches in diameter. Cover the drainage hole with a piece of broken pot or screen. Then fill the container with best-quality potting soil.

Purchase potted tulips already in bud in plastic pots. Rap the plastic pot hard a couple of times and tip it on its side to gently remove the tulips. Plant and fill in around them with the toadflax and pansies.

Enjoy this beautiful planting for a month or two. When temperatures consistently hit the 80s, the plants, which need cool weather, will start to brown and fade. At that time, replant with warm-season annuals, such as marigolds and salvia.

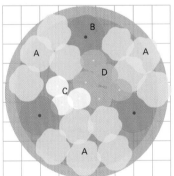

Each square = 3 inches

PLANT LIST

A. **13 Pansies** *(Viola × wittrockiana)* such as 'Panola Pink Shade': Zones 5–11

B. **3 Toadflax** *(Linaria maroccana)* such as 'Fantasy Speckled Pink': Annual

C. **3 White tulips** *(Tulipa 'Diana')*: Zones 3–8

D. **5 Pink and white tulips** *(Tulipa 'Diamond')*: Zones 3–8

BHG REGIONAL NOTE

BULBS IN POTS

You'd think you could plant bulbs in pots in fall, just like you would when planting bulbs in the ground. But it's not quite that simple.

In the northern half of the U.S., the soil and bulbs in pots will freeze. In roughly the southern half of the U.S., it doesn't get cold long enough for most spring-blooming bulbs to develop. So buy and plant prechilled bulbs, or chill them yourself in bags in the fridge. USDA Zone 7 (see page 216) is the only region of the country were you can reliably plant spring-blooming bulbs in pots in fall and enjoy their blooms in spring.

Anywhere else, in spring purchase bulbs that are already started in pots and transplant them to your container.

A Bounty Of Bulbs

Sit under a tree and enjoy the sights and scents of spring with this bulb combo.

GREET SPRING WITH A RIOT OF EARLY COLOR—RED TULIPS, YELLOW DAFFODILS, PURPLE GRAPE HYACINTHS, AND TOUCHES OF FRAGRANT DUTCH HYACINTHS.

Carve out a pleasant niche in your garden with two comfy chairs surrounded by bulbs in full bloom.

This garden is filled primarily with tulips and daffodils, but it also includes grape hyacinths—minor bulbs with flowers that resemble tiny clusters of grapes. They come back reliably year after year.

They're teamed with Dutch hyacinths, which grow 8 to 10 inches tall with large, oblong flower heads that are extremely fragrant. (If you have more than one or two blooming in a pot in a room, the scent will be too intense for most people.) If you're really into fragrance, substitute more Dutch hyacinths for the tulips.

The boulders are a natural way to add structure to the garden, but they are optional. Fill in with more bulbs or plant shrubs in those spots instead, if you prefer. Or substitute a small flowering shrub or two in those spots in the plan.

PLANT LIST

A.   **5 Hyacinths** *(Hyacinthus orientalis)*: Zones 4–8

B.   **50 Grape hyacinths** *(Muscari armeniacum)*: (10 groups of 5 each): Zones 3–8

C.   **70 Daffodils** *(Narcissus)* such as 'King Alfred' (14 groups of 5 each): Zones 3–10

D.   **40 Darwin hybrid tulips** *(Tulipa)* such as 'Red Apeldoorn' (8 groups of 5 each): Zones 4–8

GARDEN SMARTER
BETTER BULBS

Good drainage is essential. **Most bulbs are natives of gravelly mountain slopes. If they are planted in heavy clay or wet spots, they'll rot. Put bulbs in raised beds or amend the soil heavily with compost.**

Plant in mid-autumn. **That's the ideal time for most spring-blooming bulbs in most regions. Work soil well with a spade, going down at least a couple of inches deeper than the actual planting depth to allow for good drainage.**

Plant pointed sides up. **Place bulbs at the depth specified on the label, measuring from the bottom of the bulb.**

Plan for replacements. **Most newly planted spring-blooming bulbs will return next year and some multiply over time. But be aware that tulips and hyacinths look best their first year, less so their second, and tend to die out in their third. Replace as needed.**

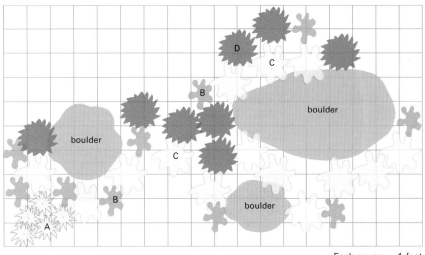

Each square = 1 foot

Sweet Scents Of Spring

Line a path with fragrant early-season bloomers to make a stroll along a walk a multisensory experience.

IT'S EASY TO FIND PLANTS THAT SMELL DELIGHTFUL IN SPRING. IT'S AS IF NATURE ITSELF REACHES OUT TO SHARE IN THE EXUBERANCE OF THE SEASON.

This garden filled with spring flowers would be wonderful in a variety of settings. It would be delightful leading out the back door to a garage or running alongside a walk leading to the front door. In fact, plant it along any walkway that leads to a gate or door. If your yard has no path, this garden is worth creating one just so you can plant this garden around it.

The garden's cornerstones are two small flowering trees, a cherry and a dogwood—both of which have a light, sweet scent. Plant richly fragrant rhododendrons underneath them. Choose your rhododendrons carefully. Only a few have good fragrance, including

'Mi Amor', 'Fragrantissimum', 'Princess Alice', and 'Countess of Sefton'.

Fill in around the trees and shrubs with fragrant bulbs. Freesia is one of the most fragrant and the basis for many perfumes. This design is rich with tulips, daffodils, and bearded irises. Some varieties of these are more fragrant than others, so read labels and catalog descriptions carefully.

Also tuck in fragrant perennials. Forget-me-not is lightly scented as is candytuft. Foxglove and Grecian windflower are included simply for their beauty.

PLANT LIST

A. **1 Flowering dogwood** (*Cornus florida*): Zones 5–8

B. **26 Forget-me-nots** (*Myosotis sylvatica*): Zones 5–9*

C. **7 Fragrant daffodils** (*Narcissis* hybrids) such as 'Thalia' or 'Replete': Zones 3–8

D. **7 Foxgloves** (*Digitalis purpurea*): Zones 4–8

E. **4 Candytufts** (*Iberis sempervirens*): Zones 5–9

F. **33 Grecian windflowers** (*Anemone coronaria*): Zones 8–10, treat as annuals elsewhere

G. **27 Fragrant tulips** (*Tulip* hybrids) see list at right: Zones 3–8

H. **6 Fragrant German bearded irises** (*Iris germanica*): Zones 3–8

I. **6 Freesias** (*Freesia* hybrids): Zones 8–11; treat as an annual elsewhere

J. **1 Sargent cherry** (*Prunus sargentii*): Zones 5–9

K. **2 Fragrant rhododendrons** (*Rhododendron* spp.): Zones 7–9

L. **10 Tall flowering tobaccos:** (*Nicotiana sylvestris*): Annual

* Reseeds freely, so can plant half as much and allow to fill in over time.

In colder regions, substitute 'Bright Lights' azaleas (Zones 4–8) for the rhododendrons. Plant woodland phlox (*Phlox divaricata*) instead of the Grecian windflower and stock (*Matthiola*) or Dutch hyacinths instead of the freesia.

PLANT SUPERSTARS
FRAGRANT TULIPS

Most tulips don't have a fragrance, but these do indeed have a light scent.

'Ad Rem'	'Christmas Marvel'	'Keizerskroon'
'Angelique'	'Couleur Cardinal'	'Monsella'
'Apricot Beauty'	'Creme Upstar'	'Oranjezon'
'Angelique'	'Daydream'	'Oxford'
'Ballerina'	'Diana'	'Peach Melba'
'Beauty Queen'	'General de Wet'	'Purissima'
'Bellona'	'Holland's Glory'	

Each square = 1 foot

Tulips and Friends

Plant tulips with companion perennials that complement the bulbs with color and style.

MAKE THE MOST OF SPRING TULIPS BY PLANTING THEM WITH OTHER COLORFUL PERENNIALS THAT TURN A PRETTY PLANTING INTO A SHOWSTOPPING DISPLAY.

In this garden, a generous planting of tulips is planted behind low-growing basket-of-gold, rock cress, dame's rocket, and snow-in-summer. The perennials are beautiful in their own right, but after they're done blooming, their foliage continues to look good into summer (just cut back the flowers when they're spent).

The tulips are another story. It's necessary to leave that browning foliage in place. The process is called "ripening." The dying foliage helps rejuvenate the bulbs for next year. Remove browning foliage only when it pulls away with no resistance, usually 4 to 8 weeks after bloom time.

Until that time, the attractive foliage of the perennials can carry the day, keeping the garden vibrant through late spring and early summer.

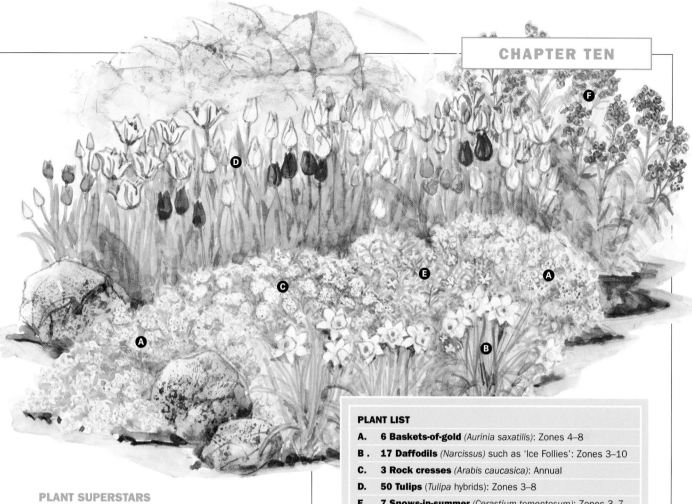

PLANT LIST

A. **6 Baskets-of-gold** (*Aurinia saxatilis*): Zones 4–8

B. **17 Daffodils** (*Narcissus*) such as 'Ice Follies': Zones 3–10

C. **3 Rock cresses** (*Arabis caucasica*): Annual

D. **50 Tulips** (*Tulipa* hybrids): Zones 3–8

E. **7 Snows-in-summer** (*Cerastium tomentosum*): Zones 3–7

F. **4 Dame's rockets** (*Hesperis matronalis*): Zones 4–9

PLANT SUPERSTARS

BULB COMPANIONS

Besides bulbs, hundreds of perennials and ephemeral wildflowers bloom with gusto in spring. Pair these lovely early bloomers with your favorite bulbs for a cheerful spring garden.

EARLY SPRING

BLOODROOT (*Sanguinaria canadensis*): White flowers. Deep to partial shade. Zones 3–8.

LENTEN ROSE (*Helleborus orientalis*): White or greenish-white flowers. Dappled shade. Zones 4–9.

PASQUE FLOWER (*Pulsatilla vulgaris*): Purple or white flowers. Full sun. Zones 4–8.

MIDSPRING

BETHLEHEM SAGE (*Pulmonaria saccharata*): Violet or white flowers. Full or partial shade. Zones 4–8.

COWSLIP (*Primula veris*): Yellow flowers. Partial shade. Zones 3–8.

WHITE WAKEROBIN (*Trillium grandiflorum*): White flowers. Deep to partial shade. Zones 5–8.

LATE SPRING

BLEEDING HEART (*Dicentra spectabilis*): Pink or white flowers. Partial shade. Zones 3–9.

BLUEBELLS (*Mertensia virginica*): Blue flowers. Full sun, midday shade. Zones 4–7.

CANADA COLUMBINE (*Aquilegia canadensis*): Red and yellow flowers. Full sun or partial shade. Zones 3–8.

CANDYTUFT (*Iberis sempervirens*): White flowers. Full sun. Zones 5–9.

SNOWDROP ANEMONE (*Anemone sylvestris*): White flowers. Full sun or partial shade. Zones 4–9.

BHG DESIGN TIP

Don't like the look of fading bulb foliage in June? Conceal the ripening foliage of tulips, daffodils, and hyacinths by tucking in perennials with tall, attractive foliage and later bloom times.

They emerge about the time the bulbs bloom, then grow rapidly to cover the dying foliage. Good choices include daylily, hosta, catmint, hardy geranium, purple coneflower, and Siberian iris.

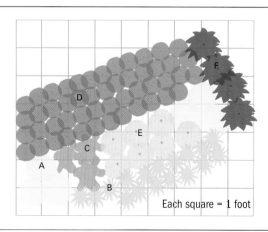

Each square = 1 foot

Try Terrific Tropicals

August's heat and humidity can make it feel like a jungle out there. It's no surprise that many tropical natives love it.

JUST WHEN SUMMER REACHES ITS WORST HEAT AND HUMIDITY, THESE NATIVES OF *REALLY* HOT, *REALLY* MUGGY REGIONS HIT THEIR VIBRANT PEAK.

Cannas are the star of this show. Natives of tropical regions in Southeast Asia, they grow 4 to 7 feet tall. Their large flowers come in yellows, oranges, peaches, reds, pinks, and creams.

The foliage is almost as amazing. 'Pretoria' has gorgeous green leaves with pale lemony stripes. Foliage of the appropriately named 'Tropicanna' has a riot of green, yellow, pink, and red stripes. 'Bengal Tiger' develops cream-and-green-striped leaves fanning out from purple stalks.

Plant cannas as large rhizomes in spring, after all danger of frost has passed. Like so many tropical plants, they're thirsty and need watering if rainfall is less than 1 inch per week.

In the warmest parts of the country, Zones 8 to 11, cannas are perennials. Everywhere else, treat them as annuals or dig and store them for winter.

Other plants in this garden play a supporting role. They play off the cannas with more hot, tropical colors—chartreuse arborvitae, deep golden black-eyed susan, and purple or bright pink spider flower.

A fountain is an excellent focal point for a tropical garden. Its splashing water brings to mind a jungle river, and it emphasizes the lush feel of this paradise.

PLANT LIST

A. **6 Orange cannas** (*Canna* hybrids) such as 'Pretoria': Zones 8–11, annual elsewhere

B. **1 Panicled hydrangea** (*Hydrangea paniculata*): Zones 4–8

C. **3 Spider flowers** (*Cleome hassleriana*): Annual

D. **4 White garden phloxes** (*Phlox paniculata*) such as 'David': Zones 4–8

E. **1 Bigleaf hydrangea** (*Hydrangea macrophylla*) such as 'All Summer Beauty': Zones 6–9

F. **8 Black-eyed susans** (*Rudbeckia fulgida*): Zones 4–9

G. **5 Siberian irises** (*Iris sibirica*): Zones 4–9

H. **1 Globe American arborvitae** (*Thuja occidentalis*) such as 'Gold Cargo': Zones 3–7

I. **1 Agave** (*Agave* spp.): Zones 4–10, depending on the species

J. **3 Daylilies** (*Hemerocallis* hybrids): Zones 3–10

K. **3 Pink garden phloxes** (*Phlox paniculata*) such as 'Eve Cullum': Zones 4–8

L. **4 Bright pink cannas** (*Canna* hybrids) such as 'Pink Futurity': Zones 8–11

Elephant's Ears

PLANT SUPERSTARS
OTHER EXOTICS

POINCIANA (*Caesalpinia pulcherrima*)
Fabulously intricate flowers in shrublike plant. Zones 8–11, annual elsewhere or dig and store for winter.

CROCOSMIA (*Crocosmia × crocosmiiflora*)
Spires of orange, red, and or yellow atop strappy foliage. Hardy Zones 5–9.

ELEPHANT'S EAR (*Alocasia macrorrhizos*)
Giant leaves in green or purplish black give this plant its name. Zones 8–11, annual elsewhere or dig and store for winter.

PASSIONFLOWER (*Passiflora incarnata*)
Climbing vine to 20 feet. Incredible, intricate flowers in blues, purples, pinks, and whites seem other-worldly. Zones 6–10.

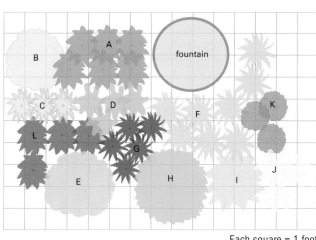

Each square = 1 foot

A Midsummer Day's Dream

Even during the long, hot days of late summer, you can have a garden that's verdant and full of color.

EVEN THOUGH THE LAST RAIN MAY BE A DISTANT MEMORY, AND THE SUN IS BEATING DOWN MERCILESSLY, THIS GARDEN COMES INTO ITS OWN IN LATE SUMMER, RIGHT WHEN YOU NEED IT MOST.

It shouldn't be surprising that native plants stand up to the tough conditions of late summer. They have adapted to thrive on the water that nature provides (or fails to provide) them and to fend off pests and disease.

While flowers that were showy in spring and early summer are now tattered and tired, the late-bloomers of summer step up and put on a show all their own.

In this garden, selections of native plants step into the spotlight: purple coneflower, blazing star, butterfly bush, aster, and tickseed. Butterfly bush rises up in back to provide drama, while hollyhock and sedum play supporting roles.

This garden is attractive to butterflies. Expect to spot them flitting from plant to plant. It's enough to give you a whole new perspective on the dog days of summer.

PLANT LIST

A.	**1 Dwarf New England aster** (*Aster novae-angliae*) such as 'Purple Dome': Zones 4–8
B.	**2 Thread-leaf tickseeds** (*Coreopsis verticillata*) such as 'Zagreb': Zones 4–9
C.	**6 Purple coneflowers** (*Echinacea purpurea*) such as 'Magnus': Zones 3–9
D.	**3 Hollyhocks** (*Alcea rosea*): Zones 3–9
E.	**6 White blazing stars** (*Liatris spicata*) such as 'Floristan White': Zones 4–9
F.	**1 Butterfly bush** (*Buddleia davidii*) such as 'Black Knight': Zones 5–9
G.	**3 Russian sages** (*Perovskia atriplicifolia*): Zones 4–9
H.	**1 Tall sedum** (*Sedum* 'Autumn Joy'): Zones 3–10

GARDEN SMARTER
WHAT'S A NATIVE?

What defines a native plant or a wildflower? What exactly does it mean when a plant has been naturalized? Here's a mini-glossary to guide you:

Native. A plant indigenous to this country, growing here long before Europeans arrived. Some plants are the natives of a particular region, such as of the Northeast or Southwest. Most natives grow in specific environments, such as woodland, swamp, desert, or prairie.

Native plant hybrids. Plants that derive from a native plant but are bred for better performance. Native goldenrod is beautiful, but it is also prone to mildew, grows very tall and rather floppy, and spreads to the point of invasiveness. Hybridized cultivars grow shorter, are more resistant to mildew, and spread slowly. If the hybrids have flowers, they are usually larger and available in a wider variety of colors and forms. The plants also usually bloom longer.

Wildflower. A loose term that encompasses native plants as well as non-native ones that are grown in a naturalistic setting. It can include hybridized native plants as well.

Naturalized. Plants that are grown in a naturalistic way and spread readily. Examples include growing crocuses in lawns or daylilies that have escaped gardens and spread into ditches.

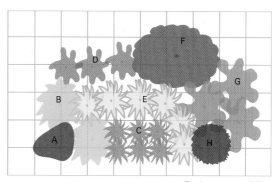

Each square = 1 foot

Fantastic Fall Color

Group the season's most brilliant bloomers next to each other for high impact and lots of color.

MANY OF THE BEST FALL-BLOOMING PLANTS ARE TOWERING GIANTS. THIS GARDEN STAYS NEATLY IN CHECK WITH DWARF VARIETIES OF LANKY FAVORITES, SUCH AS ASTERS, GOLDENROD, AND GRASSES.

This autumn garden stays tidily within bounds with smaller plants, making it easier to manage.

Many asters reach 4 to 6 feet tall and spread prolifically. However, cushion types, such as the popular 'Purple Dome' used in this garden, remain under 2 feet and stay easily in bounds.

The same is true with ornamental grasses. Some can grow 8 feet tall and be invasive, but silver-gray blue fescue stays about 12 inches high and wide. Dwarf goldenrod can be difficult to find, but is worth it. Most goldenrod varieties reach 4 feet or more and can some are invasive. The types recommended here are better behaved and so low-growing that they can be used as groundcovers.

This design would be ideal tucked into a larger border or set apart on its own. Try it as a front garden or a section of a backyard landscape. When the rest of the garden is winding down, this garden comes to life.

PLANT SUPERSTARS
MORE OUTSTANDING FALL BLOOMERS

Autumn crocus
Boltonia
Dahlia
False sunflower
Joe-pye weed
Ornamental cabbage
Ornamental grass
Ornamental kale
Pansy

PLANT LIST

A. **5 Spike speedwells** (*Veronica spicata*) such as 'Goodness Grows': Zones 3–8

B. **2 Yarrows** (*Achillea* spp.) such as 'Moonbeam': Zones 4–8

C. **5 Chrysanthemums** such as 'Foxy Nana': Zones 5–9

D. **2 'Purple Dome' asters** (*Aster noveae-angliae* 'Purple Dome'): Zones 4–6

E. **1 Dwarf white aster** (*Aster* hybrids), such as 'Snow Flurry': Zones 4–8

F. **3 Dwarf goldenrods** (*Solidago* hybrids) such as 'Golden Baby' or 'Golden Fleece': Zones 5–9

G. **1 Blue fescue** (*Festuca glauca*) such as 'Elijah Blue': Zones 4–8

H. **1 Lamb's-ears** (*Stachys byzantina*): Zones 4–8

I. **1 Pink New England aster** (*Aster novi-belgii*) such as 'Alma Potschke': Zones 4–8

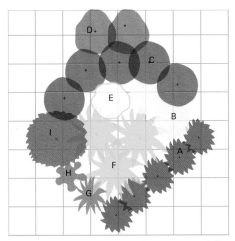

Each square = 1 foot

GARDEN SMARTER
PINCH MORE THAN AN INCH

Mums and asters are gorgeous flowers, but they'll be more attractive if you do some smart pruning in early summer.

With mums, pinch off the developing flower heads until the Fourth of July. This will ensure a more bushy, full plant with better, larger flowers that bloom a little later during cooler weather, when they'll last longer.

With tall types of asters (those that grow 3 feet or more) cut them back by about one-third to one-half in late spring, when the plants are a foot or so tall. This will ensure a bushier, stronger plant that is less prone to flopping.

Fall For Country Casual

This generously sized autumn planting is nicely suited to a rural, cottage, or otherwise relaxed garden.

IN THIS GARDEN, TALL GRASSES SPRAWL OVER A DECIDUOUS AZALEA, WHICH MERGES INTO A STAND OF BLACK-EYED SUSAN, SURROUNDED BY SWEET ALYSSUM, PANSIES, ASTERS, AND SEDUM.

Flowerbeds are a little like houses. Some people like theirs well-kept and orderly while others love a casual, relaxed feel. This garden is definitely the latter. It rises and sprawls, mingles and melts, in a design that is both exuberant and relaxed.

Pansies add bright spots of clear color, while evergreens stay fresh right through the first snow and into spring, giving this garden seasonal staying power.

The birdbath is the focal point of this garden, but as with other focal points and garden art in planting plans, you can substitute freely. Consider a sundial, reflecting ball, globe, or other accent. Since the flowers in this garden attract birds and butterflies, it would be fun to include a birdhouse on a pedestal or a small platform-type birdfeeder.

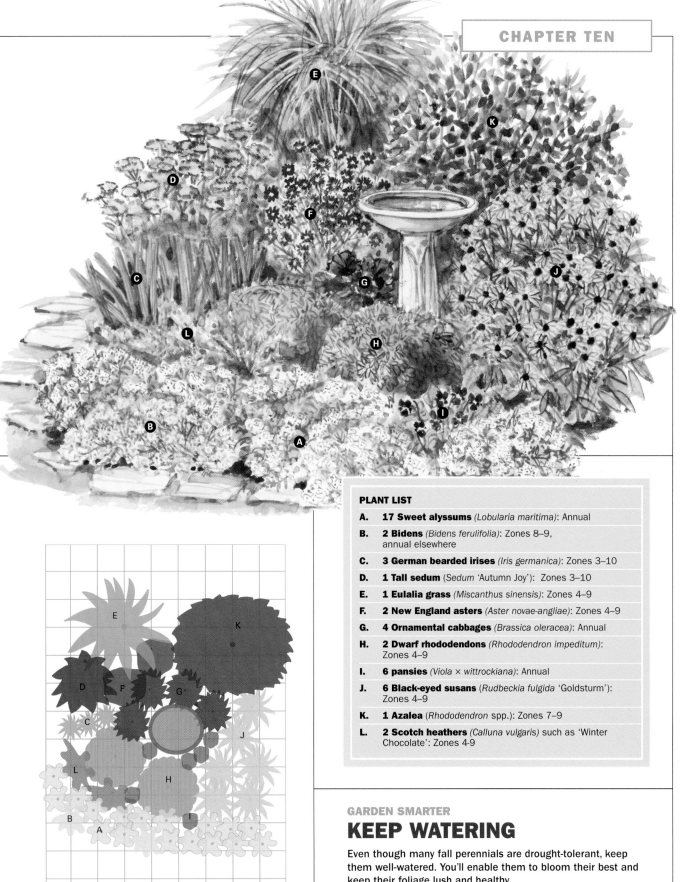

PLANT LIST

A. **17 Sweet alyssums** *(Lobularia maritima)*: Annual

B. **2 Bidens** *(Bidens ferulifolia)*: Zones 8–9, annual elsewhere

C. **3 German bearded irises** *(Iris germanica)*: Zones 3–10

D. **1 Tall sedum** *(Sedum 'Autumn Joy')*: Zones 3–10

E. **1 Eulalia grass** *(Miscanthus sinensis)*: Zones 4–9

F. **2 New England asters** *(Aster novae-angliae)*: Zones 4–9

G. **4 Ornamental cabbages** *(Brassica oleracea)*: Annual

H. **2 Dwarf rhododendons** *(Rhododendron impeditum)*: Zones 4–9

I. **6 pansies** *(Viola × wittrockiana)*: Annual

J. **6 Black-eyed susans** *(Rudbeckia fulgida 'Goldsturm')*: Zones 4–9

K. **1 Azalea** *(Rhododendron spp.)*: Zones 7–9

L. **2 Scotch heathers** *(Calluna vulgaris)* such as 'Winter Chocolate': Zones 4-9

Each square = 1 foot

GARDEN SMARTER
KEEP WATERING

Even though many fall perennials are drought-tolerant, keep them well-watered. You'll enable them to bloom their best and keep their foliage lush and healthy.

Keep an eye on shrubs and other plantings too. Many plants need to go into winter well-hydrated. If not, they're more susceptible to winter damage.

Swayed by Grasses

Valued for their graceful lines and striking seed heads, ornamental grasses add movement to a fall garden.

UNLIKE ANY OTHER PLANT, ORNAMENTAL GRASSES ADD ELEGANCE, GRACE, MOTION, AND A NATURAL EASE TO THE LANDSCAPE. THIS PLANTING USES THEM AS A BACKDROP FOR BRIGHT PERENNIALS.

Use tall, upright ornamental grasses, such as the eulalia grass shown here, in the back of fall gardens to add a vertical element. Add sprawling types of ornamental grasses, such as the pennisetum in this design, in the middle, and shorter grasses, such as blue fescue, at the front of the border or in containers.

Ornamental grasses are excellent next to water features. Their soothing motion and cascading blades mimic the rhythmn and flow of water, making them a natural combination. Any grass looks good near a water feature, but right along the edge, consider grasses that trail over, such as golden hakone grass (*Hakonechloa macra* 'Aureola').

In this fall garden, anchored by grasses, other fall flowers fill in at the front, adding splashes of color. Dwarf azalea, New Zealand flax, mums, black-eyed susans, asters, and blanket flower add color and a variety of shapes and textures.

It's a design that definitely saves the best for last.

GARDEN SMARTER

WISE WAYS WITH ORNAMENTAL GRASSES

Choose carefully. Ornamental grasses come in two types: clumping or spreading. The clumping types are better behaved while the spreaders can be runaways. Plant rapidly spreading types in areas contained by walks, driveways, or other barriers.

Check the hardiness zone. Hardiness varies widely among grasses. Purple fountain grass, for example, is a perennial in some regions but an annual in others. (See page 216.)

Use seedheads in arrangements. Those beautiful plumes are gorgeous in a vase, either solo or mixed in with branches of autumn leaves or fall flowers.

Enjoy grasses throughout the winter. Leave them standing until spring. Their dried leaves and seedheads are beautiful.

Prune the easy way. In spring, before it starts to send out new growth, it's time to cut it back perennial grass—a tough task. Invest in an inexpensive electric hedge trimmer to slice off the fibrous stalks in minutes with no blisters.

PLANT LIST

A.   **1 Eulalia grass** (*Miscanthus sinensis*): Zones 4–9

B.   **1 Dwarf Indica azalea** (*Rhododendron eriocarpum*): Zones 6–9

C.   **1 New Zealand flax** (*Phormium tenax*): Zones 7–11*

D.   **1 Chrysanthemum** (*Chrysanthemum × moriflorum*): Zones 4–9

E.   **1 Gloriosa daisy** (*Rudbeckia hirta*): Zones 5–10

F.   **1 Fountain grass** (*Pennisetum alopecuroides*) such as 'Hameln': Zones 6–9

G.   **1 New York aster** (*Aster novi-belgi*): Zones 4–6

H.   **1 Blanket flower** (*Gaillardia × grandiflora*): Zones 3–8

* In colder regions, substitute variegated German bearded iris.

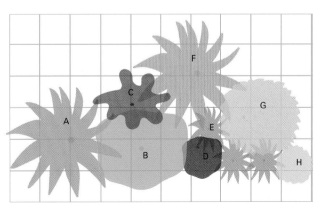

Each square = 1 foot

Welcome Wildlife!

Who doesn't enjoy the sight of butterflies flitting from plant to plant on a sunny day? Or the spectacle of birds tending a nest of babies? Or a symphony of birds singing their hearts out right in your own yard?

From birds and butterflies to toads and turtles, if you plant it, they will come. Fill your garden with flowers, herbs, and shrubs that will attract birds with their seeds and butterflies with their nectar. Then sit back and enjoy the show!

Attract Birds and Butterflies To Your Garden

Fill your garden with a vareity of seed- and nectar-bearing plants and you'll also fill it with butterflies, hummingbirds, and songbirds.

Take your cue from hummingbird feeders. Hummingbirds love bright red and pink flowers with tubular shapes.

With the right flowers, your garden on will be filled with multiple butterflies on a sunny summer day.

Attracting wildlife to your garden is easy. Simply by planting a landscape filled with a variety of trees, shrubs, and flowers you're likely to attract birds, butterflies, and hummingbirds that will be drawn to the shelter and food supply. You can attract particular types of birds and butterflies by selecting their favorite plants.

Provide shelter. Trees give excellent shelter. Plant a tree or two, and the birds will start flocking to your yard. In more limited spaces, create shelter with large shrubs and vines. Both make good spots for nesting and fleeing from predators. Birdhouses add a nice touch too. (Clean them out in late winter or early spring to encourage returning birds.)

Provide water. Water attracts birds and other animals. A basic birdbath will do. The most attractive water setup, however, is in a shallow (just an inch or less) basin or pool where water falls or bubbles up from a fountain. The splashing sound attracts many types of wildlife. Birds love to bathe in the shallow pool, and butterflies will drink from moist spots along the edge.

Provide food. Many flowers naturally provide good food for wildlife, especially if you let the flowers go to seed or develop into fruits—a real bird treat.

Go for color. As a rule, birds, butterflies, and hummingbirds are most drawn to clear reds and brilliant pinks. Red zinnias, for example, attract more butterflies than white ones. And magenta morning glories are more alluring to hummingbirds than blue ones.

It's helpful if the planting is large. A large stand of favorites is like a highway billboard to butterflies and birds, beckoning them to stop in.

Use chemicals sparingly, if at all—especially insecticides. Many insecticides, even organic ones, kill helpful insects as well as harmful ones. (The larvae of butterflies are caterpillars.)

Be messy. When it comes to gardening for wildlife, be casual about maintenance. Birds love to feast on the seed heads created by flowers left to ripen on the stem. They adore tall grass and thrive in tall, unpruned shrubs. They like to rummage for worms among the leaf litter under a tree.

Think about how a forest or meadow looks—filled with fallen trees, tall plants gone to seed, a wide variety of plant life, and layers of dead plants on the ground. That's wildlife's ideal environment, so use it as your model.

While most birds are attracted to seeds, Baltimore orioles love half oranges set out for them.

GARDEN SMARTER
BIRD BUFFET

A bird feeder attracts many winged visitors. A flat-tray bird feeder filled with a general blend of seed draws the widest variety of birds. To lure specific types of birds, check with your local seed and bird feeder supplier. Goldfinches, for example, love niger thistle seed delivered from a tube feeder.

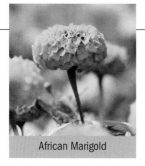

African Marigold

Gladiolus

Purple Coneflower

PLANT SUPERSTARS
TOP FLOWERS TO ATTRACT SONG BIRDS

African marigold
  (*Tagetes erecta*)
Black-eyed susan
  (*Rudbeckia* spp.)
Cosmos (*Cosmos* spp.)
Giant sunflower
  (*Helianthus giganteus*)
Goldenrod (*Solidago* spp.)
Honeysuckle (*Lonicera* spp.)
Ornamental grasses
Purple coneflower
  (*Echinacea purpurea*)
Tall zinnias (*Zinnia elegans*)
Tickseed (*Coreopsis* spp.)

PLANT SUPERSTARS
TOP FLOWERS TO ATTRACT HUMMERS

Canna (*Canna* × *generalis*)
Dahlia (*Dahlia pinnata*)
Flowering tobacco
  (*Nicotiana* spp.)
Floxglove (*Digitalis*)
Fuchsia (*Fuchsia* × *hybrida*)
Gladiolus (*Gladiolus* hybrids)
Honeysuckle (*Lonicera* spp.)
Lantana (*Lantana* spp.)
Morning glory (*Ipomoea*)
Petunia (*Petunia* × *hybrida*)
Red salvia (*Salvia splendens*)
Snapdragon
  (*Antirrhinum majus*)
Weigela (*Weigela florida*)

PLANT SUPERSTARS
TOP PLANTS TO ATTRACT BUTTERFLIES

Aster (*Aster* spp.)
Bee balm (*Monarda didyma*)
Butterfly bush
  (*Buddleia davidii*)
Butterfly plant
  (*Schizanthus pinnatus*)
Dill (*Anethum graveolens*)
Joe-pye weed
  (*Eupatorium* spp.)
Lantana (*Lantana* spp.)
Marigold (*Tagetes* spp.)
Nasturtium (*Tropaeolum*)
Parsley
  (*Petroselinum crispum*)
Purple coneflower
  (*Echinacea purpurea*)
Salvia (*Salvia* spp., annual
  and perennial types)
Sedum (*Sedum* spp.)
Spicebush (*Lindera benzoin*)
Tickseed (*Coreopsis* spp.)
Wisteria (*Wisteria* spp.)
Zinnias (*Zinnia* spp.)

A Fascination With Fountains

Draw birds and butterflies to your garden with the sound of splashing water.

PLANT LIST

A.	**3 Impatiens** *(Impatiens walleriana)*: Annual
B.	**3 European wild gingers** *(Asarum europaeum)*: Zones 4–9
C.	**2 Big blue lilyturfs** *(Liriope muscari)*: Zones 5–10
D.	**1 Kangaroo paw** *(Anigozanthos* 'Bush Gem'): Zones 9–10
E.	**1 Coleus** *(Solenostemon scutellarioides)*: Annual
F.	**1 Hummingbird mint** *(Agastache cana)* such as 'Purple Pygmy': Zones 5–10

BIRDS LOVE SPLASHING WATER FOR BATHING AND DRINKING. BUTTERFLIES LOVE SHALLOW WATER AND STONES FOR SUNNING AND SIPPING. GIVE BOTH THE BEST OF ALL WORLDS WITH THIS ONE-OF-A-KIND FOUNTAIN.

Birds have long been attracted to birdbaths, but it's the sound of splashing or dripping water that they really love. And this fountain delivers. It's powered with a tiny fountain pump, available at most better-stocked garden centers and nurseries.

Butterflies, who love to suck salts out of muds and porous stone, will enjoy alighting on the pebbles for deliciously long drinks. Because the stones absorb heat, butterflies bask in their radiant warmth.

The fountain itself is easy and inexpensive to make (see directions on the opposite page). Tuck the fountain into this garden or other location for an instant, soothing water feature.

MAKE THIS FOUNTAIN

Materials
30-inch-diameter, 7-inch-tall, terra-cotta bowl with
   drainage hole in bottom
Pond liner
9-inch-wide terra-cotta saucer
Small grounded submersible pump capable of
   pumping 60 to 80 gallons of water an hour
12- to 16-inch terra-cotta sphere
Flexible plastic tubing
Bag of ¼- to ½-inch rounded pebbles

Tools
String
Heavy-duty shears
Drill
Carbide-tip, masonry, or diamond drill bit
   (slightly larger than tubing)
Goggles
Bucket to wash gravel

Step 1. Using string, measure from the top edge of
the bowl across the bottom to the top of the other side,
allowing the string to conform to the bowl's shape. Cut
a piece of pond liner to a slightly larger diameter. Place
liner in the bowl, letting excess drape over the edge.
Don't trim excess liner until the fountain is assembled.

Step 2. Set the saucer upside down on the liner in
bottom of bowl. (Confirm that pump will fit under the
saucer with liner in place.) Remove saucer; drill several
holes in bottom for drainage. Drill one hole in center
large enough to house the plastic tubing and a hole
along the edge for the pump's electrical cord.

Step 3. Using a drill bit slightly larger than the
diameter of plastic tubing, make a hole in the top center
of the sphere. Wear goggles to protect your eyes.

Step 4. From inside the sphere, feed one end of tubing
through the hole in the top. Place the saucer upside
down and feed the other end of tubing through the
central hole; take care not to pull the tubing loose from
the sphere.

Step 5. Center the sphere on the upside-down saucer.
Connect tubing coming from the saucer to the pump
outlet; set saucer and sphere in the bowl. Gently tug
on tubing so it runs straight up from the pump, through
the saucer, and out the sphere's top. Check the pump
by filling bowl with water and plugging in the unit. If
everything works, trim the end of plastic tubing flush
with the sphere.

Step 6. Wash pebbles to remove silt and grit. Fill bowl
with pebbles. Adjust liner so it is laid evenly, with no low
spots along the edge. Trim excess to the edge of the
bowl. Conceal the liner with pebbles.

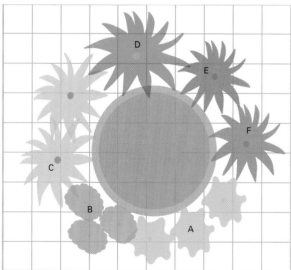

Each square = 6 inches

Kangaroo paw is hardy only in the
southernmost regions of the U.S. In
colder regions, substitute daylilies for a
similar effect.

Go With Grasses

Create a bird haven with ornamental grasses, a good source of food, nesting material, and shelter.

PEOPLE LOVE ORNAMENTAL GRASSES FOR THEIR GRACEFUL FOLIAGE, RUSTLING GENTLY IN THE WIND. IN LATE SUMMER AND FALL, THEY SEND UP ELEGANT PLUMES, WHICH RIPEN INTO TASTY SEEDHEADS FOR BIRDS.

Depending on the bird, the grass, the season, and the region, grass seed heads play an important role in a bird's diet.

Whenever possible, plant grasses native to your region since those seedheads are perfectly timed to local birds' nutritional needs and eating preferences. Be sure to leave those seedheads standing through the winter, when the birds appreciate them most.

A variety of birds use dried ornamental grass leaves for nesting material come spring. For this reason (and to enjoy their sculptural effect in winter) leave ornamental grasses standing until spring. Cut back the plant only once you see new growth pushing up from the ground. Toss the leaves on top of the compost heap or other open area. You'll be treated by a bird, tugging out a choice length of dried grass to build a nest.

PLANT LIST

A. **12 Black-eyed susans** (*Rudbeckia* spp.): Zones 3–9,

B. **2 Maiden grasses** (*Miscanthus sinensis* 'Gracillimus'): Zones 4–9

C. **1 Variegated eulalia grass** (*Miscanthus sinensis* 'Variegatus'): Zones 4–9

D. **2 Tall sedums** (*Sedum* 'Autumn Joy'): Zones 3–10

E. **1 Silver variegated Japanese sedge** (*Carex morrowii* 'Variegata'): Zones 5–9

F. **6 Tall zinnias** (*Zinnia elegans*): Annual

G. **1 Low-growing sedum** such as *Sedum sieboldii*: Zones 6–9

H. **1 Prickly pear** (*Opuntia compressa*): Zones 6–8

I. **4 Pink tickseeds** (*Coreopsis rosea*): Zones 3–9

J. **2 Japanese blood grasses** (*Imperata cylindrica* 'Red Baron'): Zones 4–9

K. **2 Fountain grasses** (*Pennisetum alopecuroides*): Zones 6–9

L. **1 Zebra grass** (*Miscanthus sinensis* 'Zebrinus'): Zones 4–9

M. **5 Daylilies** (*Hemerocallis* spp.): Zones 3–10

N. **8 Hollyhocks** (*Alcea rosea*): Zones 3–9

Each square = 1 foot

Build a Bird Buffet

A birdbath makes a pretty and practical focal point for a garden designed to attract feathered visitors.

JUST LIKE PEOPLE, BIRDS NEED BOTH FOOD AND WATER NEAR THEIR HOMES. PROVIDE THE FOOD WITH PLANTS AND THE WATER WITH AN ATTRACTIVE BIRDBATH.

This mix of annuals, perennials, and shrubs assures a good blend of shelter, seeds, berries, and insects for visiting birds.

Some annuals in this plan, such as the marigolds and zinnias, set seed in the late summer, offering tasty treats for birds.

Native plants, such as Jacob's ladder, provide cover for birds as they forage for food, as does the shrubby cinquefoil. Sweet alyssum and fleabane attract insects that birds devour. Both also set and drop seed that birds will nibble. The seeds they miss will germinate for more plants next year.

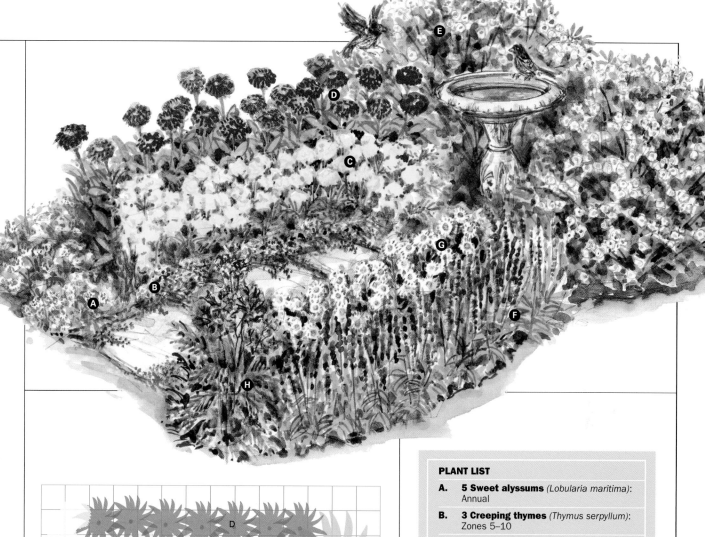

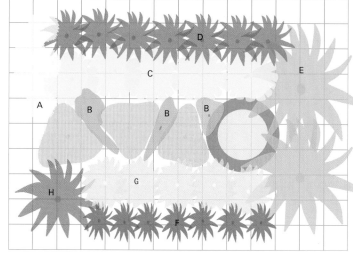

Each square = 1 foot

PLANT LIST

A. **5 Sweet alyssums** (*Lobularia maritima*): Annual

B. **3 Creeping thymes** (*Thymus serpyllum*): Zones 5–10

C. **5 African marigolds** (*Tagetes erecta* 'Inca'): Annual

D. **7 Compact zinnias** (*Zinnia* spp.) such as the Profusion series: Annual

E. **2 Shrubby cinquefoils** (*Potentilla fruticosa*) such as 'Abbottswood': Zones 2–6

F. **7 Mealycup sages** (*Salvia farinacea*): Zones 7–11; annual elsewhere

G. **5 Daisy fleabanes** (*Erigeron annuus*): Annual that reseeds freely

H. **1 Jacob's ladder** (*Polemonium caeruleum*) such as 'Stairway to Heaven': Zones 3–7

GARDEN SMARTER
BETTER BIRD BATHING

Choose a birdbath that when filled will provide water no more than 2 inches deep. Locate it near shrubs or low-hanging trees so birds have ready branches for preening and drying off. Also, some like the sense of shelter provided by shrubs.

Birds dislike stagnant water. Change water in the birdbath daily. If algae builds up, pour out the water and scrub the birdbath with a mixture of hot soapy water and bleach. Rinse well. (The flagstones in this plan make for easy access to the bath, a good idea no matter what your design.)

To attract more birds, consider purchasing a dripper for your birdbath. Birds are attracted to the sound of dripping water.

In winter, keep the birdbath open for business by installing a water heater. Overwintering birds will flock to it!

Plant a Hub For Hummers

This colorful, sun-loving planting attracts hummingbirds and butterflies.

A PATH PROVIDES ACCESS TO THIS SMALL, MEANDERING GARDEN. IT CURVES THROUGH THE PLANTING GRACEFULLY, ALLOWING YOU TO ENJOY THE GARDEN MORE FULLY.

This casual planting's vibrant forms peak in mid- to late-summer, yet there's something of interest from spring onward. (For early spring interest, tuck in tulips and daffodils among the perennials.)

This design is filled with a mix of plants that attract hummingbirds but also song birds and butterflies. Bee balm has sweet nectar that hummingbirds adore, as does Brazilian vervain and crocosmia.

This garden also invites butterflies. That's because the same plants that attract hummingbirds often attract butterflies as well. And borage is an excellent host plant for butterfly larvae.

A bonus of this garden is that once established, it needs little additional water to keep it looking its best. Spread mulch in spring to suppress weeds and to conserve moisture.

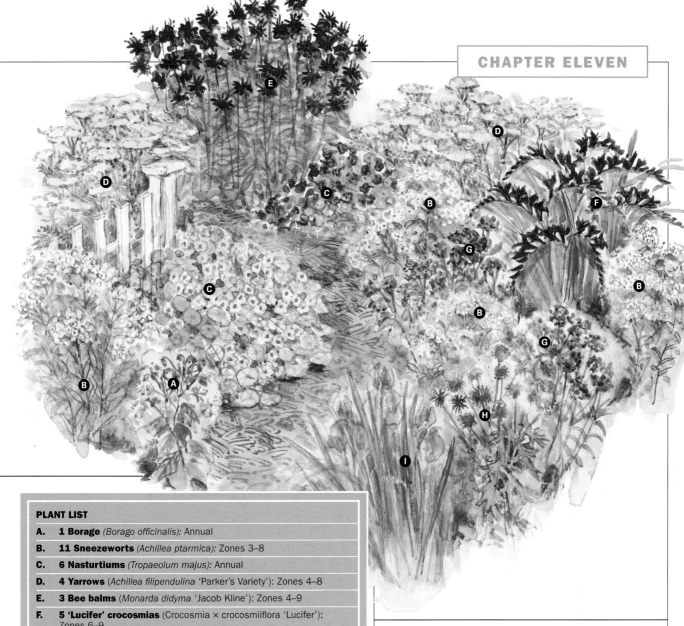

PLANT LIST

A. **1 Borage** *(Borago officinalis)*: Annual

B. **11 Sneezeworts** *(Achillea ptarmica)*: Zones 3–8

C. **6 Nasturtiums** *(Tropaeolum majus)*: Annual

D. **4 Yarrows** *(Achillea filipendulina* 'Parker's Variety'*)*: Zones 4–8

E. **3 Bee balms** *(Monarda didyma* 'Jacob Kline'*)*: Zones 4–9

F. **5 'Lucifer' crocosmias** (Crocosmia × crocosmiiflora 'Lucifer'): Zones 6–9

G. **3 Brazilian vervains** *(Verbena bonariensis)* Zones 7–11; annual elsewhere

H. **2 Globethistles** *(Echinops ritro)*: Zones 3–9

I. **1 Siberian iris** *(Iris sibirica)*: Zones 3–9, depending on species

GARDEN SMARTER

BELOVED BEES

Many of the plants that attract butterflies with their delectable nectar also attract bees. This worries some gardeners, but remember that bees sting only if provoked. And they play a hugely valuable role as they pollinate most of the flowering plants on this planet.

Bee populations are in danger for unknown reasons, so welcome them to your garden. They're key to the ecosystem and without them, humans probably couldn't exist!

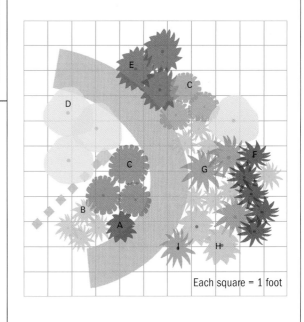

Each square = 1 foot

Lure Butterflies With Annuals

In just weeks, you can have butterflies flitting through your garden by planting easy, inexpensive annuals.

THIS GARDEN DRAWS BUTTERFLIES WITH A COLORFUL MIX OF NECTAR-RICH ANNUAL FLOWERS. BEST OF ALL, YOU CAN START MANY OF THESE FLOWERS FROM SEED FOR BIG SAVINGS AND BIG REWARDS.

Butterflies love the bright colors and nectar provided by the annuals in this garden—pentas, zinnia, sage, cosmos, Mexican sunflower, and marigolds.

Butterflies also need water. Unlike birds, butterflies don't drink from open water sources but rely instead on dew or wet soil. They enjoy sipping the salts out of sandy or muddy riverbanks and puddles. This garden replicates that with a saucer filled with wet sand set into the design.

To make this garden even more butterfly-friendly, tuck in some plants for butterfly larvae. Cater to caterpillars (a.k.a. butterfly larvae) by planting good host plants, such as milkweed, parsley, dill, fennel, basil, and oregano. These host plants are favored by butterflies to lay eggs on. The eggs develop into caterpillars—so be tolerant when they happily munch the leaves!

PLANT LIST

A. **3 Star flowers** *(Pentas lanceolata)*: Zones 9–10; annual elsewhere

B. **5 Creeping zinnias** *(Sanvitalia procumbens)*: Annual

C. **5 Mealycup sages** *(Salvia farinacea)*, such as 'Victoria Blue': Zones 7–11; annual elsewhere

D. **8 Cosmoses,** such as *Cosmos sulfureus* 'Little Ladybird': Annual

E. **2 Spider flowers** *(Cleome hasslerana)*, such as 'Rose Queen': Annual

F. **3 Mexican sunflowers** *(Tithonia rotundifolia)*: Annual

G. **11 Tall zinnias** *(Zinnia elegans)* such as 'Cut and Come Again': Annual

H. **6 Compact zinnias** *(Zinna* spp.), such as the Profusion series: Annual

I. **7 French marigolds** *(Tagetes patula)*, such as 'Yellow Boy': Annual

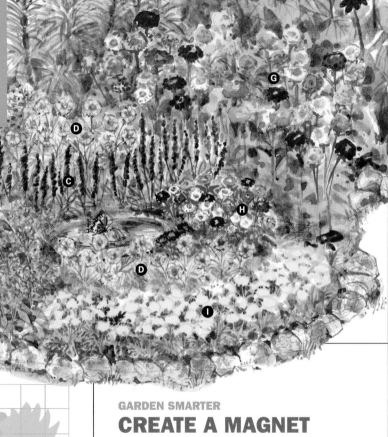

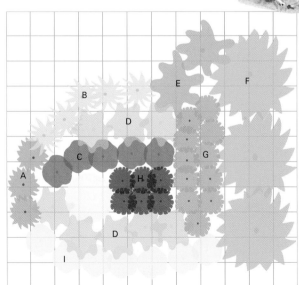

Each square = 1 foot

GARDEN SMARTER

CREATE A MAGNET FOR BUTTERFLIES

Attract more butterflies with these techniques:

Avoid pesticides. **Sprays kill butterfly larvae along with other less-desired caterpillars.**

Include red and hot pink. **Butterflies gravitate toward these colors in your garden.**

Plant in large drifts. **Group a couple dozen favorite annuals or a dozen perennials. Butterflies are more likely to notice them.**

Plant in full sun. **Most butterfly-attracting plants require full sun. Butterflies bask in the warming rays of the sun to pump warmth into their bodies.**

Add stones. **Stones that catch morning sun are especially useful. Butterflies are attracted to the radiant heat of the rocks.**

USDA Plant Hardiness Zone Map

A plant's ability to withstand cold temperatures is designated as a hardiness rating. The lowest range of temperatures at which it survives is its hardiness zone. The Zone Map on the facing page shows the geographical breakdown of hardiness zones.

Knowing your hardiness rating will help you grow plants that can withtstand your area's winters.

PLANTING FOR YOUR ZONE

There are 11 zones from Canada to Mexico, and each zone represents the lowest expected winter temperature in that area. Each zone is based on a 10-degree difference in minimum temperatures. Once you know your hardiness zone, you can choose plants for your garden that will flourish. Look for the hardiness zone on the plant tags of the perennials, trees, and shrubs you buy.

MICROCLIMATES IN YOUR YARD

Not all areas in your yard are the same. Depending on your geography, trees, and structures, some spots may receive different sunlight and wind and consequently experience temperature differences. Take a look around your yard and you may notice that the same plant comes up sooner in one place than another. This is the microclimate concept in action. A microclimate is an area in your yard that is slightly different (cooler or hotter) than the other areas of your yard.

CREATE A MICROCLIMATE

Once you're aware of your yard's microclimates, you can use them to your advantage. For example, you may be able to grow plants in a sheltered, southern-facing garden bed that you can't grow elsewhere in your yard. You can create a microclimate by planting evergreens on the north side of a property to block prevailing winds. Or plant deciduous trees on the south side to provide shade in summer.

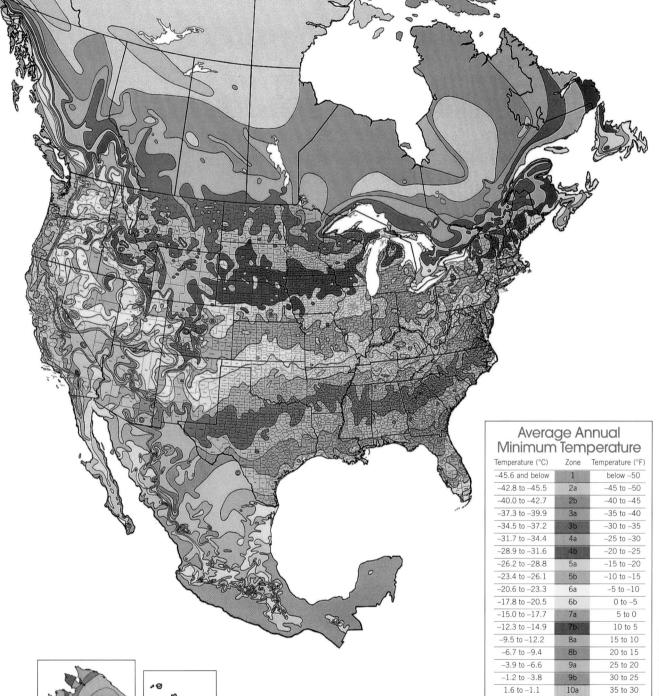

Average Annual Minimum Temperature

Temperature (°C)	Zone	Temperature (°F)
−45.6 and below	1	below −50
−42.8 to −45.5	2a	−45 to −50
−40.0 to −42.7	2b	−40 to −45
−37.3 to −39.9	3a	−35 to −40
−34.5 to −37.2	3b	−30 to −35
−31.7 to −34.4	4a	−25 to −30
−28.9 to −31.6	4b	−20 to −25
−26.2 to −28.8	5a	−15 to −20
−23.4 to −26.1	5b	−10 to −15
−20.6 to −23.3	6a	−5 to −10
−17.8 to −20.5	6b	0 to −5
−15.0 to −17.7	7a	5 to 0
−12.3 to −14.9	7b	10 to 5
−9.5 to −12.2	8a	15 to 10
−6.7 to −9.4	8b	20 to 15
−3.9 to −6.6	9a	25 to 20
−1.2 to −3.8	9b	30 to 25
1.6 to −1.1	10a	35 to 30
4.4 to 1.7	10b	40 to 35
4.5 and above	11	40 and above

Source: U.S. Department of Agriculture

Page numbers in italic type indicate photographs or illustrations.

N

Nasturtium *(Tropaeolum majus)*
  for fence plantings, 123
  for front entrances, 153
  for planter boxes, 35, 178, 179
  size, 12
  for wildlife, 205, 213
Native plants
  glossary of terms, 195
  for hell strips, *54–55*, 54–55
  for raised beds, 64
  for summer gardens, *194–195*, 194–195
  for wildlife, 194, 208–209, 210–211
New Zealand flax *(Phormium tenax)*, 159, 201
Nigella, *74*

O

Obedient plant *(Physostegia virginiana)*, 25, *25*, 129
October daphne *(Sedum sieboldii)*, 119, 209
Oleander, 75
Onion *(Allium)*, 171
  giant ornamental *(A. giganteum)*, 113, 119
Oregano *(Origanum vulgare)*, 175

P

Pansy *(Viola × wittrockiana)*
  blue, 85
  for container gardens, 185
  for cottage gardens, 111
  for fall borders, 197, 198, 199
  for front entrances, 161
  for pondside plantings, 67
Parrot's beak *(Lotus berthelotii)*, 35
Parsley *(Petroselinum crispum)*, 173, 175, 205
Parterres or potagers, 180, *180–181*
Pasque flower *(Pulsatilla vulgaris)*, 191
Passalong plants, *128–129*, 128–129
Passionflower *(Passiflora incarnata)*, 193
Paths and sidewalks
  cottage-style, *106–107*, 106–107
  formal made fun, *14–15*, 14–15
  front walks, *150–151*, 150–151
  lining with roses, *100–101*, 100–101
  materials for, 136, 144
  mirror-image plantings, *132*, 132
  for potagers, 180
  stepping stones, 134
  steps, 158, *158–159*
Patio gardens, *110–111, 176–177*
Peas *(Pisum sativum)*, 178, 179, 180
Pennisetum. *See* Fountain grass
Penstemon or beardstongue *(Penstemon)*, 16, 17, 57, 117
  dwarf hairy *(P. hirsutus)*, 59
  firecracker *(P. eatonii)*, 57
  foothill *(P. heterophyllus)*, 59

P. barbatus, 57
P. serratus, 57
  pineleaf *(P. pinifolius)*, 57
Peony *(Paeonia lactiflora)*, 78–79, 83, 127, 129, 151, 163
Peppers, bell and hot *(Capsicum annuum)*, 173, 178, 179, 180
Perennial plants
  with bulbs, *190–191*, 190–191
  for cold climates, *62–63*, 62–63, 81
  for container gardens, 38
  cost-saving tips, 113
  distinguished from annuals, 15
  drought-tolerant, *56–57*, 56–57
  for edible gardens, 173
  for hell strips, *54–55*, 54–55
  for light shade, *24–25*, 24–25
  passalong plants, *128–129*, 128–129
  with roses, 102, *102–103*
  for shady areas, 22, 45, 45
  for wildlife, 210–211
Persian shield *(Strobilanthes dyerianus)*, 28, 29
Peruvian lily *(Alstroemeria)*, 114, 115
Pesticides, wildlife killed by, 204, 215
Petunia *(Petunia)*
  for birds, 205
  for front entrances, 151
  for hummingbirds, 16, 17
  for knot gardens, 139
  'Purple Wave', 13, 15
  red, 81
  for slopes, 63
  for window boxes, 40
Phlox *(Phlox)*
  annual *(P. drummondii)*, 61
  garden *(P. paniculata)*, 55, 57, 193
  moss or creeping *(P. subulata)*, 67, 77, 115, 165
  woodland *(P. divaricata)*, 189
Pincushion flower *(Scabiosa columbaria)*, 59, 61, 107, 119
Pine *(Pinus)*
  standard dwarf, 109
Pinks *(Dianthus)*, 63, 69, 119
  China *(D. chinensis)*, 13, 39, 129
  maiden *(D. deltoides)*, 77
Plantain, purple-leaf *(Plantago major 'Rubrifolia')*, 119
Poles and flagpoles, planting around, 13
Polka-dot plant *(Hypoestes phyllostachya)*, 18, 19, 19
Ponds, planting around, *66–67*, 68, *68–69*
Poppy *(Papaver)*
  corn *(P. rhoeas)*, 65, 108, *109*, 109
  Iceland *(P. nudicaule)*, 161
  opium *(P. somniferum)*, 137
  Oriental *(P. orientale)*, 11, 63, 113
Potagers or parterres, 180, *180–181*
Potentilla *(Potentilla)*, 75

Potting soil
  for container gardens, 30
  for raised beds, 65, 178
Prickly pear *(Opuntia compressa)*, 209
Primrose *(Primula)*, 37
  English *(P. vulgaris)*, 37
  German *(P. obconica)*, *37*, 37, 39
  Japanese *(P. japonica)*, 36, 37
  polyanthus *(P. × polyantha)*, 36, 37, 37
Pruning plants
  container gardens, 40
  for long-lasting blooms, 121
  ornamental grasses, 201
  shearing hedges, 139
  summer pruning, 197
Pumpkin, space required for, 179

R

Rain gauges, 6
Raised beds
  benefits of, 6
  deck planter boxes, *34–35*, 34–35
  for front entrances, 150–151, *150–151*
  for herbs, 174
  for high-altitude gardens, 64, *64–65*
  soil for, 65, 178
  square of greens, *168–169*, 169
  for sunny side yards, 170–171, *170–171*
  for vegetables, *178–179*
Redbud *(Cercis canadensis)*, 162, 163
Retaining walls, for slopes, 60, *60–61*
Rhododendron *(Rhododendron)*, 165
  dwarf *(R. impeditum)*, 199
  fragrant varieties, 189
Rhubarb *(Rheum rhabarbarum)*, 173
Ribbon grass *(Phalaris arundinacea picta)*, 67
Rock cress *(Arabis caucasica)*, 191
Rock rose *(Cistus creticus)*, 115
Rose campion *(Lychnis coronaria)*, 71, 109, 157
Rose *(Rosa)*, 91
  antique, 93
  arbor planting, *96–97*, 96–97
  Canadian Explorer, 93
  choosing, 92
  for circular garden, *102–103*, 102–103
  with clematis, *98–99*, 98–99
  climbing, 94, 95, 96–97, *98–99*, 98–99, 102, 170, 171
  for cold climates, 93, 115
  for color, 75
  for container gardens, 31, *108–109*,
  for cottage gardens, 111
  for cutting gardens, 93, 134, 135
  David Austin, 93, 103, 155
  Earthkind, 93
  easy-care combination bed, *94–95*,
  for edging borders, 132
  for fence plantings, 123